New
Progress
to Proficiency

....

Student's Book

Leo Jones

CAMBRIDGE
UNIVERSITY PRESS

PUBLISHED BY THE PRESS SYNDICATE OF THE UNIVERSITY OF CAMBRIDGE
The Pitt Building, Trumpington Street, Cambridge, United Kingdom

CAMBRIDGE UNIVERSITY PRESS
The Edinburgh Building, Cambridge CB2 2RU, UK
40 West 20th Street, New York, NY 10011–4211, USA
477 Williamstown Road, Port Melbourne, VIC 3207, Australia
Ruiz de Alarcón 13, 28014 Madrid, Spain
Dock House, The Waterfront, Cape Town 8001, South Africa

http://www.cambridge.org

First published 1986
Second edition 1993
Third edition 2002
Reprinted 2002

Printed in Italy by G. Canale & C. S.p.A

Typeface: New Baskerville 10/12pt.   *System:* QuarkXPress® (Apple Macintosh)

A catalogue record for this book is available from the British Library

ISBN 0 521 63553 5 Student's Book
ISBN 0 521 00789 5 Self-study Student's Book
ISBN 0 521 63552 7 Teacher's Book
ISBN 0 521 63551 9 Cassette set

Contents

Thanks . . .

to everyone who helped with this book:
  Charlotte Adams, Annie Cornford and Alison Silver
The teachers who commented on the first draft of *New Progress to Proficiency*:
  Annie Broadhead, Christine Barton, Anne Gutch, Elizabeth Kilbey, Patricia O'Sullivan and Clare West.
The people who kindly agreed to be interviewed:
  Shazia Afridi, William Boyd, James Charles, Allison Curbishley, Jayne Evans, Ray Gambell,
  Tessa Holman, Amanda Hooper, Claudine Kouzel, Karen Lewis, Christine Massey, Alastair Miller,
  Michael Newman, Simon Russell Beale, Beth Titchener, and Sarah Wilson
The actors who took part in the studio recordings.

Interviews by Susie Fairfax
Recording produced by James Richardson at The Soundhouse studio assisted by Darrin Bowen
Picture research and permissions by Hilary Fletcher
Proof-read by Ruth Carim
Designed by Caroline Spindler at Oxford Designers & Illustrators

From the second edition

I'd like to thank everyone who generously gave their advice and made comments and suggestions which have
helped to shape this New Edition of *Progress to Proficiency*.

Heartfelt thanks to Jeanne McCarten, who started the ball rolling and kept the project moving along. Her
discerning ideas and wise advice encouraged me to incorporate countless improvements.

Thank you to the teachers who provided feedback on the first edition:
  Craig Andrew, Liz Charbit, Anne Cosker, Marina Donald & Margery Sanderson, Shirley Downs, Brian Edmonds,
  Hilary Glasscock & Jenny Henderson, Cecilia Holcomb, Ian Jasper, Anne Koulourioti & Ourania Petrakis,
  Sheila Levy, Vicki Lynwoodlast, P.L. Nelson-Xarhoulakou, Steve Norman, Bruce Pye, Michael Roche,
  Cristina Sanjuan Alvarez, and Jennie Weldon

I'm particularly grateful to everyone who wrote detailed reports on the first edition, and recommended particular
improvements and changes:
  Margaret Bell, Jennie Henderson, Ruth Jimack, Jill Mountain, and Clare West

The New Edition was greatly enriched with ideas, criticisms and suggestions from:
  Ruth Jimack Jenny Johnson Rosie McAndrew Laura Matthews Pam Murphy Jill Neville Madeline Oliphant
  Alison Silver Bertha Weighill Clare West

And thanks to the following people for their contributions and assistance:
  Peter Taylor, who devoted so much time and effort to collecting the authentic interviews, and who produced
  and edited all the recorded material, with the help of Studio AVP.
  The actors who took part in the studio recordings, and who talked about their own experiences and attitudes.
  The people who generously agreed to be interviewed.
  Lindsay White, Amanda Ogden, Ruth Carim, Nick Newton, and Peter Ducker.
  Alison Silver guided the project smoothly, efficiently and cheerfully towards its publication. Her eye for detail and
  thoroughness enhanced the book enormously. Working with her was, as always, such a pleasure.

Finally, thanks to Sue, Zoë and Thomas for everything.

From the first edition

My special thanks to Christine Cairns and Alison Silver for all their hard work, friendly encouragement and
editorial expertise.

Thanks also to all the teachers and students at the following schools and institutes who used the pilot edition of
this book and made so many helpful comments and suggestions: The Bell School in Cambridge, the British
Council Institute in Barcelona, The British School in Florence, the College of Arts and Technology in Newcastle
upon Tyne, the Eurocentre in Cambridge, Godmer House in Oxford, the Hampstead Garden Suburb Institute in
London, Inlingua Brighton & Hove, International House in Arezzo, Klubschule Migros in St Gallen, The Moraitis
School in Athens, the Moustakis School of English in Athens, the Newnham Language Centre in Cambridge, VHS
Aachen, VHS Heidelberg, VHS Karlsruhe, the Wimbledon School of English in London and Ray Thomson in
Switzerland. Without their help and reassurance this book could not have taken shape.

Acknowledgements

The author and publishers are grateful to the authors, publishers and others who have given permission for the use of copyright material identified in the text. It has not been possible to identify the sources of all the material used and in such cases the publishers would welcome information from copyright owners.

1.3 ©David Stafford (1.0.91) and *The Guardian*; *The Guardian* for the use of the following articles, all ©*The Guardian*: 1.6 Vivek Chudhary (23.6.99), 3.1 Margaret Horsfield (2.4.91), 5.6 Paul Brown (18.9.97), 8.3 Leader (1.9.97), 9.7 Andrew Northedge (24.9.91), 11.7 Stephen Burgen (28.1.91), 14.6 Anita Chaudhury (14.6.2000), 14.8 Nicholas Bannister (24.7.99), 16.5 Roger Dobson (15.7.97), 18.1 Will Englund (22.6.2000), 18.1 Michael Ellison (22.6.2000), 18.1 Jamie Wilson (22.7.99), 18.1 David Sharrock (18.2.92); *The Observer* for the use of the following articles, all ©*The Observer*. 1.7 John Henderson (27.6.99), 4.5 Alexander Garrett (29.6.97); 2.1 ©Punch (Feb 1984); 2.4 Estate of Peter Fleming for the extract from *Brazilian Adventure* by Peter Fleming; 3.6 Jake Bowers-Burbridge (8.3.2000) and *The Guardian*; 3.8 Estate of James MacGibbon for the poem from *The Collected Poems of Stevie Smith* (Penguin 20th Century Classics) ©1972 Stevie Smith. *"Not Waving But Drowning"* by Stevie Smith, from *Collected Poems of Stevie Smith*, copyright ©1972 by Stevie Smith. Reprinted by permission of New Directions Publishing Corp. 3.8 *'BloodyMen'* from *Serious Concerns* by Wendy Cope. Reprinted with permission of PFD on behalf of Wendy Cope ©1993 Wendy Cope; 4.3 ©The Estate of Anthony Burgess, Artellus Ltd for the extract from *'Language Made Plain'* by Anthony Burgess; 5.2 ©Telegraph Group Limited 1989; 5.3 ©John Henley (10.3.2000) and *The Guardian*; 6.2, CA4, CA16 extract from *Towers of Trebizond* by Rose Macaulay reprinted by permission of the PFD on behalf of The Estate of Rose Macaulay ©Rose Macaulay 1956; 6.5 extract from *'Hunting Mr Heartbreak'* by Jonathan Raban, reprinted with permission of Gillon Aitken Associates ©1991 by Jonathan Raban. Submitted Excerpt, pages 68-69 from *Hunting Mister Heartbreak* by Jonathan Raban. Copyright ©1990 by Jonathan Raban. Reprinted by permission of HarperCollins Publishers, Inc; 6.6 ©Tourism Saskatchewan; 7.2 ©The Economist (2.11.96); 7.3 Dave Hill and The Independent/Syndication; 7.9 ©Telegraph Group Limited 1995; 8.5 ©Telegraph Group Limited 1998; 8.10, CA8, CA17, CA27 extracts from *'Bad Time For Talking'* by Paul Sussman *'Death by Spaghetti'*, ©1993-6 The Big Issue/©1996 Paul Sussman; 9.3 ©M A Udom; 9.9 extract from web page reprinted with permission of the Head Master, Summerhill School. ©Summerhill School. www.summerhill2000.com; 10.3 extract from *Rise And Fall Of The Third Chimpanzee* by Jared Diamond published by Hutchinson. Used by permission of The Random House Group Limited. Submitted extract from *Rise And Fall Of The Third Chimpanzee* by Jared Diamond. Copyright ©1992 by Jared Diamond. Reprinted by permission of HarperCollins Publishers, Inc; 10.5 extract from *The Stationary Ark* by Gerald Durrell. Reproduced with permission of Curtis Brown Ltd, London, on behalf of the Estate of Gerald Durrell, ©Gerald Durrell; 10.7 ©The Economist (13.6.92); 10.10 extract from *Life on Earth* by David Attenborough, reprinted with permission of HarperCollins Publishers Ltd; 10.11 extracts from *'Save the Earth'* by Dorling Kindersley Limited. ©Joe Miller for the use of his poem 'If the Earth were...'; 11.3 extract from *Brazzaville Beach* by William Boyd, published by Sinclair-Stevenson. Used by permission of The Random House Group Ltd. Also used by permission of The Agency Ltd, London; 11.3 extract from *A Dark Adapted Eye* by Barbara Vine used by permission of Penguin Books Ltd; 11.3 extract from *Nice Work* by David Lodge reproduced with permission of Curtis Brown Ltd, London, on behalf of David Lodge. Copyright ©David Lodge 1988; 11.9 extract from *A Farewell to Arms* by Ernest Hemingway ©Hemingway Foreign Rights Trust; 11.9 William Heinemann Ltd and Viking Penguin for the extract from *The Grapes Of Wrath* by John Steinbeck. "Chapter 1", from *The Grapes of Wrath* by John Steinbeck, copyright 1939, renewed ©1967 by John Steinbeck. Used by permission of Viking Penguin, a division of Penguin Putman Inc; 11.9 The Wylie Agency, London for the extract from *The Mosquito Coast* by Paul Theroux; 12.3 ©1998. Extract *Design Flaws* from *Notes From A Big Country*, published by Black Swan, a division of Transworld Publishers. All rights reserved. *Notes From A Big Country* (Published in the U.S. as *I'm A Stranger Her Myself*) by Bill Bryson, reprinted with permission of The Doubleday Broadway Publishing Group; 12.4 ©Telegraph Group Limited 1997; 12.8 From *The Psychology of Everyday Things* by Donald A.Norman. Copyright ©1988 by Donald A.Norman. Reprinted by permission of Basic Books, a member of Perseus Books, L.L.C; 13.3 extract from *My Family And Other Animals* by Gerald Durrell, reproduced with permission of Curtis Brown Ltd, London, on behalf of the Estate of Gerald Durrell. ©Gerald Durrell; 13.3 extract from *The Cement Garden* by Ian McEwan published by Jonathan Cape. Used by permission of The Random House Group Limited. *The Cement Garden*, by Ian McEwan. Copyright ©1978 by Ian McEwan. Reprinted by permission of Georges Borchardt, Inc; 13.3 The Wylie Agency for the extract from *My Secret History* by Paul Theroux; 13.5 extract from *Wilt* by Tom Sharpe published by Secker & Warburg. Used by permission of The Random House Group Limited. Also by permission of Sheil Land Associates Ltd Copyright ©Tom Sharpe 1976; 13.5 Faber and Faber Ltd, Nigel Williams Ltd for the extract from *The Wimbledon Poisoner* by Nigel Williams, also by permission of Gillon Aitken Associates; 13.7 extract from *The Millstone* by Margaret Drabble, published by Weidenfeld and Nicolson. Reprinted by permission of The Orion Publishing Group Ltd; 14.5 ©Mark Honigsbaum; 15.1 ©Raj Persaud and *The Guardian*, 15.9 Reproduced from *The Art Book* ©1994 Phaidon Press Limited; 15.5 extract from *The Shock Of The New* by Robert Hughes reproduced with the permission of BBC Worldwide Limited. Copyright ©Robert Hughes. Alfred Knopf; 15.6, 15.8 extract from web page reproduced with permission of Empireonline.co.uk; 16.9 *Taking The Waters* ©Jane Clarke Author and Nutritionist; 16.11 ©The Economist; 17.1 extract from *Europe A History* by Norman Davies published by Pimlico. Used by permission of The Random House Group Limited. From *Europe: A History* by Norman Davies, copyright ©1993 by Norman Davies. Used by permission of Oxford University Press, Inc; 17.2 the poem *The Soldier* by Rupert Brooke; 17.2 *Futility* by Wilfred Owen is reprinted from *Wilfred Owen, The Complete Poems and Fragments* edited by John Stallworthy and published by Chatto and Windus; 17.2 the poem *The General* by Siegried Sassoon, copyright Siegfried Sassoon by kind permission of George Sassoon. *"The General"*, from *Collected Poems of Siegfried Sassoon* by Siegrfried Sassoon, copyright 1918, 1920 by E.P.Dutton. Copyright 1936, 1946, 1947, 1948 by Siegrfried Sassoon. Used by permission of Viking Penguin, a division of Penguin Putnam Inc; 17.4 extract from *Goodbye To All That* by Robert Graves, reprinted with permission of Carcanet Press Limited; 18.4 ©1998. Extract *Why No One Walks* from *Notes From A Big Country*, published by Black Swan, a division of Transworld Publishers. All rights reserved.

Introduction

New Progress to Proficiency is for students who are preparing for the University of Cambridge Certificate of Proficiency in English examination ('CPE' or 'Proficiency', for short), or for an examination of similar level and scope. Each unit is based on a different topic, and contains sections which will help you to develop and improve your reading, writing, listening and speaking skills in English.

Using *New Progress to Proficiency* . . .
• will make your learning an enjoyable experience
• will be intellectually stimulating and thought-provoking
• will help you do your very best in the exam
• will enable you to perfect your English for professional, academic and social purposes — not just for an exam, but for real life too

The exercises and activities in *New Progress to Proficiency* focus on different aspects of English:
• developing and increasing your vocabulary
• helping you to understand, enjoy and appreciate reading passages
• revising grammar
• studying more advanced grammar points
• improving your writing skills and composition writing
• idioms and phrasal verbs
• improving your listening comprehension
• developing your speaking skills
• Proficiency examination skills

As you work through the units, you'll be building your proficiency in English PROGRESSIVELY. You'll notice a gradual change in the nature and style of the exercises and activities as you progress through the book. At the beginning, they help you to improve your English by giving you guidance, encouraging you to enjoy learning and giving you opportunities to use English creatively. Towards the end, you'll be concentrating more on acquiring and refining the special skills needed for the examination.

Many of the exercises and activities are designed to be done in co-operation with other students, working in pairs or small groups. You'll find that by sharing ideas you can learn a great deal from each other.

Working through *New Progress to Proficiency* will help you to make progress, but it's YOUR TEACHER who can help you to improve the specific aspects of English in which you're weakest, and can guide you towards particular exercises that seem most valuable for you and your class. Your teacher may decide to leave out some exercises if the limited amount of time available can be more profitably devoted to other exercises – you may decide to do some of these omitted exercises as extra homework.

But remember that the most important person in the learning process is YOU! You are the person who is most responsible for your progress: by asking questions, seeking advice and working to expand your vocabulary – and by reading English for pleasure, talking English and listening to English whenever you can.

A lot of this work will need to be done on your own outside class: preparing material for each lesson, regularly reviewing what you have covered in class, learning new vocabulary, and doing all the written tasks that you are set.

You'll need a good English–English dictionary, as well as a comprehensive grammar reference book, because no coursebook can answer all your questions on vocabulary and grammar, and your teacher is only available when you're in class.

Symbols

👤→👤 means 'Join another person to form a pair'

👥 means 'Work in pairs'

👥→👥 means 'Join another pair to form a group'

👥👤 means 'Work in groups of three'

👥👥 means 'Work in groups of three or four'

> Examination advice and study tips are given in notes like this at the side or at the bottom of the page.

Enjoy using New Progress to Proficiency !

Leo Jones

The Proficiency exam

The University of Cambridge Local Examinations Syndicate (UCLES) **Certificate of Proficiency in English (CPE)** examination is held twice a year: in June and in December.

Paper 1 Reading – 1 hour 30 minutes

Part 1 Three short texts (total 375–500 words), each with 6 gaps. There is a choice of four possible answers for each gap.

You have to choose the best .... to fit in each gap in the text.
A guess **B** idea **C** thing **D** word ✓

Part 2 Four short texts on the same theme (total 600–900 words) with two multiple-choice comprehension questions per text. You have to choose the best answer.

How many texts are there in Part 2?
A one **B** two **C** three **D** four ✓

Part 3 One long text (800–1100 words) from which seven paragraphs have been removed and placed in jumbled order on the next page. You have to decide from where in the text the paragraphs have been removed. There is one paragraph which doesnít fit anywhere.

Part 4 One long text (700–850 words) with seven multiple-choice comprehension questions.

(Total: 40 questions = 40 marks)

Paper 2 Writing – 2 hours

In both parts of the Writing Paper you have to write 300–350 words. Each part carries equal marks.

Part 1 This part is compulsory. After reading the instructions, you read a short text (maybe a short letter, article or advertisement) and then write an article, essay, letter or proposal. The focus is on presenting and developing arguments, expressing and supporting opinions, and evaluating ideas.

Part 2 There are four questions from which you choose one. One of the choices includes a question on each of the set texts. The following formats are included here: an article, an essay, a letter, a report or a review. The tasks may involve any of the following functions: describing, evaluating, giving information, making recommendations, narrating, persuading, summarising.

(Examiners' marks scaled to 40 marks)

Paper 3 Use of English – 1 hour 30 minutes

Part 1 One text with 15 gaps to fill, testing grammar and vocabulary. You have to think of a suitable word to fill each gap. (15 questions, each worth 1 mark)

Part 2 One text with 10 gaps to fill. Each gap corresponds to a word. The 'stems' of the missing words are given beside the text and you have to transform them to provide the missing word. (10 questions, each worth 1 mark)

This part tests your KNOWLEDGE of word formation.   **KNOW**

Part 3 Six groups of three sentences, each with a word missing. You have to decide which single word fits into all three gaps. This tests collocation, phrasal verbs, idioms and meanings. (6 questions, each worth 2 marks)

Part 4   Eight key word transformations. You have to rewrite each sentence using the word so that it has a similar meaning. You mustn't change the word given and you must use between three and eight words only. (8 questions, each worth 2 marks)

> This is an example of a key word transformation sentence.
> **kind**
> This is an example *of the kind of sentence* you may have to transform.

Part 5   Two short texts with two questions on each, and one summary task. The questions focus on the style and tone of the text, and on vocabulary. For the summary you have to select relevant information from both texts and write 50 to 70 words. (4 questions, each worth 2 marks. Summary, worth 14 marks)

(Total: 75 marks, scaled to 40)

Paper 4   Listening – about 40 minutes

Each text is heard twice. You have time to read the questions and to check your answers afterwards.

Part 1   You hear four short extracts, with two multiple-choice questions per extract. You have to choose the best of three alternative answers for each question. (8 questions)

Part 2   You hear a monologue or interview. You have to complete gaps in sentences with information from the recording. Each sentence has to be completed with a word or short phrase. One longer extract with nine sentence completion questions. (9 questions)

Part 3   You hear a discussion or interview. There are five multiple-choice questions. You have to choose the best of four alternative answers for each question. (5 questions)

Part 4   You hear a discussion between two people. You have to match each of a list of six opinions or statements to the names of the speakers, according to who said what. If they agreed about something you write both names. (6 questions)

(Total: 28 marks, scaled to 40)

Paper 5   Speaking – about 20 minutes

There are two candidates and two examiners. One is the assessor (who listens and assesses but doesn't join in) and the other is the interlocutor (who sets up the task, joins in sometimes, and also assesses). The interlocutor also has to make sure that one candidate doesn't dominate the conversations, so that you both have an equal amount of time to show how good you are at speaking English.

Part 1   The interlocutor encourages each candidate in turn to give information about themselves and to express personal opinions. This part involves general interaction and social language. (3 minutes)

Part 2   The candidates are given visual and spoken prompts, which generate a discussion between them. You'll have pictures to talk about (but not actually describe): the interlocutor will tell you what you have to do. This part involves comparing, decision making, evaluating, giving opinions and speculating. The interlocutor only joins in if one candidate is speaking too much. (4 minutes)

Part 3   Each candidate in turn is given a written question to respond to. You have to talk for two minutes on the theme of the question, uninterrupted. After each candidate has spoken, the interlocutor asks you questions to encourage a discussion on the same topic. This part involves organising a larger unit of discourse, developing topics, and expressing and justifying opinions. (12 minutes)

(Assessors' marks scaled to 40 marks)

For more information, visit the UCLES website: www.cambridge-efl.org.uk

9

1

Time to spare?

1.1   In my spare time . . .

A 👥 **Work in pairs. Discuss these questions with your partner:**

- What do you think is going on in the photos? What do the people seem to be doing?
- What's your favourite sport? Why do you enjoy playing or watching it?
- Do you have a hobby? If so, why do you enjoy it? If not, why not?

B 1 👥 **Before you listen to the recording, find out what your partner thinks are the attractions (or otherwise) of these hobbies and interests:**

When you meet someone for the first time (and in the Proficiency Speaking test), you may well be asked about your hobbies and interests. Saying 'I don't have time for any' is a conversation killer. It may be better to pretend that you *are* interested in a couple of sports or hobbies, adding later that you regret how little time you have to pursue them.

2 🔊 **You'll hear Ruth, Bill, Sarah, Emma and Jonathan describing their hobbies or interests. As you listen, note down:**

a the name of each person's hobby or interest
b the reasons why they enjoy it and find it rewarding.

3 👥 **Compare your notes with a partner. Listen to the recording again to settle any points of disagreement, or to fill any gaps in your notes.**

4 **Discuss which of the activities sounded most and least attractive.**

C 1 👥 **Write down THREE more examples for each of the following lists:**

Hobbies:	collecting stamps carpentry
Interests:	listening to music dancing going to the cinema
Indoor games:	chess backgammon
Team sports:	soccer rugby
Individual competitive sports:	boxing motor-racing tennis
Non-competitive sports:	aerobics windsurfing skateboarding
Outdoor activities:	bird-watching fishing hunting

2 **Join another pair. Compare your lists and then find out:**
- which of the activities your partners participate in or watch
- which of the activities they dislike or disapprove of – and why
- what hobbies or sports they might take up if they had more time

1.2 Comparing and contrasting GRAMMAR REVIEW

These **Grammar review** sections will help you to revise the main 'problem areas' of English grammar, giving you a chance to consolidate what you already know and to discover what you still need to learn. The **Advanced grammar** sections will introduce you to more advanced structures.

But they are no substitute for a good, comprehensive grammar reference book, to which you should refer for more detail and further examples.

A **Match each sentence on the left with the sentence on the right that has the same meaning or implication.**

1	Water-skiing is less difficult than sailing.	Both sports are equally hard.
	Sailing is as difficult as water-skiing.	Sailing is harder than water-skiing.
2	Like you, I wish I could play the piano.	Neither of us can play the piano.
	I wish I could play the piano like you.	You can play the piano well, I can't.
3	Your essay was most interesting.	Nobody's essay was better than yours.
	Your essay was the most interesting.	It was a very interesting essay.
4	The cliff was too hard for us to climb.	We were able to climb it.
	The cliff was very hard for us to climb.	We were unable to climb it.
5	She is a much better pianist than her brother.	They both play quite well.
	Her brother is a much worse pianist than she is.	Neither of them plays well.
6	She swims as well as she runs.	She is equally good at both sports.
	She swims as well as runs.	She takes part in both sports.
7	Bob isn't as bright as his father.	Bob is less intelligent than his father.
	Bob's father is bright, but Bob isn't that bright.	His father is more intelligent than Bob.
	Bob isn't all that bright, like his father.	Neither of them is particularly intelligent.

B **Fill each of the blanks with a suitable word or phrase. Think of TWO different ways of completing each sentence, as in the example:**

1 His sister .... that she can beat everyone in her age group.
    a *plays tennis so well*   **b** *is such a brilliant tennis player*
2 Track and field athletics .... jogging.
3 Learning English .... learning to drive a car.
4 On Saturday night .... than stay at home studying.
5 She's a very good runner: she can run ....
6 Fishing .... energetic .... swimming.
7 Collecting antiques is .... that I can think of.

C **Find the mistakes in these sentences, and correct them.**

1 *It isn't true to say that London is as large than Tokyo.*
2 *He's no expert on cars: to him a Mercedes and a BMW are like.*
3 *Her talk was most enjoyable and much more informative as we expected.*
4 *Don't you think that the more something is difficult,*
   the less it is enjoyable?
5 *Less people watched the last Olympics on TV than watched*
   the soccer World Cup.
6 *Who is the less popular political leader of the world?*
7 *My country is quite other than Britain.*
8 *She's such a faster runner as I can't keep up with her.*

D   Compare and contrast the activities shown here. What are the similarities and differences between them? Look at the example first.

1 Riding a bike or riding a motorbike both require a good sense of balance. As far as safety is concerned, neither cyclists nor motorcyclists are as safe as people in cars. A new bike costs much less than a motorbike and riding one is good exercise. However, you can go much faster on a motorbike.

1.3 Learning a musical instrument   READING

A   Work in groups and discuss these questions:

- Do you know anyone who plays any of these instruments?
- Which of them would you like to be able to play? Give your reasons.
- What are the rewards of learning a musical instrument?
- Look at the title of the article opposite: what do you think it's going to be about? Is it likely to be serious or humorous? Why?

B 1 Read the article opposite and note down your answers to these questions. Highlight the relevant information in the text.

1 Nine instruments are mentioned: what are they?
2 Three rewards of learning an instrument are mentioned: what are they?
3 Four kinds of pain are mentioned: what are they?
4 What is the difference between the two symptoms of 'Lipchitz's Dilemma'?
5 What reasons does the writer give for advising the reader NOT to take up eight of the nine instruments he mentions?
6 Which of the instruments seems to have the fewest drawbacks?
7 What happened at the end of the imaginary evening out with a drummer?

2   Join a partner. Compare and discuss your answers to the questions.

C 1 Highlight these words in the text – the paragraph number is shown with ¶.

¶1 grudge   ¶5 syndrome   ¶6 maudlin   ¶8 endeavour
¶12 be misled   physical co-ordination   nuance
¶14 unruffled equanimity   ¶17 charisma

2 Match their meanings to these words and phrases, using a dictionary if necessary:

*charm and magnetism   condition   control of one's movements   dislike   effort
get the wrong idea   perfect calmness   self-pitying   subtle variation*

Tinkling the ivories, jangling the nerves

EXCEPT perhaps for learning a foreign language and getting your teeth properly sorted out once and for all, there is nothing more rewarding than learning a musical instrument. It provides a sense of accomplishment, a creative outlet and an absorbing pastime to while away the tedious hours between being born and dying. Musical "At Homes" can be a fine way of entertaining friends, especially if you have a bitter grudge against them. Instrumental tuition is widely available publicly, privately and by post.

Before choosing an instrument to learn you should ask yourself five questions. How much does it cost? How easy is it to play? How much does it weigh? Will playing it make me a more attractive human being? How much does it hurt? All musical instruments, if played properly, hurt.

The least you can expect is low back pain and shoulder strain, in some cases there may also be bleeding and unsightly swelling. Various relaxation methods such as meditation can help.

The most popular instrument for beginners is the piano though I don't know why this should be so. The piano is expensive, it's fiendishly difficult to play, it weighs a ton and it hasn't been sexy since Liszt died. If you sit at the keyboard in the approved position for more than a few minutes, the pain is such that you are liable to break down and betray the secrets of your closest friends. The only good thing you can say about the piano is that it provides you with a bit of extra shelf space around the house.

Being difficult to play means that learning the piano could make you vulnerable to a syndrome known as Lipchitz's Dilemma. Lipchitz was an Austrian behavioural psychologist who observed that setting out to acquire a difficult skill leads to one of just two alternative results.

Either, because of lack of talent or lack of application, you reach only a low to average level of attainment, which leads to general dissatisfaction and maudlin sessions of wandering aimlessly about the house, gently kicking the furniture and muttering, "I'm hopeless at everything."

Or you reach a very high attainment level but, because you spend anything up to 18 hours a day reaching and maintaining this level, other aspects of your personality do not develop properly, which leads to general dissatisfaction and maudlin sessions of wandering aimlessly about the house, gently kicking the furniture and muttering, "Up the Villa."

Having thus established that no good at all can come of any sort of endeavour, Lipchitz himself gave up behavioural psychology and took a job in a Post Office as the person who runs out of things.

The violin is definitely a Lipchitz's Dilemma instrument, but it does have certain advantages over the piano. It is portable and need not be all that expensive to buy. You might not be able to get as good a sound out of a cheap instrument as an expensive one but since it is notoriously difficult to get much of a sound out of any sort of violin your best advice is to forget the whole idea and take up something easier.

The maraca is a hollowed out gourd half filled with beads or dried lentils or some such. Shaken, it makes a rattling sound. Small babies find this mildly entertaining but nobody else is interested.

The harmonica is similar. You buy it. You blow it. You suck it. You put it in a drawer. You lie on the sofa and you turn the telly on.

Some people think that the drums are easy to play and assume it must be fun, thrashing about like that. Do not be misled. Even basic rock'n'roll drumming requires a high level of musical understanding and physical co-ordination. Years of practice are needed to acquire a fluent technique, sufficient stamina and command of rhythmic and dynamic nuance and yet, after all that trouble, people still come up and say, "Must be fun thrashing about like that." This is why drummers often contract some of the more amusing personality disorders from the Encyclopaedia Psychopathics.

An evening out with a drummer can be diverting but be prepared for it to end with lines such as, "Leave it, Terry!" "For God's sake, he was only joking!" and "OH, CHRIST, WHAT A MESS!" Otherwise take my mother's advice and don't have anything to do with drums or drummers.

Brass instruments are much more fun. Professional brass players always wear an expression of bewildered good cheer. This is because they have discovered one of life's most wonderful secrets: you can earn a living making rude noises down a metal pipe. It is a secret that enables them to steer through all life's uncertainties and absurdities with unruffled equanimity.

I have played the guitar for more than 30 years, but I would not advise others to do the same. Far too many other people play the guitar and you will probably find, as I have, that they do it better than you.

A friend once invited me for tea. He had also invited a chap from the pub. The chap from the pub brought his accordion with him. It was an electric accordion which plugged into an amplifier. The living room was small: the amplifier large. He played Lady Of Spain and The Sabre Dance. The International Court of Human Rights has my report on the incident and is considering my recommendations.

For sheer sex appeal you can't do better than a saxophone. Just holding a saxophone gives you a late night charisma, enables you to drink whisky and smoke with authority. But if you wish to maintain credibility, it's as well to have a good stock of excuses ready for when you're asked actually to put the thing to your lips and blow, especially if your best shot is "Oh, The Camptown Ladies Sing This Song, Doo Dah Doo Dah." Otherwise be prepared for maudlin sessions of aimless wandering, gentle furniture kicking, and muttering, "I'm hopeless at everything."

DAVID STAFFORD

D **1** Highlight three sentences which amused you in the text.

2 Discuss your reactions to the humour of the text.

E **1** Look at the six tips given here. There's one word missing from each tip – can you guess the missing words?

2 Discuss which recommendations seem to be most useful for you personally. Highlight the most important pieces of advice given.

Learning new vocabulary

1 If you come across a potentially useful new word or phrase in a text, use a dictionary to look it up. Pay particular _____ to the example sentences given and any information given about collocations*.

2 If a word or phrase seems specialised, obscure or recondite*, you shouldn't necessarily try to remember it – often you can guess its _____ from the context anyway. Make your own choices about whether new words and phrases are 'useful' or not.

3 Highlight useful new words so that they stand out whenever you flip through* the book. Flip through the units you have covered so far at least once a week – you could do this on the bus on your way to or from class, for example. This will help you to assimilate* the words so that eventually you can incorporate them into your own active vocabulary, and use them in your _____ and conversation.

4 Writing new words in a notebook will help you to memorise new words, particularly their _____. If you put words in categories, rather than making a chronological* list, it will be easier to find them again later. New words can be stored under topic headings: Free time, Sport, Music, Literature, etc. Or you may prefer to build up a 'personal dictionary' where each fresh page lists words beginning with A, B, C, and so on.

5 Use a loose-leaf 'personal organiser' or Filofax as your vocabulary notebook. New pages can be inserted when you run out of _____ in each category. Or use a notebook computer.

6 When writing new words in your notebook, write an _____ of each word in a sentence, as well as a definition. If it's a difficult word to pronounce, make a note of its pronunciation too. Leave a line space between each entry* in case you want to add more information at a later date.

* If you don't understand these words, look them up now. Decide which of them are worth highlighting and remembering.

1.4 'You've got to be selfish'

LISTENING

A **1** Allison Curbishley is a professional athlete. Before listening to the recording, look at the questions and pencil in any information you can guess.

2 Note down your answers to these questions with information from the recording.

1 What are Allison's track events?

| | 1 |

2 How long does a typical training session take?

| | 2 |

3 Why are her afternoons 'easy-going' and 'lazy'?

| | 3 |

4 How did she feel before the relay at the Olympics? `[        4]`

5 How did she feel after the relay? `[      5]`

6 Which of these things does she love? Tick (✓) the things she mentions:
winning ☐   flying ☐   training ☐   travelling ☐   socialising ☐
standing on the winners' podium ☐   being applauded by the crowd ☐

7 What is the worst part of her job? `[      7]`

8 What adjectives does she use to describe herself? `[      8]`

B   👥 **Compare your answers. Then discuss these questions:**

• What kinds of attributes or qualities does an athlete need to have?
• Which of these adjectives would you use to describe Allison Curbishley?

aggressive   arrogant   brave   charismatic   compassionate   competitive   confident
consistent   dedicated   determined   dignified   disciplined   easy-going   emotional
extrovert   exuberant   fearless   humorous   impetuous   intelligent   introvert
knowledgeable   methodical   modest   persistent   proud   resourceful   ruthless
self-assured   selfish   single-minded   sociable   stubborn   temperamental

1.5   Adjective + noun collocations

A   👥 **Work in pairs. Look at the odd-looking phrases below: replace the crossed-out adjectives with ones which really do collocate with the nouns.**

a ~~high~~ (great) pleasure   a ~~major~~ (heavy) cold   a ~~profound~~ lake   a ~~nearby~~ friend   a ~~close~~ shop
a ~~loud~~ room overlooking the street   a ~~silent~~ room overlooking the garden
a ~~noisy~~ noise   a ~~quiet~~ silence   an ~~expensive~~ piece of advice   a ~~dear~~ meal   a ~~deep~~ book

B **1** 👥 **Decide together which of the adjectives on the left can be used to describe the nouns on the right.**

a/an   absorbing   attractive   beautiful
breathtaking   catchy   close   delicious
delightful   entertaining   exciting
ferocious   funny   gifted   great
handsome   hard-working   naughty
pretty   serious   slight   talented   thrilling

adventure   animal   athlete
book   boy   game   interest
meal   painting
photographer   place
problem   song   story
student   talk   view   woman

2 👥 **Write down ANOTHER adjective that can be used with each of the nouns above. Use a dictionary if you need to. Look at the examples first:**

a cuddly / wild / furry animal   a fine / readable / long / best-selling book

C   **Here are some adjectives which have similar meanings. Fill the gaps with suitable nouns, using a dictionary from time to time if necessary. Look at the examples first:**

A good English-to-English dictionary is indispensable when learning new vocabulary. Understanding the basic meaning of unfamiliar new words isn't enough – you have to be able to use them in appropriate contexts and collocations.

1 a light <u>summer coat</u>   a pale <u>face</u>   a bright <u>sunny day</u>   a colourless <u>liquid</u>
2 a famous _____   a well-known _____   a notorious _____
   an infamous _____   a distinguished _____
3 an extensive _____   a long _____   a wide _____   a broad _____
4 an old _____   an elderly _____   an ancient _____   an old-fashioned _____
5 a new _____   a modern _____   an up-to-date _____
   a recent _____   a fresh _____
6 a major _____   a strong _____   an important _____
   a significant _____   a vital _____   an essential _____
7 an insignificant _____   a minor _____   a small _____
   a little _____   a trivial _____
8 a strange _____   an unusual _____   a rare _____
   a peculiar _____   an uncommon _____

1.6 Tennis stars

A 1 Choose the best word or phrase to fill each gap in this article:

1 **A** worrying	**B** biggest	**C** large	**D** strange
2 **A** new	**B** recent	**C** unknown	**D** anonymous
3 **A** previous	**B** former	**C** past	**D** n other
4 **A** passionate	**B** emotional	**C** unaccustomed	**D** temperamental
5 **A** large	**B** huge	**C** great	**D** major
6 **A** hard	**B** severe	**C** careful	**D** some
7 **A** following	**B** next	**C** subsequent	**D** successive
8 **A** constant	**B** regular	**C** gentle	**D** familiar
9 **A** most youthful	**B** youngest-ever	**C** most junior	**D** most immature
10 **A** family	**B** educational	**C** sporting	**D** professional

Hingis beaten by girl wonder from down under

Wimbledon witnessed one of the _____ ¹ upsets in its 122-year history after top seed and world number one Martina Hingis was defeated in her opening game by the _____ ² Australian Jelena Dokic, ranked 129th in the world.

A packed court No 1 watched in amazement as Dokic, 16, won 6-2, 6-0, making her the lowest ranked player in modern tennis history to defeat a No 1 seed in a grand slam event.

Dokic, who is of Serbian origin, only made it to Wimbledon by winning a _____ ³ qualifying tournament.

She said after her victory: "I still can't believe I've beaten her. It's a big win for me, especially in the first round, coming from qualifying, but I thought I played quite well and I'm happy that I've won." Moments after her defeat, Hingis revealed she was buckling under the _____ ⁴ strain and pressure faced by young tennis professionals and indicated that she needed a break from the game.

Hingis also revealed that she had decided to attend Wimbledon without her mother and coach Melanie Molitor because the two needed some time apart given the pressures of the last few weeks.

Yesterday's match was the first time that the Swiss player's mother was not present at a _____ ⁵ tournament where her daughter was playing. Ms Molitor has driven her daughter throughout her career.

Hingis, aged 18, who has earned around $10m during her career, said: "I think I need to take some time off. Take a break and recover again."

"I think it has been a great life so far. I mean, I really like it, and I just probably… I need a break. It would really suit me right now." Hingis came to Wimbledon under _____ [6] scrutiny and criticism from the public and fellow professionals following her tantrum at the final of the French Open last month.

When on the verge of losing the match to Steffi Graf she served under-hand twice, entered the crowd and then stormed off court.

She was eventually persuaded to return by her mother, but was criticised for her impetuous, childish outbursts.

Hingis said yesterday that the events at the French Open and the _____ [7] criticism and a temporary separation from her mother had affected her.

She added: "I was probably too nervous, not much believing what I can do or not and didn't really see… I want to try it by myself here [at Wimbledon] and she [my mother] wanted to do more about her private life, to do the things she wanted to do, and the same for me.

"We decided to have a little bit of distance, as I said before, and probably work a bit more on our private lives and see how it is going to go in the future." News of the separation is being seen as a further indicator of Hingis's alleged emotional problems and the severe pressures faced by young women tennis professionals.

Many like Hingis have known little else other than tennis throughout their lives and are under _____ [8] pressure from pushy parents and coaches to compete at tournaments and win.

Hingis began playing tennis at the age of seven and was the _____ [9] player to win a grand slam tournament when she became the Australian Open champion at the age of 16. She won her first major title aged 12 when she won the French Open junior championship in 1993.

Despite the defeat, Hingis denied she wanted to break off all _____ [10] links with her mother and find a new coach. She said: "We are going to talk about it and then we will do some more decisions. But right now, I need a break."

Vivek Chaudhary

2 🏃 **Find the answers to these questions in the article:**

1 Martina Hingis was beaten by Jelena Dokic in . . .
   A the Wimbledon final
   B the final of the Australian Open
   C the first match of Wimbledon
   D the first match in Australia
2 Martina blamed her defeat on the . . .
   A absence of her mother
   B presence of her mother
   C stress of being No 1 seed
   D skill of her opponent
3 Martina was criticised after the French Open for . . .
   A unsporting behaviour
   B shouting at the crowd
   C shouting at the umpire
   D refusing to finish the match
4 Martina seems to have a . . . relationship with her mother.
   A caring   B childish   C stable   D tempestuous
5 After the French Open Martina and her mother agreed to . . .
   A work more closely together
   B focus on their individual private lives
   C end their professional relationship
   D spend more time together socially
6 When Martina won her first adult international tournament she was . . .
   A seven   B twelve   C sixteen   D eighteen

When using a dictionary, remember that the examples given are often more helpful than the definitions. The examples show some of the contexts in which the words occur, and their collocations. If you and your partner have different dictionaries, there are even more examples at your disposal.

"Damn! Trust me to get a seat behind the umpire!"

B Five paragraphs have been removed from this article. Choose the most suitable paragraph from the list A–E for each gap (1–5) in the article.

The ladies' man

Jon Henderson lifts the latch to discover Phil De Picciotto's Advantage in tennis

The big house on the hill overlooking the All England club, where the management company who look after Martina Hingis set up camp for the two weeks of Wimbledon, might not have been a good place to visit last Tuesday after the world No 1 had suffered one of the greatest upsets in a singles match since David loaded up a sling.

1

On the contrary, the front door was ajar and I let myself in to be cheerily greeted by a member of Advantage International's management team, who wondered if I had 'come to talk about Anna'. The queen is dead, long live the queen. In fact my appointment to meet Phil de Picciotto, the president of Advantage's athlete representation operation, had been made before the afternoon's drama to discuss the attractions of a company who have lured such a lustrous line-up. Now, though, a few specific questions about Hingis – and Kournikova – did seem in order.

2

He is sensitive about stories that she and her mother, Melanie Molitor, who was so unexpectedly absent from the Dokic defeat, have fallen out. 'There is no split,' he says. 'Martina's very honest and open with these things. She's a very nice girl who doesn't have any pretences whatsoever, and I think she'll become very much appreciated for this over time. When one doesn't have any pretences in a world where many other people do and when one is young and is the best at one's craft, it's a combination that can lead to instances like this.'

3

Who decided that Molitor should forsake her customary courtside perch? 'Ultimately it's the athlete who makes the final decisions,' says De Picciotto, given an opportunity to discourse on his management techniques. 'We're there to educate, advise and present the options. Whether it's a tennis, business or family decision, we believe that each player is in the best position to make that decision.' But Hingis might have received some guidance from you? 'That's right,' he agrees, guardedly.

4

Dokic, too, comes complete with a ready-made parental problem – 'Damir the Dad from Hell', as one headline described the 16-year-old's father, who had been thrown out of a tournament two weeks ago for supporting his daughter too boisterously. De Picciotto is wary of fanning this one. 'I think there will be no difficulty coping with the father,' he says. 'Everyone is entitled to one bad tournament – on or off the court.'

5

'The point is the media are only interested in anyone over an extended period, and so it is in the interests of the women's tour and each player to eliminate or minimise the distractions so they can extend their careers. They'll all have better stories to tell if they do.'

A

Having recently interviewed Mark McCormack, the autocratic head of International Management Group, Advantage's great competitors (although neither company would admit a rivalry existed), the informality of the big house on the hill was striking. So was the difference between McCormack and De Picciotto. I had interviewed the besuited McCormack in an impressive office overlooking the Thames; I spoke to the casually dressed De Picciotto, a 44-year-old lawyer, under a tree in the garden. He helped to found Advantage in 1983 and, unsurprisingly, he has a different perspective on Hingis than the 'spoilt brat' portrayal in some newspapers.

B

However, in this case they were representing both Goliath and the David of the piece – the Serbian sparrow Jelena Dokic, now an Australian citizen. There were other clients from the company's starry cast list still to be attended to, including Anna Kournikova, Steffi Graf, Jana Novotna, Conchita Martinez and Amanda Coetzer. No drawn curtains, then.

C

Perhaps Advantage's greatest coup was being approached by Kournikova, previously represented by McCormack's IMG. 'We began working with Anna less than a year ago,' says De Picciotto, 'and at that point the tabloid media were creating whatever image of her they wanted. It was the image of the day, completely inconsistent and very difficult to manage. The only way is not just to curtail interviews but eliminate them, except for the obligation, which Anna handles very professionally, to give conferences after her matches.'

D

The story of Hingis and her mother provides a classic dilemma for De Picciotto and his Advantage team: the media are invaluable allies in establishing an athlete's name but they can also make life very difficult. 'It is unfortunate that everything is so public,' he says. 'It's always easier to work through any relationship issue if the discussions can remain entirely among the people concerned. At Wimbledon, though, not only is there an open window to these tennis players' lives, but the window has different filters on it depending on who writes the story. What the public decides depends largely on the way the information is presented to them.'

E

Was he, like the rest of us, unaware that Hingis's mother would be missing? 'We wouldn't be doing our job very well and the relationship wouldn't be very good if there were any surprises.'

C **Work in groups. Discuss these questions:**

- Which of the adjectives in **1.4 B** would best describe Martina and Phil?
- What kinds of sacrifices does a top athlete or sportsperson have to make?
- Do you know anyone who is a keen athlete? Describe them.
- What is your attitude to commercial sponsorship of sports events?
- How are professional sportspeople different from amateurs?
- Do you take part in sports for enjoyment, for exercise – or to win? Give your reasons.

1.7 Using participles   ADVANCED GRAMMAR

A Working in pairs, explain the difference in meaning (or emphasis) between these pairs of sentences:

1 Standing at the top of the hill, I could see my friends in the distance.
  I could see my friends in the distance standing at the top of the hill.
2 While preparing the meal, he listened to the radio.
  While listening to the radio, he prepared the meal.
3 Finding the window broken, we realised someone had broken into the flat.
  We realised someone had broken into the flat, finding the window broken.
4 Before preparing the meal he consulted a recipe book.
  After consulting a recipe book he prepared the meal.
5 Crawling across the road, I saw a large green snake.
  I saw a large green snake crawling across the road.

B **Study these examples before doing the exercises on the next page:**

1 There are two forms of **active participles**:
   You find yourself thinking about what you are going to have for dinner or singing to yourself.
   Having thus established that no good at all can come of any sort of endeavour . . .

   and three forms of **passive participles**:
   Being warned about the approaching storm, they made for the coast.
   Warned about the imminent storm, they prepared for the worst.
   Having been warned about the impending storm, they foolishly pressed on.

2 Participles are used to describe **simultaneous** or **consecutive actions**:
   We sat on the beach watching the windsurfers falling into the water.
   When writing new words in your notebook, write an example in a sentence.
   Dressed in his smartest clothes, he arrived early for the interview.
   Getting to the beach, we looked for an uncrowded spot.
   [BUT NOT: We looked for an uncrowded spot, getting to the beach. ✗]
   Having got to the beach, we found some sunbeds to lie on.
   Having recently interviewed Mark McCormack . . .

   and to explain **reasons** or causes:
   Not being an expert, I can't teach you how to windsurf.
   Being a poor swimmer, I don't go out beyond my depth.

Participles tend to be used more in formal written style than in colloquial English.

3 Participles can also be used after these words:

after   as   before   if   on   once   since   when   whenever   unless   until

After losing the match, she was heart-broken.
All musical instruments, if played properly, hurt.
Once opened, this product should be consumed within 24 hours.
When using a dictionary, remember that the examples given are often more
   helpful than the definitions.

4 Normally the **subject** of a participle is the same as the subject of the main verb:

Waiting for the bus, I saw him in his new car.
(= I was waiting for the bus when I saw him in his new car.)

But in some cases the context makes the meaning clear:

Being difficult to play means that learning the piano could make you vulnerable to a
   syndrome known as Lipchitz's Dilemma.

C Using participles of these verbs, complete the sentences below:

arrange   arrive   complete   finish   lift   reach   require   shake

1 As .... , we'll meet outside the cinema at 8 o'clock.
2 He has been feeling terribly homesick ever since .... in this country.
3 On .... home, I went straight to my room.
4 .... by her indifference, he burst into tears.
5 Having .... the game, they shook hands.
6 Unless .... later, the key should be returned to the reception desk.
7 Remember to use block capitals when .... the application form.
8 Remember to bend your knees, not your back, whenever ....
something heavy.

D Finish these sentences, with each one still meaning the same as the one before it:

1 I haven't got a car, which is why I usually travel by bus.   **Not** ....
2 The demonstrators chanted loudly as they marched into the square. **Chanting** ....
3 They turned back when they found their way blocked by the police. **Finding** ....
4 I heard that he collects butterflies and asked him to tell me about it. **Having** ....
5 None of her friends turned up outside the cinema, so she went home. **Finding** ....
6 As I don't know much about art, I can't comment on your painting. **Not** ....
7 If you drink coffee too quickly, it can give you hiccups.   **Drunk** ....
8 I went to bed early because I felt a bit under the weather.   **Feeling** ....

E Having spotted the mistakes in these sentences, rewrite them correctly:

1 *Looking out of my window, there was a crowd of people in the street.*
2 *Wearing bright yellow trousers, we thought he looked ridiculous.*
3 *Being rather tall for his age, his father treats him like an adult.*
4 *Having been giving such a warm welcome he felt very pleased.*
5 *Sitting together I saw three old men playing cards.*
6 *If washing in hot water this garment will shrink.*

F 1 Using your own ideas, add suitable participles to this story:

On [____]¹ my eyes, I knew that I was in a strange, dark room. [____]² that I might
still be dreaming, I pinched myself to see if I was still asleep, but, [____]³ that I really
was awake I began to feel afraid. I felt my way to the door, but it was locked. I tried to
call for help but, after [____]⁴ for several minutes, I knew no one could hear me.
[____]⁵ to the window, and cautiously [____]⁶ the shutters, I discovered that the
window was barred and, [____]⁷ outside, all I could see was darkness. My heart sank.
[____]⁸ with an apparently hopeless situation, I sat down [____]⁹ what to do. I
remained there [____]¹⁰ on the bed in silent desperation for several minutes.

Suddenly, [____]¹¹ a key being turned in the lock, I . . .

2 Add THREE more sentences, continuing the story with your own ideas . . .

A 1 👥 Rearrange these steps into a more sensible order – and decide which of them you would OMIT. If any vital steps are missing, ADD them to the list.

GOLDEN RULES
FOR WRITING A COMPOSITION

Jot down all the points you might make.

Take a break.

Analyse your notes, deciding which points to emphasise and which to omit.

Show your first draft to someone else and get feedback from them.

Edit your first draft, noting any changes you want to make.

Proof-read the first draft: eliminate errors in grammar, spelling and punctuation.

Do any necessary research.

Proof-read your final version, eliminating any mistakes you spot.

Discuss with someone else what you're going to write.

Write a first draft, perhaps in pencil.

Look carefully at the instructions.

Write a plan, rearranging the points in the order you intend to make them.

Use a dictionary to look up suitable words and expressions and write them down.

Think about what you're going to write.

Get feedback from other students on your final version (they are 'your readers').

Look again at the instructions.

Have a rest.

Write your final version.

> Try to follow these steps every time you do written work during this course. In the exam, a well-planned, well-thought-out composition is always given better marks than an unplanned one that's dashed off quickly.

2 Decide which of the steps would NOT be feasible when working against the clock under exam conditions.

If you do writing tasks on a computer, decide which of the steps you'd still have to do on paper.

B Choose one of these topics and write an article (300–350 words).

Describe your own favourite hobby or sport, explaining its attractions and drawbacks.

or Write about a sport or hobby that you'd like to take up one day – when you eventually have enough time.

or Write about a hobby or sport you dislike, explaining what it is you don't like about it.

1 ✒ Follow the 'Golden rules' you discussed earlier. Before you begin writing, MAKE NOTES of the points you might make. In 320 words, you're unlikely to have enough room to mention them all, so you'll have to select the most important or most interesting ones.

2 👥 Show your finished composition to a partner and ask for feedback.

← When writing compositions, leave a wide margin on either side of your work and leave a couple of lines space between each paragraph. This will leave you room to add extra ideas – and even to rewrite complete sentences later, if necessary. →

Maybe write on alternate lines of the paper – or print your work out double spaced . . .

. . . and there'll also be more space for your teacher to add comments later too!

Adventure   Exploration   Extreme sports

2

A sense of adventure

2.1 **Eight Feet in the Andes** TOPIC VOCABULARY AND READING

A **1** 👥👥👥👥 **Discuss these questions with your partners:**

- Are you an adventurous person – or do you tend to play safe and avoid risks?
- What kinds of adventures or dangerous activities do you avoid at all costs?
- What kind of people do adventurers or travellers need to be? Which of the following qualities do you think are the ten most important – and why?

arrogance   boldness   charisma   compassion   confidence   courage   curiosity
dedication   determination   dignity   a good sense of direction   enthusiasm   fearlessness
humility   a sense of humour   intelligence   knowledge   linguistic skills   modesty
obstinacy   patience   persistence   resilience   resourcefulness   ruthlessness   stamina
tolerance   willpower

2 Look at the people in this photo –
what kind of people do they look like?

B   The text below is a review of *Eight Feet in the Andes* by Dervla Murphy. As you read it, find the answers to these questions:

1 Whose were the eight feet?
2 Who is the heroine of the story?
3 How long was the journey?
4 Where did they sleep?

C **1** Highlight these words and phrases in the article:

¶1 saunter   ¶3 madcap schemes   ¶4 frolic   heartening   ¶6 overenthusiastically
day one   ¶7 fretting   coveted   ¶9 homespun   ¶12 sticky moments
¶13 trusting soul

2 Match their meanings to these words and phrases:

amusing game   crazy plans   stroll   encouraging   without restraint   the beginning
dangerous incidents   fussing and worrying   envied and wanted   unsophisticated
someone who believes other people are honest

ONCE upon a time, with travel writing, the rewards won related to the risks taken. No longer. Travel writers travel by public transport; often they just hop in the car. They travel round British seaside resorts; they saunter up low mountains in the Lake District. Greatly daring, they visit islands off the coast. There is no point in travelling hopefully; far better to arrive as quickly as possible and collect your multinational publisher's advance.

Dervla Murphy had never heard of such a thing when she decided, after the death of her invalid mother, to travel from Ireland to India – on a bicycle.

Motherhood usually puts paid to such madcap schemes but for Miss Murphy only temporarily. She waited for the child to reach a reasonable age and then took it with her.

Rachel was five when they travelled together in South India, six when they went through Baltistan with a pony, and nine when, in this book, she crossed the Peruvian Andes from Cajamarca to Cuzco with her mother and a mule – a 2,000 kilometre journey of which she did 1,500 on foot. This Andean frolic – her mother's term – was to be her last before settling down to school, though it is hard to see what there can be left for her to learn. To read about Rachel is heartening for parents of a generation which seems to be losing the use of its legs.

She is an ideal travelling companion, settling down on a ledge overlooking the world to read Watership Down or write poems after ten hours up one mountain and down the next. "We're seeing clouds being born," she says once. She is thrilled to find a baby scorpion under her sleeping bag. After three months of travelling up and down vertical slopes of

3,300 metres her mother notes almost absently that she never once complained; and she herself only once questions the wisdom of asking a nine-year-old to walk 35 kilometres at an altitude of 4,000 metres on half a tin of sardines.

Rachel confides in her diary: "I got the whole of my upper left arm punctured by lots of slightly poisonous thorns . . . Mummy is in an exceedingly impatient mood . . . I think this is a very pretty place, at least in looks . . . We had to sit down while we thought about what to do next . . . " She has a much better sense of direction and indeed of responsibility than her mother who tends to join overenthusiastically in all religious festivals and who has dreadful blisters from day one in a hopeless pair of walking shoes.

The Murphys clearly see not Rachel but Juana, their beautiful glossy mule, as the heroine of the story. She cost £130 and they fuss over her like a film star, fretting about her diet, her looks, her mood. Juana is coveted by all; as the journey proceeds it is shadowed by the parting from her. There is a terrible moment when she falls over a precipice to certain death but for a divinely placed single eucalyptus tree in her path.

From Cajamarca to Cuzco they follow in the hoofprints of Pizarro and the conquistadores, often camping in the same place, almost always surveying the same timeless unchanging scene.

Miss Murphy's philosophy may be homespun – "I know and always have known that we twentieth-century humans need to escape at intervals from that alien world which has so abruptly replaced the environment that bred us" – but she has an enviable gift for communicating her passion for the road. No heat or cold is too extreme, no drama too intense for her to sit on the edge of some mountain and tell us about it that evening in her diary. Sometimes the view is too exciting for her to eat her raw potatoes and sardines.

There is very little food; everyone goes hungry. The pair arrive at sizeable towns and find nothing to buy but noodles and stock cubes and bottles of Inca Cola; the restaurant offers hot water to add to your own coffee. There is always worry about alfalfa for the choosy Juana. They are shocked at the poverty they see, and find it mystifying that the Indians can tolerate such a life.

She and Rachel share it wherever possible. They stop, make friends, join in. They accept all invitations, are ready to sleep with hens roosting on their legs, eat anything, drink anything no matter what floats on top of it and they repay hospitality (when permitted) with tins of sardines. She worries that religion is so little comfort to the Peruvian Indian, that the babies chew wads of coca, that the boys Rachel plays football with on their sloping pitches have no future, that she cannot repay kindnesses: the ancient shepherdess who shared her picnic lunch of cold potato stew on a cabbage leaf, the old man who set his dog to guard their tent at night.

There are sticky moments, always near towns. Within a day of Cuzco, Juana is stolen but all ends happily and they reach the Inca city with feelings of anti-climax at journey's end. They took a week less than the conquistadores but then the conquistadores had battles to fight.

The Murphys, mother and daughter, know no fear just as they know no discomfort, and their remarkable journey shows that the trusting soul is still free to wander at will.

Maureen CLEAVE

D **Now note down your answers to these questions, referring back to the article as necessary.**

1 What is the writer's attitude to most modern travel writers?
2 When was the *reasonable age* that Rachel first got taken on a journey with Dervla?
3 Why was this journey to be their last one together?
4 How did Dervla behave in a less grown-up way than her daughter?
5 When the writer describes Miss Murphy's philosophy as *homespun* (¶9), is this pejorative or complimentary?
6 What did they eat on their journey?
7 What happened to Juana at the end of their journey?
8 What was their worst experience? What was their best experience?

E **Looking at the first paragraph again, highlight the words or phrases which show sarcasm or irony. Which of these, if any, do YOU find amusing? (The first is *Once upon a time* – normally used to start a children's story.)**

F 👤👤👤👤 **Discuss your reactions to the text.**

- What risks was Dervla Murphy running by taking Rachel on her journey?
- What aspects of their journey would you find most difficult and rewarding?
- Where in the world is it safe for *the trusting soul* to *wander at will*, do you think?

2.2 Articles and determiners GRAMMAR REVIEW

A 👥 **Match the sentences on the left with the ones on the right that mean the same:**

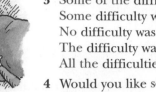

1 What was the mule like?
  What are mules like?

  What is a mule like?
  Could you describe their mule?

2 Do you like tea now?
  Do you like the tea now?

  Is the tea all right for you now?
  Have you overcome your dislike of tea?

3 Some of the difficulties were foreseen.
  Some difficulty was foreseen.
  No difficulty was foreseen.
  The difficulty was foreseen.
  All the difficulties were foreseen.

  We expected a certain amount of difficulty.
  We didn't expect any difficulty.
  Every difficulty was foreseen.
  We expected a particular difficulty.
  Not all of the difficulties were foreseen.

4 Would you like some coffee now?
  Would you like your coffee now?

  Would you like a coffee now?
  Would you like the coffee now?

B **1 Look at these examples:**

Some nouns are normally **uncountable**:

advice   applause   behaviour   clothing   fun   information   laughter   luggage
music   news   progress   rain   research   snow   spaghetti   teaching   transport
travel   wealth

Music helps me to relax.   Travel broadens the mind.

But when referring to a **particular** example, a different **countable** word or phrase must be used:

What a pretty song!   What a catchy tune!   What a lovely piece of music!
Did you enjoy your trip?   We had a great journey.

2 Match these countable words or phrases to the uncountable nouns above:

a/an action   analysis   article   asset   car   chuckle   class   coat   fact
      fortune   game   hint   improvement   joke   journey   laugh   lesson
      possession   report   shirt   song   suitcase   tip   train   trip   tune

a/an article   dish   drop   fall   flake   item   means   piece
      plate   round   **of . . .**

C **1 Study these examples:**

Some nouns are **uncountable** if used with a **general** meaning:

ABSTRACT NOUNS   adventure   atmosphere   business   confidence   death   education
            environment   experience   failure   fear   history   imagination
            industry   kindness   knowledge   life   love   philosophy
            pleasure   success   thought

MASS NOUNS   butter   cheese   coffee   juice   metal   milk   pasta   plastic
          poison   soup   sugar   tea   wine   wood

Business is booming.   Do you know much about business?
I have orange juice and coffee with milk for breakfast.

But they are **countable** if they refer to **particular** things or examples:
Some businesses are more profitable than others.
Running a business is a great responsibility.
I'd like an orange juice please.   Lead is a heavier metal than aluminium.

2 Fill the gaps with suitable nouns from the lists above:

1 A thorough .... of English is required.
2 It was an unforgettable ....
3 The journey was a great ....
4 Oak is a harder .... than pine.
5 She had a thrilling ....
6 It was a great .... to meet them.
7 He has a very vivid ....
8 The trip was an utter ....
9 This is a very salty ....
10 Cheddar is a very tasty ....
11 He has a great .... of music.
12 I'd like a strong black .... , please.

The use of articles is often determined by the context, and depends on information given earlier in a text or conversation, as in this example:

Last year I bought a computer from a mail order company. The computer has gone wrong but I can't get it fixed because the company's gone out of business.

D Fill the gaps in these extracts with a, an, the, his, her, their, or ∅ (no article) – in some cases more than one answer is possible. Afterwards, refer back to paragraphs 7 and 11 of the article in 2.1.

The Murphys clearly see not Rachel but Juana, ¹ beautiful glossy mule, as ² heroine of ³ story. She cost £130 and they fuss over her like ⁴ film star, fretting about ⁵ diet, ⁶ looks, ⁷ mood. Juana is coveted by all; as ⁸ journey proceeds it is shadowed by ⁹ parting from her. There is ¹⁰ terrible moment when she falls over ¹¹ precipice to ¹² certain death but for ¹³ divinely placed single eucalyptus tree in ¹⁴ path.

She worries that ¹⁵ religion is so little comfort to ¹⁶ Peruvian Indian, that ¹⁷ babies chew ¹⁸ wads of ¹⁹ coca, that ²⁰ boys Rachel plays ²¹ football with on ²² sloping pitches have no future, that she cannot repay ²³ kindnesses: ²⁴ ancient shepherdess who shared ²⁵ picnic lunch of ²⁶ cold potato stew on ²⁷ cabbage leaf, ²⁸ old man who set ²⁹ dog to guard ³⁰ tent at night.

E Correct the errors in these sentences:

1 Politics don't interest him, except when election takes place.
2 Grapefruits are my favourite fruits, but I don't like the banana.
3 The news are depressing today: two aircrafts have crashed.
4 There are crossroads at top of hill.
5 Mathematics were most difficult subject at the school for me.
6 Hague is capital of Netherlands, but Amsterdam is largest city.
7 The women are usually safer drivers than the men.
8 We missed bus and had to walk all the way home – it was quite adventure!

F Rewrite these sayings and quotations, inserting the or a, where appropriate:

1 Travel broadens mind.   Travel broadens the mind.
2 Love makes world go round.
3 Greatest adventure of all is life itself.
4 Friend in need is friend indeed.
5 Absence makes heart grow fonder.
6 While cat's away, mice will play.
7 Out of sight out of mind – as saying goes.
8 Woman without man is like fish without bicycle.

2.3 Words easily confused   VOCABULARY DEVELOPMENT

A Study the pairs of words below and discuss the difference in meaning between them – putting them in sentences may be helpful. If you're unsure about any, use a dictionary. Look at the example first:

actual = existing as a real fact   Well, I've heard about it but I haven't read the actual article.
current = (most) up to date   Have you seen that article in the current issue of The Economist?

actual · current	in fact · indeed	pretend · intend
advice · opinion	in front of · opposite	propaganda · advertising
control · check	large · wide	remember · remind
editor · publisher	lend · borrow	rob · steal
experience · experiment	lose · miss	savage · wild
fault · mistake	occasion · bargain	sympathise with · like
hear · listen	presently · at the moment	sympathetic · likeable

B **1** 👥 **Decide which of the words below fit in the gaps, and which don't. Tick the ones that fit.**

1 The immigration officer .... their passports suspiciously.
checked ✓   controlled   examined ✓   restrained   stamped

2 Her parents had a big .... and now they're not on speaking terms.
discussion   argument   debate   fight   quarrel   row   talk

3 Don't take any notice of him, he's just being ....
sensible   sensitive   difficult   touchy   emotional   moody

4 How many people .... the performance?
assisted   attended   participated   took part   helped   served

5 Please go away and stop .... me!
annoying   bothering   disturbing   harassing   pestering   infuriating

6 We arranged to meet at 7.30 and I made a note in my .... to that effect.
agenda   notebook   exercise book   diary   schedule   timetable

7 Please forgive him for forgetting, he's getting rather .... as he gets older.
distracted   absent-minded   forgettable   forgetful   preoccupied

8 What are the .... of studying when you could be enjoying yourself?
benefits   profits   advantages   prizes   rewards   prices

9 It's a(n) .... club to which only members are admitted.
exclusive   idiomatic   particular   personal   private   secluded

10 They didn't foresee the .... result of their irresponsible behaviour.
eventual   possible   imminent   feasible   plausible

11 At the end of her .... she had to sit a stiff exam.
career   course   education   training   upbringing   experience

12 I'm getting tired; how much .... is it to the summit?
further   furthermore   farther   far   faraway   far away   father

2 Highlight any words in this section that you had difficulty with. Check their meanings in a dictionary. Pay particular attention to the EXAMPLES in the dictionary, not just the definitions. Sometimes the difference is in the context a word is used, rather than its basic meaning.

2.4 **Brazilian Adventure**   **READING**

In Part 5 of the Use of English paper you'll have to read two texts and write short answers to four questions. Then you have to write a 50–70 word summary, based on the two texts. You should avoid quoting word-for-word and use your own words instead. This is easier said than done, and may require a lot of practice.

In later units, we'll practise some of the techniques you can use to avoid quoting from the text: using synonyms or opposites, using a different grammatical structure, etc.

A **Find the answers to these questions in the following text :**

1 Apart from the writer, how many other people are mentioned in the text?
2 Which of them did the writer trust most – and who did he trust least?
3 How confident was the writer that the expedition would ever leave London?
4 Did Major Pingle really exist?

Brazilian Adventure

PETER FLEMING

Outlook Unsettled

THERE are, I suppose, expeditions and expeditions. I must say that during those six weeks in London it looked as if ours was not going to qualify for either category. Our official leader (hereinafter referred to as Bob) had just the right air of intrepidity. Our Organizer, on the other hand, appeared to have been miscast, in spite of his professional-looking beard. A man of great charm, he was nevertheless a little imprecise. He had once done some shooting in Brazil, and we used to gaze with respect at his photographs of unimaginable fish and the corpses (or, as it turned out later, corpse) of the jaguars he had killed. But when pressed for details of our own itinerary he could only refer us to a huge, brightly-coloured, and obsolete map of South America, on which the railway line between Rio and Sao Paulo had been heavily marked in ink. 'From Sao Paulo,' he would say, 'we shall go up-country by lorry. It is cheaper and quicker than the train.' Or, alternatively: 'The railway will take us right into the interior. It costs less than going by road, and we shall save time, too.' It was clear that Bob, for all his intrepidity, viewed our Organizer's vagueness with apprehension.

At the other end – in Brazil, that is to say – the expedition's interests were said to be in capable hands. Captain John Holman, a British resident of Sao Paulo whose knowledge of the interior is equalled by few Europeans, had expressed his willingness to do all in his power to assist us. On our arrival in Brazil, as you will hear, this gentleman proved a powerful, indeed an indispensable ally; but at this early stage of the expedition's history our Organizer hardly made the most of him, and Captain Holman was handicapped by the scanty information which he received with regard to our intentions. In London we were given to understand that the man who really mattered was a Major Pingle – George Lewy Pingle. (That is not his name. You can regard him as an imaginary character, if you like. He is no longer quite real to me.)

Major Pingle is an American citizen, holding – or claiming to hold – a commission in the Peruvian army. He has had an active and a varied career. According to his own story, he ran away from his home in Kentucky at the age of 15; joined a circus which was touring the Southern States: found his way across the Mexican border: worked for some time on a ranch near Monterey: accompanied an archaeological expedition into Yucatan, where he nearly died of fever: went north to convalesce in California: joined the ground staff of an aerodrome there and became (of all things) a professional parachutist: went into partnership with a German, whose ambition it was to start an airline in South America: and since then had travelled widely in Colombia, Peru, Chile, and Brazil. All this, of course, we found out later. All we knew, or thought we knew, in London was that Major Pingle was a man of wide experience and sterling worth who had once accompanied our Organizer on a sporting expedition in Brazil, and who was even now preparing for our arrival in Brazil – buying stores, hiring guides, and doing everything possible to facilitate our journey. A great deal, obviously, was going to depend on Major Pingle. 'This Major Pingle,' I used to tell people, 'is going to be the Key Man.'

It was difficult to visualize Major Pingle, all those miles away. The only thing we knew for certain about him was that he was not very good at answering cables. This, we were told, was because he must have gone up-country already, to get things ready. Whatever the cause, however, very imperfect liaison existed between his headquarters in Sao Paulo and ours in London; and when a letter did at last reach London from Brazil, our Organizer lost it. So it was impossible to find out definitely whether Major Pingle's preparations were being made in the light of our plans, or whether our plans were being made to fit his preparations or neither, or both. It was all rather uncertain.

from Brazilian Adventure by Peter Fleming

B **1** ✐ **Write your answers to these questions. Highlight the relevant information in the text, but wherever possible, use YOUR OWN WORDS instead of quoting verbatim from the text.**

1 How did Bob, the leader, inspire confidence?
   Quote: *'He had just the right air of intrepidity.'* (line 3)
   Own words: *He looked suitably brave.*
2 How much shooting had the Organizer done on his previous trip to Brazil?
3 What were the Organizer's plans for travel to the interior?
4 How did Bob feel about the Organizer's vagueness?
5 What kind of man does Major Pingle seem to be?
6 Whilst still in London, who did the writer consider their most valuable contact in Brazil?
7 Where, according to the Organizer, was Major Pingle?
8 How had they tried to get in touch with Major Pingle?
9 How many letters from Major Pingle were the party shown?
10 What preparations was Major Pingle believed to be making for the expedition?
11 Judging by what the writer tells us, how is the expedition likely to turn out?

C **Find the words in red in the text and highlight them there. Then fill the gaps.**

1 Expeditions and expeditions (line 1) means that there are many different ....
2 Miscast (line 3) is normally used when talking about .... , not explorers.
3 A little imprecise (line 4) is an example of ....
4 When pressed (line 6) implies that the Organizer was .... to answer questions.
5 An obsolete map (line 7) is one that is no longer ....
6 An indispensable ally (line 16) is someone whose help ....
7 If you have scanty information (line 18), you have ....
8 According to his own story (line 22) suggests the story is ....

D **Discuss these questions:**

- When do you think the text was written?
- How would you describe the TONE of the writing?
- Does it make you want to read more about the adventure? Why (not)?
- If you had been leader of the expedition, what steps would *you* have taken to ensure that all the necessary preparations were made?
- What do you think the expedition found when they actually did arrive in Brazil?

E ✎ **Write a paragraph (about 60 words) summarising the air of uncertainty surrounding the expedition 'during those six weeks in London'.**

First of all, highlight the relevant information in the text. Try to use your own words, rather than quoting directly from the text.

2.5 **'If something goes wrong . . .'** **LISTENING**

A 👥 **Alastair Miller was a member of an expedition to Everest. Before you listen to the interview, look at the questions he was asked. What answers do you think he gave?**

1 What do you enjoy about climbing mountains?
2 Do you ever find yourself in situations where you're frightened?
3 What is it like taking part in an expedition to climb Everest?

B 🔊 **In the first part of the interview, Alastair deals with the first two points. Note down your answers to these questions.**

1 What are the FOUR things he says he enjoys about climbing – and what are the reasons he gives for enjoying each of them?
2 What are the two kinds of fear he describes?
3 Why did the accident in Yosemite Valley frighten his companion more than Alastair?
4 Why did he have to be *philosophical* during the thunderstorm on the Aiguille du Midi?
5 Why didn't they go back down the mountain when the storm broke?

C 🔊 **The second part of the interview is about the Everest expedition. Fill the gaps in these sentences with information from the interview:**

1 On a large expedition there is a ' .... effect': there are .... people at the bottom of the mountain and .... or .... people trying to reach the summit. This means that .... have to be carried up the mountain.
2 Approaching Everest from the .... , there were no .... to carry their equipment. So it was carried by yaks, and above Camp One, by ....
3 It was exciting for Alastair when he went above .... for the first time, even though he was on .... ropes and was entirely ....
4 Above Camp One they didn't .... or .... , they only cleaned their ....
5 Snow holes are .... but they are .... and ....

D 👥 **Compare your reactions to the interview. What impressed you most? What surprised you most? Would you like to be a mountaineer and rock-climber? Give your reasons.**

A   **Read the composition below on this topic:**

Write a letter to a friend describing an exciting or frightening experience you have had (300–350 words).

1 Decide which features of the writing help to keep your interest as a reader, and which features don't. Consider these aspects in particular:

choice of vocabulary   humour   sentence structure

> It had been a long, tiring journey to S_____. The ferry, which should have taken at most five hours, had had engine trouble and didn't arrive till 2 a.m. As the harbour itself was several miles from the main town - the only place where accommodation was available - and much too far to walk even by daylight, we hoped against hope that the local bus service would still be running. Sure enough one tiny, ancient blue bus was waiting on the quayside but imagine our dismay when we saw that about 98 other passengers were also disembarking with the same destination. We fought our way onto the bus and waited for the driver to appear. A man staggered out of the bar nearby and groped his way into the driving seat - presumably he'd been drinking since early evening when the ship was supposed to arrive.
>
> We were very frightened. Most of the passengers hadn't seen the driver come out of the bar. The bus went very slowly up the steep road. On one side the cliffs dropped vertically down to the sea hundreds of metres below. We arrived in the town at 3 a.m., but there was no accommodation. We found a taxi to take us to the other side of the island. We slept on the beach.
>
> As it began to get light and the sun rose over the sea, waking us from our dreams, we realised that it had all really happened and that we were lucky to be alive.

250 words

2 Although the first paragraph is fairly interesting, the rest is pretty dull – and the letter is too short! Rewrite the second half, incorporating any improvements you think are necessary, so that the total length is 300–350 words.

B **1** Here are some phrases that can be used when telling a story. Complete them in your own words.

1 There was nothing I could do but ....
2 It was only after .... that I ....
3 My big mistake was to ....
4 All I could do was ....
5 You can imagine how I felt when ....
6 It all started when ....
7 To my utter amazement ....
8 To our surprise ....
9 Slowly opening the door, I ....
10 After a while ....
11 Without thinking I ....
12 I held my breath as ....

2 Write the first two paragraphs (no more than half a page) of a letter to a friend, telling the story of an exciting or frightening experience YOU have had.

3 Read each other's stories and guess what happened next in your partner's story and how the story might have ended.

2.7 Position of adverbs

ADVANCED GRAMMAR

A 👥 Discuss the differences in meaning or emphasis in these sentences. How would you complete the last two?

1 Tricia only wants to help.　　　　　　　　　　Only Peter wants to help.
2 Pam doesn't really feel well.　　　　　　　　Jack really doesn't feel well.
　 Anne doesn't feel really well.
3 Tony and Jane still aren't married.　　　　　Still, Sue and Bob aren't married.
　 Olivia and Paul aren't still married, are they?
4 I don't particularly want to see Lisa.　　　　I particularly don't want to see Tim.
5 I enjoy eating normally.　　　　　　　　　　 I normally enjoy eating.
　 Normally, I enjoy eating.　　　　　　　　　 I enjoy eating – normally!
6 Carefully, I lifted the lid of the box.　　　　 I carefully lifted the lid of the box.
　 I lifted the lid of the box carefully.
7 Paul just doesn't like flying, he . . .　　　　　Olivia doesn't just like flying, she . . .

B Look at the examples and fill the gaps with suitable adverbs or phrases from the lists.

1 Some adverbs are almost always placed **in front of the main verb** in a sentence (or after the verb *to be*) – but not usually at the beginning or end of the sentence:

*almost　already　always　ever　hardly ever　just　nearly　never　often
practically　quite　rarely　seldom　utterly　virtually*

Have you ever been to South America? ✓✓
Ever have you been to South America? ✗
Have you been ever to South America? ✗

a We have .... finished our work.
b I .... disagree with what you said.
c It is .... as cold as this.

2 Some adverbs are usually placed **in front of the main verb** OR **after the object** – but not normally at the beginning of the sentence:

*constantly　continually　perpetually　regularly　sporadically
absolutely　altogether　completely　enormously　entirely
exactly　greatly　more or less　perfectly*

He constantly asks questions. ✓✓
He asks questions constantly. ✓✓

a I don't .... agree with her.
b Your work has .... improved.
c He isn't .... brilliant.
d I enjoyed the show ....

3 Adverbs consisting of **more than one word** are usually placed at the **end** of the sentence, or at the **beginning** – but NOT in front of the main verb:

*again and again　all the time　every so often　from time to time　many times
most of the time　once a week　once every four years　once in a while　over and over again
several times　twice a day*

*at the moment　at one time　a fortnight ago　before breakfast　before long
every day　in a moment　in the evening　in the past　the following week
the previous day　within the hour*

Most of the time I try to avoid risks. ✓✓
I try to avoid risks most of the time. ✓✓

a The Olympic Games are held ....
b I don't have the information .... , so I'll call you back ....
c .... I agree with what she says, but .... we don't see eye to eye.
d Although she had washed her hair .... , she washed it again ....

Remember that adverbs almost never go between a verb and a direct object:

He ate quickly his sandwiches. ✗
She took gently his hand. ✗
He dropped accidentally the vase. ✗

4 Some very common adverbs can be placed at the **beginning** of the sentence, or **in front of** the main verb, or **after** the main verb or the object:

normally   occasionally   periodically   sometimes   usually
afterwards   at once   clearly   eventually   immediately   later   obviously   presently
shortly   soon   suddenly   probably   presumably

Usually I wash my hair twice a week. ✓   I usually wash my hair twice a week. ✓✓
I wash my hair twice a week usually. ✓

  a I can't give you my answer .... , but I'll let you know ....
  b Let me know .... what you thought of the film.
  c It will .... be time to go home, so you'll have to finish the work ....

5 Most **adverbs of manner**, which describe **how** people act or speak, are commonly placed **after** the main verb or its object – though other positions are often possible:

accidentally   anxiously   apprehensively   automatically   carefully   discreetly   easily
fiercely   fluently   foolishly   frankly   gently   gloomily   gratefully   hurriedly   innocently
instinctively   lovingly   oddly   proudly   reassuringly   reluctantly   sensibly   sincerely
strangely   thoughtfully   violently   warmly

He reacted violently to my comments. ✓✓
He reacted to my comments violently. ✓

  a She was behaving very ....
  b He held up the prize .... and thanked everyone ....
  c She took his hand .... and looked .... into his eyes.
  d I raised my hand .... to protect my face.

6 Adverbs which 'comment' on the **whole** sentence are usually placed at the very beginning of a sentence before a comma – though other positions are often possible.

Fortunately   Funnily enough   Hopefully   Luckily   Strangely enough   Surprisingly
Unfortunately

Unfortunately, Elizabeth lost the race. ✓✓   Elizabeth unfortunately lost the race. ✓
Elizabeth lost the race, unfortunately. ✓

  a .... , I found my wallet in the car.
  b .... , she didn't get the job.
  c .... , I'll have finished the work soon.
  d .... , they're getting married.

C   **Find the mistakes in these sentences and correct them:**

1 *I have seen him seldom so furious and I was shocked absolutely by his reaction.*
2 *He from time to time loses his temper but he is most of the time in a good mood.*
3 *Discreetly all enquiries will be handled and you may write in confidence to us.*
4 *'Don't worry,' she quietly said, taking my hand and squeezing it reassuringly.*
5 *She many times told them to take care but they ignored repeatedly her advice.*
6 *The door burst suddenly open and we all looked in surprise up.*
7 *I do every day my homework and it takes me usually an hour.*
8 *He just doesn't like ice cream he loves it so much that he eats every day it.*

D   **Rewrite the sentences using the words in red, but without changing the meaning:**

1 They eventually replied to my letter.	after a while
2 I'm afraid that's a mistake I frequently make.	again and again
3 There are many occasions when I eat out in the evenings.	often
4 Soon I'll have finished writing this report.	practically
5 They helped me although they seemed unwilling.	reluctantly
6 There's nothing I'd like to do less than go for a walk.	particularly
7 Each branch of the company is a separate operation.	independently
8 I expect that he will be feeling apprehensive.	presumably
9 You should pay constant attention to your spelling.	always
10 She gave me a worried look.	anxiously

Adverb position is a very difficult area of English usage, and it's often best to rely on your *feelings* for what seems right and what seems wrong. Pay special attention to any corrections you are given. There are no hard-and-fast rules, unfortunately.

2.8 **Be prepared!**

A **1** You'll hear an expert giving some advice. Before you listen to the recording, try to guess or deduce what information seems to be missing here:

Walking in the mountains

TAKE THE RIGHT PRECAUTIONS:

1. DO have at least _____ people in your party. DON'T *go alone.* .

2. DO be _____ . DON'T do anything you're not _____ to do.

3. DO expect the weather to _____ . DON'T rely on _____ .

4. DO allow yourself plenty of _____ . DON'T let _____ catch up with you.

5. DO walk at the _____ of the _____ member of the group.
   DON'T leave anyone _____ .

6. DO _____ if fog or low clouds come down.

7. DO find _____ where you can sit and wait for _____ .
   DON'T _____ in case you walk over a _____ !

TAKE THE RIGHT EQUIPMENT:

1. *A map* _____ – You must _____ your _____ before setting off.

2. A _____ in case there are no _____ or the sun is obscured,
   and make sure you know _____ – DON'T just follow _____ and rely on your .

3. A rucksack, containing _____ and _____ clothing.

4. Footwear: _____ , not _____ or _____ .

5. Emergency _____ in your rucksack: _____ , _____ , _____ .

6. A _____ in case you get caught in the dark.

7. A _____ or a _____ in case you have to spend the night in the open.

And . . .

Before setting out, DO _____ and _____ ,
and DON'T forget to _____ when you get back.

2 🔊 Listen to the recording, filling in the missing information above.

3 👥 After listening to the recording, discuss these questions:

- What important precautions and equipment did the speaker NOT mention?
- Which of his advice do you disagree with?

B 👥👥 Make a list of your own safety rules for TWO of these activities:

sailing   windsurfing
swimming in the sea   skiing
driving in remote areas   going out at night alone
cycling in heavy traffic   climbing a ladder

C 🖊 Write a letter to a friend, telling the story of a walk in the mountains where you ignored the advice given in the recording but where, despite a number of close shaves, you arrived home safely (300–350 words).

Make notes before you start writing.

(If you prefer, you could write about one of the activities you discussed in B, where you ignored your own safety rules.)

A Which of the following would you *keep* and which would you *hold*?

a diary   a meeting   a promise   a straight face   hands with someone
in touch with someone   quiet   someone company   someone in the dark
someone responsible   your breath   your eyes open   your fingers crossed
your head high   your temper   yourself to yourself

B Find synonyms for the phrases in red, or explain their meaning. Use a dictionary if necessary.

1 She walked so fast that I couldn't keep up with her.
2 There's no point in trying to keep up with the Joneses.
3 You've done a lot of good work this month. I hope you can keep it up.
4 They're getting married next month! Keep it to yourself, though.
5 I'll keep my fingers crossed for you on the day of your interview.
6 I'm sorry for what I did, I hope you won't hold it against me.
7 Their reasoning just didn't hold up.
8 They explained what happened, but I feel they were holding something back.
9 We got held up in the traffic.
10 Hold on a moment, I haven't got a pen. Could you hold the line, please?

C Fill the gaps in these sentences with suitable forms of the phrasal verbs below:

1 The clouds look pretty ominous, I don't .... much hope of sunny weather.
2 Fortunately, their supplies .... till the rescue party got to them.
3 You'd better .... the subject of his first marriage, otherwise he'll get upset.
4 They managed to .... their costs .... by employing part-time workers.
5 It was a private argument, so I thought it best to .... it.
6 She felt that her boss's attitude was .... her .... in her career.
7 If she wants to get on, she'll have to .... her boss, not disagree with him.
8 Tell me exactly what you think – don't .... anything ....
9 They didn't think our offer was high enough, so they .... more.
10 As they climbed up the cliff, the leader told them to .... tight.

hold back   hold back   hold on   hold out   hold out   hold out for
keep down   keep in with   keep off   keep out of

3

Everyone's different!

3.1 Getting away from it all

READING

A 1 Read the article opposite, preferably before the lesson. Note down THREE reasons why you might envy the writer and THREE reasons why you wouldn't envy her.

2 👥 Compare the reasons you've noted down. Then discuss these questions:

- Do you like to be alone – or do you feel lonely when you haven't got company?
- Do you enjoy the pace of life in a big city? Or do you find it stressful?
- If you wanted to 'get away from it all' where would you go?

B 1 Make notes on each of the visits to the homestead, in the order the people arrived. Note their name(s), who they were and how they got there. The writer's information is given as an example.

	NAME(S)	WHO THEY WERE	MEANS OF TRANSPORTATION
	Margaret	the writer	float plane
a)			
b)			
c)			
d)			
e)			

2 Who were her friends or acquaintances who *didn't* come to visit? Note down who they were – and the reason why you think she was relieved they didn't come.

	WHO THEY WERE	WHY MARGARET WAS RELIEVED
a)		
b)		
c)		

3 Note down your answers to these questions (¶ shows the paragraph number):

a Who were Don, Bill and Liz?
b Why is the friend described as *heroic* (¶14) and *alarmingly cheerful* (¶24)?
c What were the THREE most rewarding aspects of her stay?

C Highlight the following words and phrases in the article:

¶4 foolproof   ¶6 unassailable   outraged   the bush   ¶8 unsolicited
¶9 positively   ¶13 blissfully   ¶15 egged on   ¶16 abhors a vacuum
¶17 came to nothing   ¶21 flagged   ¶25 tentatively   ¶29 bustle

Then match them to their OPPOSITES below:

calm   civilisation   confidently   continued   did happen   discouraged   invited
loves an empty space   not in the least   precarious   unhappily   unruffled   vulnerable

D 👥👥 Discuss these questions:

- When have you spent time alone? Describe your own experience of solitude, loneliness or isolation. Or imagine what it would be like.
- Have you ever lived in a small community or village? What was it / would it be like?

The great escape

LOOKING around the small wooden cabin, I counted seven people. Or it might have been eight. The lighthouse keeper's wife was the last to arrive. She dropped out of the sky, unannounced, courtesy of a Coast Guard helicopter that landed on the gravel beach right in front of the cabin.

"Hi, I'm Lise," she shouted as the chopper disappeared. "I thought I'd drop in for a visit." Looking around, she added: "Hey, I thought you were here on your own!"

I'd stopped thinking that days ago.

"I want to be alone," I had declared on leaving London. I was tired, dog tired, of people and telephones and deadlines and crowds. So I planned a great escape, a Big Sleep, a magnificent foolproof Fortress of Solitude, where for three whole weeks I planned to hibernate like a bear in the middle of nowhere.

Everything seemed perfect. A friend in Canada needed a house-sitter for his remote homestead on the far coast of Vancouver Island, the silvery western edge of Canada. Here, the map ends and the open Pacific begins. Huge silent forests swell in the heavy winter rains, growing dense and impenetrable right down to the water's edge.

I knew I could be entirely alone here. No roads go near this part of the coast. The only way in is by boat or small plane. I would have no telephone, no electricity, no television, no interruptions. I felt unassailable. Friends and family were outraged. "What do you mean, you want to be alone? Out in the bush like that? No one wants to be that alone."

"Oh yeah?" I thought. I said nothing. They kept talking.

And then came the unsolicited offers. No fewer than 15 people offered to come and stay with me. For my own good, of course.

Some of the offers were positively scary. "Is it OK if I bring the boys?" These boys are aged two and four, television junkies from the womb. Their mother has never lived out of range of a washing machine or a dishwasher in her entire life.

"Frank and I will both come – he's much better after his operation."

"I'll bring my guitar."

"I've been really depressed, I need solitude too."

But despite all these offers, when the tiny float plane at last landed in the inlet near the cabin, and I clambered out with my heavy boxes of books and groceries, I was blissfully alone. My first few days were entirely peaceful. A long-dreamed-of silence surrounded me, and vast space. It didn't last long.

The depressed friend arrived first. She was heroically prepared to stay for 10 days. "Don't worry about me – I won't get in your way."

"Oh yeah?" I thought. This friend had been egged on by numerous other friends. "What is that woman doing out there they're all asking? I'm supposed to report back."

It was really very simple. I wasn't doing much at all. I was sleeping and reading and chopping wood and beachcombing and watching the eagles and looking out for other wildlife. The problem for everyone else seemed to be that I was doing it alone. Human nature, I decided, abhors a vacuum. It was clear that I would have to settle for semi-solitude. And in the end I found I didn't really mind. Which is just as well.

No one else arrived from "outside". The threat of "the boys", the guitar and the post-operative Frank came to nothing. But as the days passed I was astonished to find myself meeting more and more people.

My nearest neighbours turned out to be Dave and Diane, living in a deserted Indian village 15 miles up the coast. Diane called me on the marine radio. "Don told us you were there all alone, so we thought we'd check in to see how you're getting on."

"Don?" I thought. I didn't know any Don.

Dave and Diane and their children came to see me in their boat. They told me where to dig for clams and that the herring run had started and that hundreds of sea lions were playing further out in the bay and that the grey whales had arrived on their annual migration.

That was the day Lise from the lighthouse arrived. All day long, the coffee pot spluttered on the woodstove and conversation never flagged. I learned about light-keeping and edible seaweeds and how to smoke mussels and where the gooseneck barnacles grow.

"Here I was worrying about you," said Lise cheerfully. "I never thought you'd have so much company."

Neither did I. But it was good company. On the day of the crowded cabin, we went out in the boat to see the grey whales spouting. Later on, we went all the way to the lighthouse, riding on the huge swells of the open Pacific, in Dave's small boat.

My depressed friend became alarmingly cheerful after all this and thought she might stay even longer. She had, however, to get back to work. As her plane took off from the water, silence returned. The guests had all left.

"Ah, solitude," I thought, tentatively. Just me and the whales and the sea lions and the eagles and the herring. The solitude lasted precisely two more days before a large, friendly person emerged from the forest announcing that he was Bob, from the logging camp down in the next inlet. He'd hiked over to see how I was doing. "Just thought I'd check in. Bill told me you were here all alone." ▶▶

26 "Bill?" I thought, and, "All alone?" Bob stayed and drank a pot of coffee. I learned a lot about trees.

27 A few days later, a strange boat anchored in front of the house and three men made their way to shore. They were from the Department of Fisheries, monitoring the herring run. "Liz told us you were out here on your own. How's it going? Aren't you lonely?"

28 "Liz?" I thought, and, "Lonely?" as I put the coffee pot on. That day I ran out of coffee and learned more about herring

29 I had visitors on 14 of my 21 days of solitude. I learned a lot, not just about herring and trees and whales, but about solitude and loneliness. In such a remote landscape, people are very aware of each other. The presence of a person – any person – matters. People are assumed to be interesting creatures, and important. In the exhausting bustle of Central London, that doesn't always seem to be the case. I have been lonely in the rush hour at Oxford Circus. I was never lonely in my days of solitude on the far coast of Canada.

30 Next year I've been asked to go back to that coast, to house-sit once again in that green, silent place. I'll go, of course. And I'll know, next time, to take more coffee.

Margaret Horsfield

3.2 Reporting – 1   GRAMMAR REVIEW

A Match these reporting verbs with the verbs with similar meanings below:

emphasise   complain   confess   disclose   forecast   infer   insinuate   order
promise   reiterate   remember   suppose   yell

*admit   gather   grumble   guarantee   guess   imply   predict   recall   repeat
reveal   shout   stress   tell*

B 1 Decide which of the endings in blue fit comfortably with these beginnings. SIX verbs don't fit with any of the endings – which are they?

> It's more interesting for a reader if you use a variety of reporting verbs – not just *he said* or *she asked.*

| They … | accused admitted advised agreed allowed apologised asked blamed couldn't decide discovered dissuaded didn't expect explained forbade forgave hoped imagined implied didn't know learned mentioned persuaded pretended promised never realised reckoned refused didn't remember reminded didn't reveal didn't say shouted suggested didn't tell threatened wanted warned wished wondered | … that we had done it. … that we should do it. … to do it. … us to do it. … when to do it. … when we should do it. … if we had done it. |

2 Write sentences using the six verbs that didn't fit with any of the endings and show them to your partner. **Highlight** the verbs in A and B1 that you want to remember.

C Change each sentence into reported speech, using suitable verbs from the list in B above. Imagine that they were said to you by different people LAST WEEK.

1 'I'll certainly give you a hand tomorrow evening.'
   He promised to help me the next evening. or
   He promised that he would help me the following evening.
2 'I'm not going to help you, you'll have to do it by yourself.'
3 'There's no point in writing it all out in longhand – it'd just be a waste of time.'
4 'It's your fault that we missed the bus, you must have misread the timetable.'
5 'Do you happen to know what time the performance starts? I don't want to be late.'
6 'Why don't you phone him up and see if he's free tonight?'
7 'Make sure that you don't start giggling during the interview.'
8 'If you type this letter out for me, I'll buy you a drink, OK? Thanks!'
9 'You're the one who borrowed my dictionary, aren't you?'
10 'If you don't move your car, I'll call the police.'
11 'All right, if you want me to, I don't mind accompanying you.'
12 'I don't really mind about your rudeness – I know you were in a bit of a state.'
13 'Haven't you finished writing the report yet?'
14 'I'm very sorry for breaking your sunglasses. I didn't mean to sit on them.'

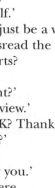

D **1** Note down SIX difficult or personal questions you want to ask your partner.

2 👥 Join a partner and ask each other your questions. Note down the answers.

3 👥 Change partners and report the conversation you had in 2 just now.

> *She asked me ... and I told her ...*
> *Then I asked her ... but she wouldn't tell me whether ...*
> *I expected her to tell me ... but I found out that ...*

When reporting something which was said in another place or a long time ago, place and time phrases may also have to be changed:

'I'll do it tomorrow.'	→ She told me that she would do it the next day.
'I was here yesterday.'	→ He said that he had been there the day before.
'Do I have to do it now?'	→ I wondered if I had to do it then/right away.
'Look at this document.'	→ She wanted me to look at the document.

3.3 Punctuation and paragraphs WRITING SKILLS

A Write down the names of each of these punctuation marks, as in the example:

? question mark ; : ! ... - — " " • ¶ * ( ) [ ] / ' .

B Add suitable punctuation in the spaces in this article. Change lower case letters to Capitals where necessary. And decide where to break the text into five paragraphs.

> A rabbit goes into a butcher's shop and asks , " Have you got any lettuce
> The butcher says   We don't sell lettuce here   You need the greengrocer's across the road
> The next day the rabbit comes into the shop and asks for some lettuce again
> The butcher tells him   Look   I told you yesterday   we don't sell lettuce   You need the greengrocer
> The rabbit comes in the next day and asks the butcher again   Have you got any lettuce
> The butcher goes mad   He says   Look   I'm sick of this   How many times do I have to tell you I don't sell lettuce   If you come in here again asking for lettuce I'm going to nail your ears to the floor
> The next day the rabbit comes in and asks the butcher   Have you got any nails
>   Nails   No
> Right   the rabbit says   Have you got any lettuce

C This job reference was typed by someone with good spelling, but poor punctuation. Proof-read it, correct the mistakes, and divide it into paragraphs.

Clear punctuation helps the reader to follow your meaning. Commas, in particular, are useful for showing the reader where one phrase or clause ends, and the next one begins. A comma can also change the meaning of a sentence. Always proof-read your own written work before handing it in.

> I have known, Jan Hall both professionally and personally, for several years, since 1998 when she first joined my department she has been a reliable, resourceful and conscientious member of my staff with a thoroughly professional attitude to her work; she has cheerfully taken on extra responsibilities and can be relied on, to take over when other staff are absent or unavailable! She particularly enjoys dealing with members of the public: and has a knack of putting people at their ease? She is particularly adept at defusing delicate situations – with an appropriate word and a smile? As her portfolio shows she is also a very, creative and talented person and her work shows great promise during her time with us her attendance has been excellent... She is an intelligent thoughtful, and imaginative person, I have no hesitation in recommending her for the post!!

D Correct the errors in these sentences and then comment on the rules of punctuation that have been broken in each:

1 *Sitting on the beach we watched the windsurfers, falling into the water.*
2 *The aspect of punctuation, which is most tricky, is the use of commas.*
3 *Could you tell me, when to use a semi-colon?*
4 *Feeling completely baffled we tried to solve the problem, with which we were faced.*
5 *He wouldnt dare say boo to a goose hes so shy.*
6 *There were surprisingly no punctuation mistakes in his work.*

3.4 Who's talking?   LISTENING

A   You're going to hear five different people talking. In each case it's not immediately obvious what they're talking about or even who they're talking to, so you'll have to pick up 'clues' to get the answers. You'll need to hear the recording more than once to get all of the clues and answers.

FIRST SPEAKER
1 How does the speaker feel and where is she?
2 Who is she talking to?
3 She says: ... *they're all over the place* ...   ← Who or what are *they*?
4 She says: ... *it's almost time to pick them up* ...   ← Who or what are *they*?
5 She says: ... *don't look like that* ...   ← How is the listener looking?
6 Why is the listener silent?

SECOND SPEAKER
7 Who is the speaker talking to?
8 Why has he started talking to her?
9 Who are all the people he refers to?
10 Why is the listener silent?

THIRD SPEAKER
11 Who is the speaker talking to?
12 She says: ... *I told her not to include me* ...   ← Who does she mean by *her*?
13 She says: ... *I got all the stuff* ...   ← What *stuff* is she referring to?
14 She says: ... *I got the bus all the way out there* ... ← What place is *there*?
15 She says: ... *they called it off* ...   ← What is *it*?

FOURTH SPEAKER
16 Who is the speaker?
17 Who is he speaking to?
18 He says: ... *it couldn't have happened* ...   ← What is *it*?
19 He ends by saying: *Nor is there any likelihood   ← Complete his sentence.
    in the future of* ...

FIFTH SPEAKER
20 What kind of person is the speaker?
21 Who is she talking to?
22 She says: ... *you can't put them back* ...   ← What are *they*?
23 Why is the listener silent?
24 She says: *Look, I'm sorry, I didn't mean* ...   ← Complete her sentence.

B 1 👥 What kind of person do you imagine each of the speakers to be? Make notes of some words you could use to describe them.

2 👥 → 👥 Describe each speaker to the other pair and ask them to guess which one you're describing.

C 1 ✐ Write five short reports, giving the GIST of what each speaker said in two or three sentences. Try to convey the essence of what they said, not a word-for-word report. Use suitable verbs from 3.2.

2 👥 Compare your reports when you've done this.

A **1** 👥 **Discuss the difference in emphasis between these sentences. One of them sounds funny because the effect is overdone – which one is it?**

1 At no level of society do women have equal rights with men.
  Women do not have equal rights with men at any level of society.

2 It occurred to me later that I had made a big mistake.
  Not until later did it occur to me that I had made a big mistake.

3 At the top of the hill stood a solitary pine tree.
  A solitary pine tree stood at the top of the hill.

4 So lonely did he feel that he went round to see his ex-wife for a chat.
  He felt so lonely that he went round to see his ex-wife for a chat.

5 Little did they know that the sheriff was about to draw his revolver.
  They didn't know that the sheriff was about to draw his revolver.

6 Bang went the door. In came Fred. On came all the lights. Out went the cat. The door opened with a bang and Fred came in. All the lights went on and the cat ran out.

7 Rarely are shy people taken as seriously as assertive people.
  Shy people are rarely taken as seriously as assertive people.

2 Highlight **the words or grammar that are used to give a special emphasis in the sentences. How have the word order and grammar been changed?**

B **Fill the gaps in these sentences with suitable words:**

1 Little .... that she would win the competition.

2 Not only .... the piano brilliantly but she .... too.

3 Never in my life .... so humiliated!

4 No sooner .... the bath than the phone ....

5 Under no circumstances .... the fire doors ....

6 Not until .... finished .... allowed to leave the room.

7 Only after .... the police able to catch the thieves.

8 Not once during her entire .... in trouble with the law.

9 Not only .... rather naive but he also .... very sensitive.

10 No sooner .... our picnic than ....

C **Rewrite these sentences more DRAMATICALLY, using structures from B above:**

1 We went out in our best clothes. The rain came down.
  Out we went in our best clothes, and down came the rain.

2 The thieves drove off with the police in hot pursuit.

3 The umbrellas went up. We went home, wet through.

4 A tall dark stranger was sitting beside her in the train.

5 A fat tabby cat lay under the table, washing itself obliviously.

6 The edge of the cliff gave way and she fell down.

7 There was a ferocious dog behind the wall, barking furiously.

8 Then I realised that I had made a very big mistake.

Inversion should be used sparingly as over-use can sound ridiculous. It can usually be avoided in conversation altogether. It does tend to come up regularly in the Use of English Paper of the exam, though.

"Boo!"

3.6 Long road to Utopia

A Six paragraphs have been removed from this article. Choose the most suitable paragraph from the list A–F for each gap (1–6) in the article.

Long road to Utopia

JUST 500 miles separates England from Sweden, but if, like me, you're a Romany traveller, the gulf in attitudes is colossal. My wife and I have recently travelled with our horse and caravan between the two countries. On our journey, we experienced not only changes in the physical landscape, but profound differences in attitudes towards many of the issues that lie at the heart of a democratic society – such as race, access to land and respect for a traditional, ecologically friendly nomadic lifestyle.

1

In 1998, I went to Sweden with my horse and wagon, in search of Romanestan. Sweden is a large country with a small population and enough living space for thousands of travellers. The roads are empty of traffic. Its law of allemänsrätt (all man's rights) is a model law protecting the "right to roam". Everybody has the right to camp and gather firewood, berries, herbs and mushrooms from the countryside. Romanies are recognised as a distinct ethnic minority by the Swedish government and even have the right to be educated in their own language.

2

There is, however, an eeriness about Sweden. The woods are suspiciously silent and empty. The thing that made us come back to England after two years was the total absence of travellers in the rural landscape. Romany communities in Sweden are concentrated in larger towns. Official policy has assimilated travellers entirely through generosity, by giving them all the benefits a well-funded welfare state can muster. It's a far cry from past policy – up until the 1960s, travellers were forcibly sterilised in Sweden – but probably a far smarter strategy.

3

Having a lifestyle like mine can give you the annoying status of an eccentric semi-celebrity. A passing tourist once photographed me peeing at 7 o'clock in the morning. Another day, while fetching some water for the horse, I saw a woman walk straight into our home as if it was a tourist attraction. I've probably been photographed and filmed at least once for every mile I've travelled on Swedish roads. The exotic appeal of your life imposes different restrictions on your freedom. But that which makes you a celebrity in Scandinavia defines you as a pariah in England.

4

The right to travel is not an issue; all you need is the vehicle. It's the right to stop that is the problem. Most of the old stopping places are gone. Those that haven't had a ditch put through them by local councils have been grabbed by farmers extending their fences or disappeared under the developers' tide of concrete. The commons we once used are gone, the verges made smaller by the widening of roads.

5

Since returning to England, I've experienced all these problems. I've met travellers who have been beaten by landowners and refused water by local villagers. At the first county line we crossed, there was a police car waiting, wanting to know our names and destination. The red carpet definitely doesn't stretch to our shores.

6

Jake Bowers-Burbridge

A

In short, Sweden is a land where Romanies have rights. It's a long way from Britain's endless fences, criminal justice act and feudal mentality towards land and class. When I first arrived, I felt as if I had found a little piece of Romanestan.

B

In the time of Henry VIII, there was a mandatory death sentence for Romanies. We have survived in an environment that is very hostile to our existence. England is one of the most densely populated countries on earth, with extremely concentrated land-ownership. That's bad news if you're a nomad needing constant access to new land for fuel and food.

C

Travelling in Britain is only possible nowadays with an extremely intimate knowledge of the countryside and a willingness to trespass in defence of the right to live as our ancestors did. We face a stark choice – settle, or engage in daily law breaking. This ongoing struggle has got to be one of the longest running and least recognised campaigns of civil disobedience this country has ever known.

D

Every nation without a homeland has its promised land. For the Kurds, it is Kurdistan; for us, it is Romanestan. But Romanestan is just an ideal, a utopia in time, if not in place. We may originally have come from India but I doubt that many of the world's 8 million Romanies would choose to go back there.

E

If our culture is to survive it must be made possible through political action. By going to Sweden I've seen glimpses of Romanestan in the forests now empty of travellers. By coming home, I hope I can bring a little bit of it back to a country so in need of its promise.

F

If Sweden can be criticised for anything it is that life is too easy. It's so good it's unreal. I've even had free cooked breakfast delivered to my caravan door. The Swedes are a rich nation but many cannot comprehend how anybody would choose to live such a basic life.

B   **Discuss these questions:**

- How much do you sympathise with the writer of the article?
- What kind of discrimination is there in your country against women (sexism), old people (agcism) and members of ethnic minorities (racism)?

3.7   Opposites   VOCABULARY DEVELOPMENT

A   **Complete these sentences with suitable words:**

1 He isn't naive, he's quite _sophisticated_
2 She isn't brave, she's ....
3 He wasn't sorry, he was ....
4 Instead of slowing down, he ....
5 She wasn't guilty, she was ....
6 They didn't help me, they ....

7 Instead of spending her money she ....
8 Instead of pulling the door open he ....
9 Instead of reassuring me she ....
10 He didn't get angry, he ....
11 *Bad* isn't an antonym of *awful*, it's a ....
12 Instead of slamming the door he ....

B 1 Decide which of these adjectives form their opposites with in– or un– :

_un_acceptable	_in_accessible	...advisable	...appropriate	...aware
...bearable	...clearly	...competent	...considerate	...consistent
...conspicuous	...conventional	...convincing	...decided	...decisive
...desirable	...dignified	...discreet	...distinct	...efficient
...eventful	...expected	...explicable	...faithful	...foreseen
...forgettable	...frequent	...grateful	...gratitude	...imaginative
...manageable	...predictable	...rewarding	...sincere	...sincerity
...sociable	...sophisticated	...stability	...stable	...sufficient
...tolerant	...trustworthy	...visible	...wanted	...welcome

2 Decide which of these words form their opposites with dis– or im–, il– or ir– :

_dis_advantage	_il_legal	...agreeable	...approve	...arm
...connect	...contented	...entangle	...legible	...legitimate
...logical	...loyal	...mature	...organised	...patient
...personal	...possible	...rational	...regular	...relevant
...respectful	...responsible	...satisfied	...similar	

3 Here are some slightly trickier ones. Think of a suitable opposite for these adjectives:

thoughtless _considerate/thoughtful_		clumsy	fearless ....
neat	noisy	proud	rare ....
restless	tactful	talkative	trivial ....

C The adjectives on the left are used pejoratively to describe someone's disposition or behaviour. Choose suitable opposites from among the words on the right.

pejorative	complimentary

pejorative

bad-tempered *good-natured*
conceited   deceitful   fussy   lazy
malicious   mean   narrow-minded
neurotic   pretentious   secretive
solitary   sullen   touchy

complimentary

cheerful   easy-going   frank   generous
good-natured   gregarious   hard-working
imaginative   kindhearted   laid back   liberal
modest   nonchalant   open   perceptive
sociable   talkative   trustworthy   truthful
unassuming

3.8 | **Not waving . . .**   R E A D I N G

A Listen to these poems read aloud. Then answer the questions below.

Not Waving but Drowning

NOBODY heard him, the dead man,
But still he lay moaning:
I was much further out than you thought
And not waving but drowning.
Poor chap, he always loved larking   5
And now he's dead
It must have been too cold for him his heart
   gave way,
They said.
Oh, no no no, it was too cold always   10
(Still the dead one lay moaning)
I was much too far out all my life
And not waving but drowning.

Stevie Smith

Bloody Men

Bloody men are like bloody buses –
You wait for about a year
And as soon as one approaches your stop
Two or three others appear.
You look at them flashing their indicators,   5
Offering you a ride.
You're trying to read the destinations,
You haven't much time to decide.
If you make a mistake, there is no turning back.
Jump off, and you'll stand there and gaze   10
While the cars and the taxis and lorries go by
And the minutes, the hours, the days.

Wendy Cope

---

1 How did the man die?
2 Which are the words spoken by the *dead man*?
3 Which words are spoken by his friends?
4 What does *larking* mean in line 5?
5 What was *too cold* in line 7? What was *too cold* in line 10?
6 In what ways was he *too far out* in line 12 and *drowning* in line 13?
7 In what ways was he *not waving* in line 12?
8 What ADJECTIVES could you use to describe the drowning man and his friends?

1 What does the poet think of men?
2 In what ways do the men she meets *flash their indicators*?
3 Why doesn't she have *much time to decide*?
4 Why is there *no turning back*?
5 What will happen if she decides to break up with a man?
6 What are *the cars and the taxis and lorries*?
7 Which words in the poem rhyme? What is the effect of this?
8 What ADJECTIVES could you use to describe the poet and the men she meets?

B **Discuss these questions:**

- What did you think of the two poems?
- Which one impressed you, or moved you, or amused you more? Why?
- What are the similarities between the two poems?
- What is the effect of expressing the ideas
  In verse,
  Rather than in prose, without
  Any line breaks?
- Are you fond of poetry – or does it leave you cold? Give your reasons.

It takes all sorts ... SPEAKING AND COMPOSITION **3**

EVERYONE'S DIFFERENT!

A **1** Note down FIVE adjectives or phrases to describe each of these people. Try to avoid the most obvious or simple words, like *nice*, *young*, *kind*, etc. Use a dictionary if necessary.

2 Follow these guidelines to describe the people in the photos:

- First impression of the person
- Appearance: clothes, age, face, hair
- Their character and the way they might behave

B A friend of yours is going to visit two people you know well*, who are quite different from each other. Your friend is nervous about meeting them for the first time. Write a letter to reassure your friend, describing the two people (300–350 words).

(* They could be two friends or relatives, for example, or someone you admire and someone you detest.)

1 First of all, make notes on the following points:

Appearance: age, clothes, complexion, eyes, face, hair
Personality and character
Family background
Past achievements
Job
Interests and hobbies
Why you like or dislike him/her
Examples of typical behaviour

2 Rearrange the notes in a suitable order. Decide which points should be left out because they are less interesting or less relevant.

3 Discuss your notes with a partner.

4 Refer back to the 'Golden rules' in 1.8. Make any necessary amendments to your notes and then write your descriptions.

5 Show your completed descriptions to a partner, and ask for comments.

4

Let's talk

4.1   Different ways of communicating   TOPIC VOCABULARY

A 1 How would you describe these people's expressions? Imagine they're about to talk to you. What are they going to say – and how will you reply?

2 → Compare your ideas.

B 1 In these sentences only THREE of the alternatives can be used to complete each sentence correctly:

1 She's going to .... about gestures and body language.
   give a lecture ✓   say ✗   speak ✓   talk ✓   tell ✗

2 If you keep on .... I won't be able to understand what you're saying.
   grumbling   mumbling   muttering   nagging   whispering

3 During a lecture I try to .... down the main points that are made.
   doodle   jot   note   scribble   sketch

4 I'm afraid I've only had time to .... the articles you recommended.
   glance at   interpret   scan   skim   study

5 When he told me about his misadventures I couldn't help ....
   chuckling   grinning   shrugging   sniggering   stammering

6 He looked at me with a .... on his face when I told him what I had done.
   frown   gasp   gulp   scowl   sneer

7 On seeing the body hanging from the apple tree she started to ....
   murmur   scream   shriek   squeak   yell

8 She went on to .... that I wasn't working hard enough.
   implicate   imply   infer   intimate   suggest

9 She used a(n) .... which I couldn't quite follow.
   clause   expression   idiom   phrase   speech

10 And her .... made me feel guilty even though I'd done nothing wrong.
   attitude   dialect   expression   idiom   tone

2 Look again at the alternatives that were wrong. Why are they wrong?

A **1** Note down some reasons why you might be tempted to buy this product. Then compare your notes with a partner.

2 You'll hear a broadcast about *The Interpreter*, another electronic translator. Tick the boxes in 1 and fill the gaps in 2–5.

1 Which of these situations are mentioned in the report?
at the airport ☐   at the chemist's ☐   at the railway station ☐   at the bank ☐
business ☐   camping ☐   complaining ☐   emergencies ☐   in the post office ☐
making friends ☐   motoring ☐   restaurants ☐   shopping ☐   sightseeing ☐

2 Which languages does *The Interpreter* speak? ....

3 What 'useful phrase' does *The Interpreter* suggest you might you use if . . .
. . . you want to know the admission charge to a museum or gallery? ....
. . . a building is on fire? ....
. . . you're trying to get a discount? ....
. . . the service in a restaurant is slow? ....

4 What useful phrase is missing from *The Interpreter*'s repertoire? ....

5 You can use *The Interpreter* in privacy, thanks to its ....

6 Its words also appear on the .... as it speaks.

B Discuss these questions:

• Which of the products would you like to have? When would you use it?
• Have you ever used a phrasebook when visiting a foreign country? What was your experience?
• Do you always assume people in another country will speak English or do you make an effort to learn some of the language before going there?
• What are the FIVE most useful phrases you'd try to learn if you were visiting another country for the very first time?
• Which do you use more often: an English-to-English dictionary or a bilingual one? Give your reasons.

C **1** Student A should look at Activity 14 on page 202, student B at 24 on page 205 and C at 31 on page 207. Each Activity contains definitions of some of these words. Together you should pool your information and discuss which dictionary seems most helpful and clear.

irony · sarcasm   collocation · cliché · platitude · proverb   slogan · jargon   accent · dialect

You should NOT read your entries out loud – that would take a very long time – but you may wish to read out BRIEF quotations.

2 Now compare the dictionary entries in all three Activities. Suppose you didn't know any of the words above: which of the entries would be most helpful?

4.3 Attitudes to language READING AND SUMMARY WRITING

A Ask your partner these questions:

- Where can you hear the 'best English' spoken?
- Where can you hear the 'best accent' of your own language spoken?

B Read this text and choose the best word or phrase to fill each gap in the text:

A language is a system of communication used within a particular social group. Inevitably, the emotions created by group loyalty get in the way of _____ [1] judgements about language. When we think we are making such a judgement, we are often merely making a statement about our prejudices. It is highly instructive to examine these occasionally. I myself have very _____ [2] prejudices about what I call Americanisms. I see red whenever I read a certain popular woman columnist in a certain popular daily paper. I wait with a kind of fascinated horror for her to use the locution 'I guess', as in 'I guess he really loves you after all' or 'I guess you'd better get yourself a new boyfriend'. I see in this form the essence of Americanism, a _____ [3] to the British Way of Life. But this is obviously nonsense, and I know it. I know that 'I guess' is at least as old as Chaucer, pure British English, something sent over in the *Mayflower*. But, like most of us, I do not really like submitting to reason; I much prefer blind prejudice. And so I stoutly _____ [4] 'I guess' as an American importation and its use by a British writer as a betrayal of the traditions of my national group.

Such condemnation can seem virtuous, because patriotism – which means _____ [5] to the national group – is a noble word. While virtue burns in the mind, adrenaline courses round the body and makes us feel good. Reason never has this exhilarating chemical effect. And so patriotic euphoria _____ [6] our contempt of foreign languages and makes us unwilling to learn them properly. Chinese is still regarded in the West as a huge joke – despite what T.S. Eliot calls its 'great intellectual dignity' – and radio comedians can even raise a snigger by speaking mock-Chinese. Russian is, of course, nothing more than a deep vodka-rich rumble bristling with 'vitch' and 'ski'. As for German – that is an ugly language, aggressively guttural. We rarely _____ [7] that it seems ugly because of two painful wars, that it is all a matter of association. Sometimes our automatic sneers at foreign languages are mitigated by _____ [8] memories – warm holidays abroad, trips to the opera. Italian can then seem beautiful, full of blue skies, vino, sexy tenors. Trippers to Paris, on the other hand, furtively visiting the *Folies Bergère*, project their own guilt on to the French language and see it as 'naughty', even 'immoral'.

1 A subjective	**B** objectionable	**C** objective	**D** prejudiced
2 A powerful	**B** extraordinary	**C** muscular	**D** educated
3 A criticism	**B** warning	**C** blame	**D** threat
4 A criticise	**B** condemn	**C** welcome	**D** treasure
5 A loyalty	**B** antipathy	**C** sympathy	**D** honesty
6 A explains	**B** matches	**C** ignores	**D** justifies
7 A reveal	**B** discover	**C** admit	**D** suggest
8 A nice	**B** pleasant	**C** amusing	**D** worthwhile

C Now read the continuation of the text and choose the best answer to the questions that follow:

Within the national group, our prejudices tend to be very mixed and, because they operate mainly on an unconscious level, not easily recognisable. We can be natives of great cities and still find a town dialect less pleasant than a country one. And yet, hearing prettiness and quaintness in a Dorset or Devon twang, we can also despise it, because we associate it with rural stupidity or backwardness. The ugly tones of Manchester or Birmingham will, because of their great civic associations, be at the same time somehow admirable. The whole business of ugliness and beauty works strangely. A BBC announcer says 'pay day'; a Cockney says 'pie die'. The former is thought to be beautiful, the latter ugly, and yet the announcer can use the Cockney sounds in a statement like 'Eat that pie and you will die' without anybody's face turning sour. In fact, terms like 'ugly' and 'beautiful' cannot really apply to languages at all. Poets can make beautiful patterns out of words, but there are no standards we can use to formulate aesthetic judgements on the words themselves. We all have our pet hates and loves among words, but these always have to be referred to associations. A person who dislikes beetroot as a vegetable is not likely to love 'beetroot' as a word. A poet who, in childhood, had a panful of hot stewed prunes spilled on him is, if he is a rather stupid poet, quite capable of writing 'And death, terrible as prunes'. We have to watch associations carefully, remembering that language is a public, not a private, medium, and that questions of word-hatred and word-love had best be tackled very coldly and rationally.

We are normally quick to observe regional variations in the use of the national language, but we feel less strongly about these than we do about class divisions in speech. If we speak with a Lancashire accent, we will often be good-humoured and only slightly derisive when we hear the accent of Wolverhampton or Tyneside. Sometimes we will even express a strong admiration of alien forms of English – the speech of the Scottish Highlands, for instance, or Canadian as opposed to American. But we feel very differently about English speech when it seems to be a badge or banner of class. The dialect known variously as the Queen's English or BBC English or Standard English was, originally, a pure regional form – so-called East Midland English, with no claim to any special intrinsic merit. But it was spoken in an area that was, and still is, socially and economically pre-eminent – the area which contains London, Oxford, and Cambridge. Thus it gained a special glamour as the language of the Court and the language of learning. It has ever since – often falsely – been associated with wealth, position, and education – the supra-regional dialect of the masters, while the regional dialects remain the property of the men. In certain industrial areas it can still excite resentment, despite the fact that it no longer necessarily goes along with power or privilege.

from *Language Made Plain* by Anthony Burgess

1 According to the writer, a rural accent may sound attractive, but it may also be . . .
  A admired   **C** funny
  B looked down on   **D** hard to understand

2 Our judgements on words we like or dislike are often based on a word's . . .
  A sound   **C** associations
  B origins   **D** beauty or ugliness

3 British accents show which region the person comes from, but may also show their . . .
  A education   **C** gender
  B age   **D** social class

4 A person with a regional accent may have less power than someone who . . .
  A has been well-educated   **C** uses Standard English
  B has no accent   **D** lives in London

5 If someone speaks with a Standard English accent (R.P.) they . . .
  A will be admired by everyone   **C** show that they are well-educated
  B show that they have power   **D** may be disliked in some regions

D   **Highlight** these words in the text and match them with the words with similar meanings below:

¶1 *objective   prejudice   instructive*   ¶3 *associations   formulate   aesthetic   pet*
¶2 *exhilarating   euphoria   mitigated*   ¶4 *derisive   badge   intrinsic   the men   excite*

arouse   artistic   bias   connotations   contemptuous   devise   emblem   favourite
happiness   impartial   inherent   moderated   revealing   workers   stimulating

E   **Discuss your reactions to the text. Do people in your country share similar prejudices about foreign languages and regional accents?**

F   **Write a summary of the British attitudes to regional accents and dialects described by the writer (50–70 words).**

4.4   **-ing and to . . .**   **GRAMMAR REVISION**

A   **Discuss the difference in meaning between these sentences. Then decide how each one might continue, as in the examples.**

1 **a** They went on running *even though they were tired.*   **b** They went on to run *five more miles.*
2 **a** We stopped to take photos but ....   **b** We stopped taking photos but ....
3 **a** Did you remember to send the fax or .... ?   **b** Do you remember sending the fax or .... ?
4 **a** I can't help you to feel better but ....   **b** I can't help feeling better, but ....
5 **a** I'm not used to using a fountain pen but ....   **b** I used to use a fountain pen but ....
6 **a** She heard him scream, but ....   **b** She heard him screaming, but ....

B **1** **Match up the verbs and phrases below to make suitable collocations.**

to answer ———————— to a letter
to call ————— a letter / the phone
to contact   someone a letter
to drop   someone a line
to get   someone on the phone
to give   someone by phone / by post
to keep   someone a ring
to reply   someone a story
to tell   through to someone on the phone
to write   in touch with someone

2 **Now use the collocations in B1 to complete each of these sentences. Add a suitable PREPOSITION if necessary. In some cases more than one version is possible.**

1 I'm sorry _not to have kept_ in touch with you. OR _for not having kept_ OR _that I didn't keep_.
2 Is there any point .... by post?
3 I regret .... her my secret. She couldn't help .... all her friends.
4 I forgot .... a birthday card.
5 Have you heard her .... about the penguin and the polar bear?
6 I strongly advise you .... his letter by return of post.
7 He never writes letters because he's so used .... on the phone.
8 Her number was engaged all day but I finally succeeded .... in the evening.
9 It may be worth .... a ring if you ever need any advice.
10 I tried .... on Sunday but there was no answer.
11 And I didn't want .... on your answering machine.
12 I'm not looking forward .... all these letters.

C **Complete each sentence with your own ideas, using -ing or to. . . :**

Remember that *to*... is also used to express intentions or plans:

He did it to help her. I phoned to warn him.

1 To get from the airport to the city centre I don't recommend ....
2 I've never been to America but I hope ....
3 After a heavy meal I can't face ....
4 The night before an important exam it's unwise to risk ....
5 After struggling to follow the first paragraph I gave up ....
6 Some people enjoy .... to Beethoven but I prefer ....
7 The first chapter was so exciting that I kept on ....
8 There was a violent thunderstorm but we carried on ....
9 After a hard day .... at the office I feel like ....
10 If I hear a baby .... I can't bear ....
11 After an enjoyable English class I don't mind ....
12 After .... ill for five days, on the sixth day I began ....
13 She probably wasn't at home when you called earlier. Why not try .... ?
14 I'd love .... a new car, but I can't afford ....
15 Someone started shouting at me but I pretended ....

4.5 **Paragraphs**   **WRITING SKILLS**

A   **There are no hard-and-fast rules for paragraphs, but here are some guidelines. Highlight the points you want to remember.**

> **PARAGRAPHS**
>
> ¶   A new paragraph signifies a new theme, or a change of direction.
> ¶   Paragraphs help the reader to follow your thought processes.
> ¶   Short paragraphs are easier to read than long ones.
> ¶   When there is dialogue, each speaker usually requires a new paragraph.
> ¶   A new paragraph gives prominence to the first sentence, setting the tone for the rest of the paragraph.
> ¶   A strong opening sentence for each paragraph keeps the reader's attention.
> ¶   The last sentence of a paragraph also has prominence and may be the pay-off line.

B 👥 **Before you read the article below, discuss these questions:**

- Do you have a mobile phone? Where do you use it? How much do you use it?
- How aware do mobile phone-users seem to be of other people around them? Have you had any amusing or annoying experiences whilst eavesdropping on them?

C **1** **Read the beginning of this article and look at the analysis of the paragraphs below.**

Why mobiles can be murder on the 8.05

THE MAN in the half-moon glasses was worried. Receivership was looming in a couple of weeks and the main shareholders didn't seem to realise the urgency.   1

'I've got three buyers lined up,' he announced, and proceeded to reel off their names.   2

Nothing particularly unusual about this conversation, you might think; except that it was taking place on a train. The other passengers may not have been very interested in the fate of a small geographical publishing company, but they didn't have much choice; the speaker – whose name we soon learnt – was oblivious to his surroundings as he candidly discussed the most sensitive details for more than an hour on his mobile phone.   3

Once upon a time, mobile phones didn't exist. Then they were used sparingly by those on trains to relay the banal message: 'I've just got on the train, darling.'   4

Nowadays, an increasing number of commuters and business travellers seem to have decided that they can carry out their duties just as successfully from a railway carriage as they can from their office. Appointments are made, files are summoned from secretaries, and political knives are inserted in backs – all from the comfort of an Inter-City window seat.   5

I once spent an hour and a half on a late-night train with one such person. The man spent the entire journey reading the names and salaries of construction workers in the Middle East into his mobile.   6

¶1 First sentence plunges the reader into the story
¶2 Still the same event as first paragraph, but direct speech
¶3 Now the writer starts to give his opinion
¶4 Change to another time
¶5 More precise description — new paragraph gives prominence to first sentence
¶6 New paragraph gives prominence to another personal experience

2 **Read the next part of the article and note the reasons** WHY **the writer chose to start and end each paragraph at the place he does.**

On another occasion, the morning rush hour journey was punctuated by a pushy woman apparently making follow-up sales calls about 'an exciting concept called the One-Stop Shop'.   7

In the usually quiet atmosphere of a railway carriage, it is difficult for the most uninterested fellow passenger to ignore such conversations, the more so if he is trying to concentrate on his own newspaper or work.   8

The problem has already prompted one railway company to introduce phone-free zones on its trains. Great Western Trains, which provides services to south Wales, the Cotswolds and the South-West, decided to ban mobile phones in some of its carriages after receiving a barrage of complaints.   9

Spokeswoman Louise Wilimot says: 'We did a three-month trial and it proved very popular. First-class passengers then asked for the same.' Great Western does not discourage passengers from working – far from it – but says that most regard a peaceful atmosphere as a prerequisite. The company also discourages passengers from holding loud meetings.   10

Other railway companies are reluctant to take steps against those who treat the carriage as their personal office space, preferring to rely upon ostracism by fellow passengers.   11

South West Trains, on one of whose trains the receivership conversation quoted took place, says the commuter-dominated nature of its business would make it difficult to introduce mobile-free zones.   12

South West's Alison Flynn says: 'We expect passengers to consider the feelings of other passengers.'   13

For those who work on the move, there is clearly a risk of breaching confidentiality. Boris Starling, of security consultancy Control Risks, spells it out: 'If you are going to sit and talk on the train, you have no idea who else is listening. They might even be journalists.   14

'Our advice is to be sensible, and simply not discuss company business on the train, particularly if it is confidential.' He points out that the risk of being overheard on a train, as opposed to another public place, such as a restaurant, is particularly acute: trains tend to be quieter.   15

ALEXANDER GARRETT

D This is the end of the same article, printed without paragraphs. Decide where to begin each new paragraph.

Mike Platt, commercial director of the business travel agency Hogg Robinson BTI, says: 'Our research among clients shows that they are increasingly using the train as an extension of the office, but they have two main concerns: one is the lack of privacy; the other is the poor signal they often get on their phone on the train.' Platt says he regards the ability to work for three hours as the second key advantage Eurostar has over the plane – the first being the ability to travel directly between city centres. Many companies take the opportunity to hold formal business meetings on Eurostar, calculating that if they book facing seats over a table, they can get away without their conversation being heard. But he adds: 'People are split down the middle about mobile phones. Half want to use them, and the other half regard them as noise pollution and say that they can't do their own work if they are next to somebody who is barking down the phone.' Last week saw the publication of yet another survey demonstrating that the British work longer hours than their European compatriots. Many of us clearly regard a train journey as an opportunity to do more work, rather than to relax and enjoy the journey. Maybe it is time we all let the train take the strain.

A 350-word composition should contain at least four paragraphs, probably more. When planning a composition, decide where each new paragraph will begin. Note down a strong opening sentence for each paragraph before you start writing.

4.6 *Wh–* clauses

ADVANCED GRAMMAR

A **1** **What you should do is (to) study these examples before doing the exercises.**

What annoys me is intolerance.	Intolerance is what annoys me.
What I need is a friend to lend a helping hand.	All I need is a friend to lend a helping hand.
Whatever she does seems to be successful.	Wherever she goes she makes friends easily.
Whoever she meets, they take a liking to her.	

It doesn't really matter whether he gets here in time or not.

Whether or not he gets here in time doesn't really matter.

2 👥 **Use your own ideas to complete each sentence.**

1 What I hate is *people being rude to me.*
2 One thing I like is ....
3 All I want is ....
4 What I feel like doing ....
5 What we need now ....
6 There's nothing I enjoy more than ....
7 I just don't want ....
8 Something that often surprises me is ....
9 What I want to do right now is ....

3 👥 **Exchange sentences with another pair. Rewrite their sentences using DIFFERENT structures:** *I hate it when people are rude to me.*

B **Match the sentences that mean the same as each other:**

1 Whatever you do, don't tell everyone.   ⌐Tell anyone anything you like.
   Make sure you don't tell everyone.   ⌐Tell anyone whatever you want.
2 Say what you like.   Speak to whoever you want.
   Talk to anyone you want to.   Say whatever you want to.
3 Whoever did you give it to?   Who in the world did you give it to?
   To whom did you give it?   Who did you give it to?
4 Why ever don't you phone him?   Why do you never phone him?
   Why don't you ever phone him?   Why on earth don't you phone him?
5 Whenever I mention it he takes offence.   When I mention it he loses his temper.
   He reacts badly every time I mention it. Each time I mention it he gets angry.

C **Rewrite these sentences without changing the meaning:**

1 He takes a phrasebook with him everywhere. Wherever ....
2 It doesn't matter when you arrive. You can ....
3 I only stuck out my tongue at her. All ....
4 You did something that was very rude. What ....
5 She just needs someone to tell her troubles to. All ....
6 You can put it anywhere you like. I don't mind ....
7 You can write or phone – as you like. Whether ....
8 I don't know what time you'll arrive, but get in touch. Whenever ....
9 He made a very impressive speech. What ....
10 I was astonished by her confidence. What ....

4.7 / The English-speaking world

SPEAKING, LISTENING AND COMPOSITION

A 👤👤👤👤 **Look at this diagram, which shows some of the differences between various national accents of English. Add two more examples to the key below.**

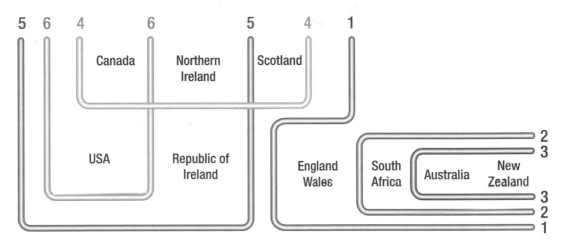

(adapted from *International English* by Peter Trudgill and Jean Hannah)

KEY

1 /r/ is pronounced at the end of *sure   mirror   far*
2 /e/ instead of /æ/ in *than   thanks   hand   cat*
3 front /aː/ instead of /ɑː/ in *part   farm   car   start*
4 no contrast between /ɒ/ in *cot   knotty   stock* and /ɔː/ in *caught   naughty   stalk*
5 /r/ is pronounced in words like *firm   bird   word*
6 no contrast between /ɒ/ in *bother* or *doctor* and /ɑː/ in *father* or *past*
+ /d/ instead of /t/ in *butter   better   hotter   shutter*
+ /æ/ instead of /ɑː/ in *can't   dance   half   banana   fast*

TWO MORE EXAMPLES

....
....
....

....
....

....
....
....

B 🔊 **You'll hear an American, a Welsh woman and an Australian discussing accents. Decide which person said what by writing USA, W or AUS in the answer boxes.**

1 There are two main accents in my country. **1** [ ]
2 A regional accent is not a badge of social class. **2** [ ]
3 People in different parts of my country find each other's accents funny. **3** [ ]
4 Some accents in my country are more pleasant to listen to than others. **4** [ ]
5 Immigration is adding to the variety of accents. **5** [ ]
6 When I was at school some children were encouraged to lose their accents. **6** [ ]
7 We used to laugh at people who spoke with an English RP accent. **7** [ ]
8 When I was at school using incorrect grammar was discouraged. **8** [ ]

C **1** 👥 **Discuss these questions about your own language. (Some of the questions may be more interesting and provocative than others. Don't discuss the questions that seem irrelevant.)**

> **1** How many people speak your language? Which countries do they live in?
>
> **2** How many different languages are spoken in your country? Is there a single 'official language'?
>
> **3** What language (and which dialect or variety) is used in schools? Do children speak the same language or dialect at home and at school?
>
> **4** Do you use a different dialect or variety of your language when talking with friends or family from the one you use with strangers or people from other parts of the country? What situations are the different varieties used in? What are some of the differences in vocabulary and grammar? Can you give any interesting examples?
>
> **5** What are the main regional accents and dialects that most people in your country can recognise? Do people in the capital regard the speakers of any of these as 'funny' or 'uneducated' or vice versa?
>
> **6** Do the people in the regions with different languages or dialects have less power than the people in the capital? Do they have TV and radio programmes in their own language or dialect?
>
> **7** Do middle-class people and working-class people talk differently? Are there any regional accents which are considered to be less 'educated' or less socially acceptable than others? What is claimed to be the 'best accent' in your language?

A report is usually for a particular audience, such as your boss or for colleagues.
A report presents information and interprets it. Reports usually have section headings.

Are there any other points not covered by the questions above that you think would help to give a clearer picture about your country and language?

2 Make notes on your answers to the questions which are most relevant to your language and the questions which are thought-provoking.

3 Rearrange the notes you've made (perhaps using arrows, lines or different colours) to make the sequence of ideas and information as coherent as possible, in preparation for writing a report for foreign visitors to your country (300–350 words):

Write a short report about the different languages, dialects and accents in your country.

4 Decide which points each paragraph of your report will contain. Write down the FIRST SENTENCE of each paragraph. Compare your sentences with a partner's.

5 ✒ Write your report. Include a sketch map or diagram if you wish.

4.8 Forming adjectives VOCABULARY DEVELOPMENT

A **Form adjectives from these VERBS and add them to the appropriate list below. Be very careful about the spelling of the adjectives you form from the verbs in red.**

accept   admire   advise   astonish   break   communicate   convince   cooperate
deceive   describe   distress   disturb   forgive   inform   inspire   instruct   obtain
overwhelm   possess   predict   prevent   produce   promise   recommend   upset

-able   *negotiable   readable   desirable*

-ing   *moving   daring   tempting   satisfying*

-ive   *repetitive   acquisitive   appreciative   decorative*

B **Form adjectives from these NOUNS and add them to the appropriate list.**

adventure   ambition   convention   curly hair   diplomat   education   enigma
experience   fiction   fortnight   function   religion   idealist   intention   long legs
magnet   malice   materialist   music   optimist   pale skin   person   pessimist
profession   proportion   quarter   realist   romance   season   secretary   sensation
space   week   year

-al   *influential   orchestral   financial   practical*

-ic   *poetic   dramatic   emphatic   systematic*

-ous   *cautious   poisonous   glamorous*

-ly   *daily   neighbourly*

-ed   *talented   red-faced*

C Fill the gaps in these sentences with suitable words from the list below:

1 Don't pick those mushrooms – they might be ....
2 She was .... when she was picked for the team.
3 This camera has .... exposure and focusing.
4 People who talk about the 'good old days' have an .... view of the past.
5 He always dresses in a .... way.
6 Small cars are more .... than powerful ones.
7 He was .... when his wife left him.
8 I'm afraid his work is only ....
9 Your signature is barely ....
10 Don't be so .... , someone has to lose – it's only a game!

astonishing • astonished   automatic • automated   childish • childlike
economical • economic   heartbreaking • heartbroken   idealistic • idealised
legible • readable   poisoned • poisonous   satisfactory • satisfying   stylish • stylistic

make and *do*   VERBS AND IDIOMS

A Which of the following would you MAKE and which would you DO?

an agreement with someone   an appointment with someone   an arrangement   your best
business with someone   certain about something   a comment about something   your duty
an excuse   a good impression   someone a favour   friends with someone   harm to someone
a lot of money   love   a mistake   a profit or a loss   progress   a reservation
sure about something   a good turn   the washing-up   wrong or right   your own thing

B Find synonyms for the phrases in red, or explain their meaning. Use a dictionary if necessary.

1 Someone was coming down the hill, but I couldn't make out who it was.
2 Adrift alone in the ocean, they knew that they were done for.
3 I don't see what this has to do with you!
4 It was a three-seater sofa, but they refused to make room for me.
5 None of it is true – I made it all up!
6 I'm sorry you had to do all the work for me, I'll make it up to you, I promise.
7 They were finding it increasingly difficult to make both ends meet.
8 How can I ever make amends for what I've done?
9 It's not very important really, you're making a mountain out of a molehill.
10 Shh, don't make a scene – we can talk about it when we get home.
11 It's a shame we were held up, but now we can make up for lost time.
12 It's a terrible portrait, it really doesn't do justice to him.

C Fill the gaps in these sentences with suitable phrases from the list below. You may need to change the form of the verbs.

1 I left my bike outside the shop and someone has .... it!
2 You've .... this room .... since my last visit. What pretty wallpaper!
3 We went out for a meal together to .... our disappointment.
4 If you're not coming back for lunch I'll .... some sandwiches for you.
5 We collected £48 for her leaving present, so I .... it .... to a round £50.
6 Your shoes need .... , otherwise you'll trip over the laces.
7 Do you agree that all examinations should be .... ?
8 You're heading in the wrong direction if you're .... the station.
9 If too many new staff are taken on, some of us older ones will be .... our jobs.
10 He threw everything on the floor, and then .... without another word.

do away with   do out of   do up
do up   make up   make for   make off
make off with   make up   make up for

"Funny how you soon forget his regional accent."

5

Bon appetit!

5.1 **To whet your appetite . . .**   TOPIC VOCABULARY

A **1**   Think of the area you live in, or the place you're studying in. Decide what is the best place locally to get the following things, and give your reasons:

fresh fruit   bread and cakes   a sandwich   a quick snack   a good, inexpensive meal
a typical local meal

2 Find out your partners' reactions to these photos:

B **1**   Write down THREE examples of each of these types of food. Try to think of some UNUSUAL examples, not the most obvious ones. Use a dictionary if necessary.

Appetisers (starters) *avocado paté*	Spices
Fish and shellfish	Dairy products
Poultry	Nuts
Game	Desserts
Herbs	Cakes and pastries

2   →   Compare your lists and then discuss these questions:

- Which are your favourite foods in each category above?
- Imagine it's your birthday – write a menu, including all your favourite foods.
- What are specialities of your region or country? What are the ingredients required and how are they made?
- How important is food in your life? Do you 'live to eat' or 'eat to live'?
- Why is the title of this unit in French?

A Read the article and decide which word (A–D) best fits each gap.

Feel free to protest

HOBSON'S CHOICE has taken on an added meaning at Berni Restaurants, the chain of more than 230 steak houses owned by Grand Metropolitan.

Nowadays if you don't like what is provided in your meal you don't pay. And that covers the service too.

Slow waitresses, soup-spilling waitresses, surly waitresses, and "please make up your mind" waitresses are out.

Under what Berni calls a customer service guarantee, diners who complain about either the meal or the service have their bill _____ ¹ up. One of the intentions is to get round the traditional British habit of not complaining, but not going back either.

A poll conducted by Berni found that 60% of dissatisfied customers said they wouldn't go back to an offending restaurant. To _____ ² down this reserve, the scheme was initiated by a group of Berni managers and tried out in the north of England, where results were sufficiently encouraging to _____ ³ the scheme to the rest of Britain.

Armed with this knowledge and thinking that it didn't seem too difficult to get a free meal, I descended on the Berni Inn at Wimbledon, where my waitress was Martha, who failed to provide me with any _____ ⁴ to use the repertoire of "Waiter, there's a fly in my soup" jokes I had rehearsed beforehand. The food proved a match for the service. Simon Smith, the manager, told me he had been pleasantly pleased at a lack of unscrupulous diners trying to take advantage of the scheme. Complaints had generally been _____ ⁵ .

In fact some people who did complain had to be _____ ⁶ to leave the bill to him. Many had not even realised the scheme was operating.

"We're finding that those who complained and had their bill torn up are returning and bringing others with them. In the first five weeks we lost £1,000 in unpaid bills, but we're getting a lot of favourable _____ ⁷ by word of mouth.

"I am sure we'll keep more customers longer this way."

James Allen

1 A broken   B brought   C thrown   D torn
2 A break   B destroy   C diminish   D reduce
3 A change   B replace   C spread   D transfer
4 A food   B opportunity C possibility D scope
5 A correct   B exaggerated C excessive   D justified
6 A forced   B ordered   C persuaded   D requested
7 A advertising B propaganda   C publicity   D publishing

B Discuss these questions:

- Could the Berni scheme operate in restaurants in your country?
- Have you ever complained (or been with someone who complained) in a restaurant? What happened?
- What other situations have you actually been in where you made a complaint?
- What are the qualities of a good restaurant? Describe a good restaurant you have been to and a bad restaurant you remember going to.

C 1 🔊 Listen to some 'Waiter, waiter!' jokes.

2 👥 Role-play a conversation between a dissatisfied customer and a courteous waiter or waitress.

"Waiter…there are no flies in my soup!"

5.3 Running a restaurant

A 👥👥👥👥 **Discuss these questions:**

- What do you think are the pros and cons of running a restaurant? Would you like to run a restaurant? Give your reasons.
- If you were going to open a restaurant or café near where you live, what kind of food would you serve? What kind of atmosphere would you try to create?
- From a restaurateur's point of view, what are the attributes of an ideal customer?
- From a customer's point of view, what are the qualities of a good restaurant?

B **Seven paragraphs have been removed from this article. Choose the most suitable paragraph from the list A–G for each gap (1–7) in the article.**

The British are coming

"A stone's throw from the Palais des Festivals," says the Michelin Guide. "Pleasant dining room, partly vaulted, recently redecorated: pearl-grey walls, plum furniture and careful lighting. Specialities: foie gras in a potato ribbon; fillet of bass in mussel soup; passion fruit sorbet."

But the bit that matters lies just to the left of that sober piece of text: a single, discreet rosette. It was awarded, last week, to a new Cannes restaurant called Neat, named after its chef, Richard. He has just become the first British restaurateur since the Second World War to win a Michelin star in France.

1 ▢

"I suppose it would have been sensible to be a little apprehensive," he says. "But to be honest, I didn't even think about it. I'm surrounded by professionals, and provided you're honest, provided you serve up a quality product for a reasonable price, you'll do well. That's always been my philosophy, and it's the same here."

2 ▢

"In a way, I'm a pure product of France," he says frankly, drawing on a post-lunch cigarette. "I've been working in France or with French people for the past 18 years. It wouldn't be honest or sensible of me to be aggressively British about anything – and I'm hardly about to bite the hand that feeds me."

Nonetheless, his rapid promotion to one-star status in France, an honour for which many French chefs spend years slaving over hot vol-au-vents, has raised eyebrows. The local press has had a field day, and even national television has made the trip down to the chic Mediterranean resort town where Neat, 33, settled with his French wife Sophie in September.

Cannes was, he says, a very deliberate choice for his new venture. It was a challenge he set himself after giving up Pied à Terre, getting married and taking off on a two-year extended honeymoon to India (during which, Neat admits, he did very little except perfect his crawl in various hotel swimming pools and become a "really rather good" amateur chess player).

3 ▢

"Cannes has a longer season than anywhere else. There are film, TV and music festivals here, conferences and congresses from January to November. And there are 150,000 Brits living within 45 minutes' drive, plus another 50,000 every summer."

4 ▢

That being no way to run a restaurant, the Frenchman was "practically on his knees, begging us to buy it" seven months later; Neat was born, and at roughly half the price its owners would have had to pay for it half a year earlier. The restaurant, redecorated by Sophie, seats 45 in winter and will take 55 when the terrace is open in summer.

Finding the right staff was no problem, Neat says – though in the end they came from a somewhat unexpected source. The first hire was Mike, an old acquaintance from the Manoir, who was on holiday in Cannes and visiting a girlfriend at the Carlton Hotel nearby.

"He recognised the name and showed up two weeks after we opened," Neat says. "He came in for a coffee and about half an hour later was asking for a job. I told him working here was different to being on holiday, but he was back in a week with his knives. It was a fait accompli."

5

A battalion of Brits behind the saucepans didn't exactly go down a bundle with the local restaurateurs, however, particularly when the sought-after star came Neat's way. The reaction from the local trade was, he concedes, "underwhelming". But his customers – the congress business, a highly enthusiastic British community, and a small but growing band of Frenchmen – are delighted.

"Sophie tells me the French who come in here are a little bit sceptical at first," Neat says. "But they take the plunge, they see it's a professional operation, they like what they eat – and they come back."

6

There are many in Britain, and a growing number in France, who will dispute the value to a restaurant of a Michelin star. The venerable red guide, which this year celebrates its 100th anniversary, is accused of favouring the traditional over the inventive, and of placing as much emphasis on the fripperies as on the food. More than one chef in both countries has turned down a star.

But Neat, unashamedly, is not one of the doubters. "I've worked in gastronomic restaurants for 13 years now," he says. "I like working in them because you can charge enough to buy the best produce, to get top personnel, and to attract the best clientele – people who really enjoy their food, are knowledgeable about what they're doing."

7

So would he like a second star? "One, two, three, I don't know," he says. "I want to run a good restaurant, but I want a life too. Right now the most important thing is that I can do that right here – and wear shorts and sunglasses 10 months of the year."

John Henley

A "It's a fact that gastronomy is judged in certain ways. Now I didn't set the goalposts, but I know what they are, and Michelin is the most creditable organisation currently giving ratings to gastronomy. I want to run a restaurant I'm proud of, and Michelin is the measure."

B "This was a good place for a lot of reasons," he says. "Sophie studied at Nice just along the coast, and the south of France is her adopted home."

C A month later came Elliot, a friend of Mike's "who does the pastry". Then Warren, Neat's old sous-chef at Pied à Terre, pitched up, and finally Jimmy, who was a good friend of Warren's. It's the best way to recruit people, Neat says: everyone can vouch for everyone else.

D Neat's three-course lunchtime menu is priced at 220 francs, and the dinner equivalent is 270 francs: good value by Cannes' standards and a downright steal by London's. The dishes, with the exception of his trademark snails with mushrooms and garlic purée, are all new since the chef's Pied à Terre days.

E Nor, he points out diplomatically, can the quality product he is serving up be described as English in any meaningful sense of the word. Having served under such French gurus as Raymond Blanc at the Manoir aux Quat' Saisons and Joel Robuchon in Paris, and spent 14 months with "the great unwashed" Marco Pierre White to boot, he is definitely more cuisinier than cook.

F It took the couple and their business partner, Frenchman Bruno Asselin, some time to find the right venue, on the Place Mérimée about 30 yards from the Congress Centre. When they first arrived, the place had just been bought by a former French textiles executive who "rather fancied running a little bistro to keep himself from getting bored in his retirement," Neat says.

G Words like coals and Newcastle may spring forcefully to mind, but Neat – formerly of the ritzy two-star London eatery Pied à Terre – insists he is not out to prove any kind of nationalist point, even if five out of the six kitchen staff in his new venture are English and it only took him six months to pick up the honour.

C 👥 **Ask your partners these questions:**

In an average week . . .
- How often do you eat lunch out? How often do you eat dinner out?
- How many meals do you prepare or help to prepare?
- How many times do you lay the table and do the washing-up?
- How often do you go shopping for food items?
- How often do you eat as a family?
- How do your habits compare with those of a 'typical person' from your country?

5.4 **The passive – 1** GRAMMAR REVIEW

A 👥 Discuss the differences in emphasis (if any) between these sentences:

1 I'm afraid all the cakes have been eaten.
  I'm afraid I've eaten all the cakes.
2 Arsenal beat Chelsea in the final.
  Spurs were beaten in the semi-finals.
  Manchester United were beaten in the quarter-finals by Southampton.
3 He thinks people are plotting against him.
  He thinks he's being plotted against.
4 The dough was rolled out and then cut into teddybear shapes.
  We rolled out the dough and then we cut it into teddybear shapes.
5 There was nothing to do.
  There was nothing to be done.
6 My wallet has been stolen!
  That man stole my wallet!
  Someone has stolen my wallet!
  I've had my wallet stolen!

B 👥 **Highlight all the passive verbs and passive participles in *Feel free to protest* on page 55. Discuss why the passive, rather than the active, has been used in each case. If each example is rewritten using an active verb, what difference does this make to the tone, style or emphasis?**

C 👥 **Rewrite these sentences using the passive: the subject can be omitted where it seems irrelevant or misleading. Your rewritten sentences should be compared with a partner's.**

1 Someone told us that the bill would include service. *understand*
  We were given to understand that service would be included.
2 A friend told me that the college has awarded you a scholarship.
3 The crash badly damaged both cars but it didn't cause the injury of anyone.
4 After the lifeguard had rescued the bather, an ambulance took him to hospital.
5 After the surgeon had operated on him, she told him to stay in bed for a week.
6 People all over the world buy McDonald's hamburgers.
7 Everton held Liverpool to a draw.
8 Thousands of demonstrators may crowd into the square tonight.
9 We expected the plane to land at noon, but something has delayed it. *schedule*
10 The rain brought about the cancellation of the tennis match. *rain off*
11 They had masses of requests for free samples of the new product. *flood*
12 Someone has seen an escaped prisoner, whom the police believe to be dangerous.

5.5 **Adjectives and participles** VOCABULARY DEVELOPMENT

A 👥 Discuss the differences in meaning between these pairs of sentences:

1 She has a talking parrot.   Have you heard her parrot talking?
2 She is an old friend.   My friend is quite old.
3 All the people concerned were there.   All the concerned people were there.
4 It wasn't a proper meeting.   The meeting proper began at 9.
5 The members of staff present.   The present members of staff.
6 Is he the person responsible?   Is he a responsible person?
7 I have a friend living in London.   She has no living relatives.
8 He is a complete idiot.   The complete meal cost a mere £5.
9 She has an elder brother.   Her brother is elderly.
10 The film had a very involved plot.   The actors involved were unconvincing.

B Study these notes, and fill the gaps in the examples:

Position of adjectives (*tasty*) and participles used as adjectives (*tired* or *tiring*).

1 **Most** adjectives and participles are normally placed **before a noun** or **after a verb**:

appetising *delicious* *delicious-looking* *frightened* *good-looking* *happy* *home-made* *lonely* *refreshing* *similar* *sleeping* *tasty* etc.

He is a very good-looking man. He is very good-looking.
That was a really ..*tasty*.. meal. Those buns look absolutely .... !

2 A few adjectives are normally only placed **before a noun** (not after a verb):

mere *sheer* *complete* *utter* *total* *downright*

It took a mere hour to finish. This is sheer madness.
The journey was a(n) .... disaster. The meal was a .... success.

3 A few adjectives are normally placed **after a verb** (not before a noun):

afloat *afraid* *alight* *alike* *aloft* *alive* *alone* *asleep* *awake* *well* *unwell* *ill* *content*

Are you awake yet? I don't feel very well.
The fire isn't .... yet. Don't leave the baby .... all night.
Shh! The baby's .... in its cot. Her two sisters look ....

4 A few adjectives are normally placed **after a noun**:

galore *manqué* *elect* *present* (= attending) *proper* (= itself)

There was food galore at the party. He is an artist manqué.
The president .... takes office next month.

5 A few adjectives and participles can sometimes be placed after a noun, rather than before it:

concerned (= affected) *responsible* (= who did it) *involved* (= included) *imaginable* (after a superlative)

All the people concerned have been notified.
That was the most disgusting meal .... !

6 A few adjectives and participles can come either **before or after a noun**:

affected *available* *required* *suggested* *obtainable*

All the people affected have complained. = All the affected people have complained.
Work expands to take up the time .... = Work expands to fill the .... time.

7 Most participles used as adjectives (ending in *-ing*, *-ed*, *-en*) and most adjectives ending in *-able* and *-ible* are placed **after a noun** when extra information is given **afterwards** – as if in a relative clause:

These are delicious cakes (which have been) made according to my own recipe.
How high are the mountains (which are) visible in the distance?
I love the smell of cakes (which are) .... in the kitchen.
The houses (which were) .... in the storm have been repaired.
A survey .... by Berni revealed some unexpected information. (see 5.2)

C Insert suitable adjectives from B before or after the nouns in green in these sentences:

1 Do you have all the ingredients?
2 I object to his rudeness.
3 Don't forget to follow the guidelines.
4 The people have all been arrested.
5 Never wake a baby.
6 In the sale there were bargains.
7 I'd love a glass of lemonade.
8 Can I try one of those cakes?
9 She is the nicest person.
10 It seems to me that he is a fool.
11 The meeting began promptly.
12 Some of the people fell asleep.

A **1** Read the report through. **Highlight** the main points.

Bottled water condemned as 'vast con'

BOTTLED water was one of the "great confidence tricks of modern times" with customers paying 700 times more in the supermarket than for the same quality from the tap, the Water Companies Association said yesterday.

Attacking the bottled water industry for being "vastly over-priced", Pamela Taylor, the chief executive, said there was little to differentiate it from tap water.

Its marketing was based on associations with sport, health and fitness which had no basis in truth, and its packaging and distribution were environmentally damaging, she said.

The difference in price between bottled water and tap water was comparable to the gap in cost between running a Ford Escort and a light aircraft. If household water supplies were charged at the same rate as bottled water, the average household bill would rise to £77,000 a year.

One of the reasons consumers believed bottled water tasted better was because they stored it in the fridge. If tap water was bottled and kept in the fridge it would be impossible to tell the difference, the association said.

Tap water was more tightly controlled than bottled water. The Drinking Water Inspectorate reported last year that 99.7% of all samples passed purity tests. Almost 2% of bottled water failed the same tests, meaning that 10 million litres of bottled water with unacceptable levels of bacteria were sold in British supermarkets each year.

The association also criticised the labelling of bottled water. Table and purified water could be and often were simply bottled tap water. Spring and natural water often had to undergo similar treatment to tap water before it could be bottled.

One of the most telling arguments against bottled water was the harm the trade caused to the environment.

Mike Walker, the association's head of policy, said: "While the bottled water industry is keen to market its product by using natural beauty and unspoilt countryside, bottled water is far more environmentally damaging than tap water. Many of the UK's major brands use plastic bottles. Most of these end their lives in landfill sites."

The transportation of water from places as far away as Israel, Japan, South Korea, and water-short countries such as India and Kenya was condemned as unnecessary and wasteful.

Robert Hayward, the director general of the British Soft Drinks Association, said bottled water was a booming business. "The growth is the result of consumer choice. Consumers buy our products because of their taste, their consistency of quality and their convenience."

Paul Brown

2 Look at the notes below. Two important points are missing from each set of notes – add these to the notes. Then decide which style of notes might be most helpful for YOU if you were going to write a similar report.

Water Companies Association say bottled water is a con:
marketing: associations with 'sport, health, fitness' – no basis in truth
price: bottled water costs 700 times more than tap water
purity: tap water more closely controlled: 99.7% of tap water passes tests. 2% of bottled water fails same tests – 10 million litres with unacceptable levels of bacteria sold each year
labelling: misleading because 'table water' + 'purified water' often just bottled tap water – 'spring water' + 'natural water' has to undergo same treatment as tap water before bottling
distribution: transportation from places overseas + water-short countries unnecessary + wasteful
British Soft Drinks Association say: 'Consumers buy bottled water because they prefer its taste, consistent quality and convenience'

Water Companies Association say bottled water a con:

marketing: associations 'sport, health, fitness' - no basis in truth

price: 700 times higher

taste: stored in fridge - tap water in fridge same

labelling misleading: 'table water' + 'purified water' bottled tap water - 'spring water' + 'natural water' same treatment as tap water before bottling

packaging: environmentally damaging - plastic bottles

British Soft Drinks Association say: Consumers prefer taste, consistent quality + convenience of bottled water

(Diagram / mind map)

"sport health fitness" → MARKETING

NO BASIS IN TRUTH

PRICE 700x more than tap water!

MARKETING → LABELLING

"table water" "purified water" = tap water in bottles

"spring water" "natural water" ← same tests as tap water

PACKAGING

DISTRIBUTION wasteful

environmentally damaging PLASTIC BOTTLES

from overseas

from water-poor countries

PURITY → TAP WATER / BOTTLED WATER

99.7% passes tests

?.?% fails tests = 10 m litres with high bacteria levels

3 👥 List the advantages and disadvantages of each type of notes. If you use a different style altogether, what are the advantages of your style of notes?

B **1** 🔊 You'll hear a radio programme about the Fairtrade scheme. MAKE NOTES on the main points that are made.

2 👥 Compare your notes with a partner's. Rewrite your notes before you write an article on this topic:

How can schemes like Fairtrade improve the quality of life for farmers in developing countries? (300–350 words)

"Fairtrade gives us several advantages. It means we can invest in our education, our health, organic farming methods and growing the highest quality coffee."
Raul del Aguila, Peru.

"Fairtrade is best - we sell to people who we believe can do us justice. My children have been going to school because of the coffee."
Paskazia Mpangu, Tanzania.

"We have seen achievements. Now I have money to buy clothes for my children, to build my house. Day by day things are improving, because of the better price."
Mario Hernandez, Nicaragua.

8.8 oz
GOURMET PERCOL
FAIRTRADE COLOMBIA
ARABICA COFFEE
FOR FILTERS & CAFETIERES

Excellent cafédirect® from the growers
ORGANIC MACHU PICCHU MOUNTAIN SPECIAL
MEDIUM ROAST
100% ARABICA   FILTER & CAFETIERE

5.7 / *should and be*

A **1** Decide which alternatives fit into the gaps – in most cases more than one alternative can be used.

1 It's important that he .... told the truth.

   is   be   should be   will be   is going to be

2 I insist that I .... my money back after such a terrible meal.

   given   be given   was given   am being given   should be given

3 This is a big problem – what do you think I .... ?

   shall do   should do   ought to do   can do

4 We were all sitting watching TV when who .... but Billy.

   could arrive   would arrive   should arrive   did arrive

5 I'm sorry that you .... upset about this.

   feel   do feel   will feel   should feel   ought to feel

B Study these examples before doing C below.

Reactions When expressing reactions, using *should* is more formal, and sounds rather less direct than a present tense:

I'm very sorry that you should feel upset.
It's a pity that she should not be on speaking terms with him.
It's interesting that they should want to visit us.
It's disgraceful that we should have to pay extra for service.
It has always worried me that he should feel lonely.

Suggestions and recommendations Using *should* or *be* + past participle tends to sound less bossy and more formal than a present tense. Compare these pairs of sentences:

I recommend that he should take up cooking as a career.
I recommend that he takes up cooking.
I suggest that she should be asked to make a speech on our behalf.
I recommend that she is asked.
I propose that she be given everything she needs.
I propose that she is given . . .

Should can also be used in **conditional** sentences like these:

If you should meet Tim, give him my regards.
Should the doors be locked, the key may be obtained from the caretaker.   (see 13.4)

C Complete these sentences, using *should* or *be* + past participle:

1 It is very important that you .... before you start writing.
2 It is absolutely essential that he .... his work on time.
3 I insist that the washing-up .... before you go out for the evening.
4 It's wrong that the government .... tax on petrol.
5 It's a nuisance that we .... so much homework at the weekend.
6 It's necessary that ....
7 I'm disappointed that ....
8 It's awfully sad that ....
9 It bothers me that ....
10 I propose that Jill .... president of the society.
11 If you .... questions, please do not hesitate to ask.

"One more notch. Room for dessert."

A **1** Before you listen to the recording, look at these diagrams, showing the process of margarine manufacture. As you can see, they are in the wrong order. Using a pencil, number the steps in what looks like the right order. The first and last steps are numbered already.

Heat and crush plant seeds

Add lecithin & monoglyceride

Deodorise by heating to melting point

React oil with hydrogen to produce hardened oils

Add skimmed milk, water & salt

Add fuller's earth to bleach oil

Add caustic soda to remove any waste as soap

Add artificial flavour, colour and vitamins

RESULT: still contaminated with gums and resins

RESULT: refined oil

RESULT: unemulsified ingredients

RESULT: blended oils

Mix with fish & animal oils

Neutralise, bleach and filter to remove waste products

Extrude into plastic tub . . . and put a lid on it

2 Listen to the recording and number the diagrams to show the correct sequence of the manufacturing process.

B **1** Students A and B look at Activity 2, C and D look at 15. Each pair has different information about the processes of making wine and brewing beer. Study the information and MAKE NOTES on the main points of the process, or highlight the important information.

2 Student A should join C and B should join D to form new pairs. Tell your new partner what you found out. Discuss what the two processes have in common, and how they are different.

C Write an article explaining either how wine is made or how beer is made.

Make notes first, and write your article WITHOUT quoting verbatim from Activity 2 or 15.

or Make notes on another culinary or non-culinary process, and write a description of the process. You may need to do some research on this.

6

See the world!

6.1 Where would you like to go?   TOPIC VOCABULARY

A **Discuss these questions:**

- Would you like to visit this place? Why/Why not?
- Which five places in the world would you like to visit one day? Why?
- And which five places have you no desire to visit ever? Why?

B Fill the gaps in this description of the illustration, using the words on the right:

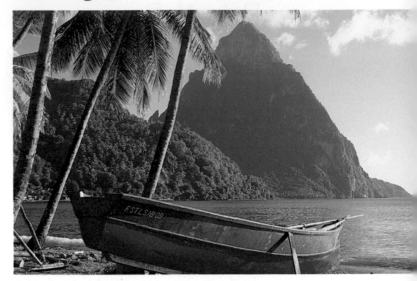

Soufrière is a small fishing   *port*   on the west ¹ of the ² of St Lucia in the Caribbean. It lies at the centre of a sheltered ³ which forms a natural ⁴.
The town is dominated by the Pitons: two mountain ⁵ which were once ⁶, covered in tropical ⁷. If you travel ⁸ up the river ⁹ you come to a ¹⁰ where there are plantations growing coconuts and tropical fruits, watered by little ¹¹ flowing down from the hills. To the north there are impressive ¹² plunging into the sea and around a ¹³ is a secluded hotel above a little ¹⁴, from where you can swim out to watch the fish around the coral ¹⁵.
The ¹⁶ from the hotel is breathtaking.
  Despite its wonderful ¹⁷, warm ¹⁸, friendly people and delicious local ¹⁹, Soufrière isn't a popular tourist destination, perhaps because it lacks the sandy ²⁰ tourists expect in a Caribbean ²¹.

bay
beaches
cliffs
climate
coast
cove
harbour
headland
inland
island
peaks
plateau
rainforest
reef
resort
seafood
setting
streams
valley
view
volcanoes

C Choose THREE words or phrases that make sense in each of the gaps:

1 Not liking crowds, I prefer going on holiday to somewhere that's ....
   abandoned   backward   derelict   deserted   dull   godforsaken   off the beaten track
   out of the way   secluded   spoiled   strange

2 I enjoy visiting places abroad where the people are ....
   churlish   courteous   easygoing   hospitable   morose   sulky   sullen

3 The Vatican in Rome is visited every year by millions of ....
   commuters   holidaymakers   passengers   pilgrims   vagrants   travellers

4 The .... takes up to four hours on the motorway, but it's quicker by train.
   crossing   drive   flight   journey   passage   track   travel   trip   voyage   way

5 I'm going overseas next week and I'll be .... for the rest of the month.
   abroad   absent-minded   away from home   missing   offshore   on the run
   out   out in the country   out of the country

D Note down SIX countries that you have visited – or might visit one day. And SIX MORE countries from which visitors to your country come. Then discuss these questions:

- What do you call a citizen of each country? What languages do they all speak?
- What are the principal cities called – and how are they pronounced?
- Which nationalities are the most frequent visitors to your country, and what are the attractions of your country to them?

6.2 Learning the language   READING AND SPEAKING

A Find the answers to these questions in the passage and <u>underline</u> or highlight the relevant information there. Then write down your answers, using your own words.

1 What did many Turks do when they encountered a non-Turkish speaker?
2 Why was the author confused at the reaction to her *useful phrase*?
3 Why was the hotel porter the first to understand her?
4 Why did Mr Yorum point to himself when they first met?
5 Why did the narrator think he was pointing to himself?
6 Why didn't the writer try to resolve the confusion with Mr Yorum?

I studied my Turkish phrase book, and learned a few of the most useful ones by heart. One was about how I did not understand Turkish well, which I copied into my note-book and carried about with me. Many Turks can't understand that anyone really does not know Turkish; they think that if they say it often enough and loud enough it will register. They did this whenever I said this phrase; it seemed to start them off asking what seemed to be questions, but I only said my piece again, and after a time they gave it up. Sometimes they said "Yorum, yorum, yorum?" as if they were asking something, but I did not know what this word meant, and I thought they were mimicking what they thought I had said.

This was all that happened about it for a few days, then one day when I said my piece to the porter he nodded, and went to the telephone and rang someone up, and presently a man came downstairs and bowed to me as I stood in the hall and said something to me in Turkish. I had better explain here that there was a misunderstanding which was my fault, for I discovered some time afterwards that I had copied the phrase in the book which was just below the one which meant "I do not understand Turkish," and the one I had copied and learnt and had been saying to everyone for days meant "Please to phone at once to Mr Yorum," though this seems a silly phrase to print in a book for the use of people who do not know Mr Yorum at all and never would want to telephone to him. But one day this Mr Yorum turned up at the hotel to stay, and the porter saw then what I wanted him to do, and he rang Mr Yorum in his room and asked him to come down. But I did not know then about my mistake, and when Mr Yorum spoke to me I said again that I did not understand Turkish, and he bowed and pointed to himself. I thought he must be offering to interpret for me, but when I tried English on him he shook his head and said, "Yok, yok," and I could see he knew none. So I looked up the Turkish for "What can I have the pleasure of doing for you?" and said it, but of course I did not understand his answer, and that is the worst of foreign languages, you understand what you say in them yourself, because you have looked it up before saying it, but very seldom what the foreigners say to you, because you have not looked up that at all. So I looked through the book till I found "Who are you, sir?" and he said in reply, "Yorum, Yorum, Yorum." I saw there was some confusion somewhere, but there is always so much confusion in Turkey that I let it go, and ordered drinks for both of us, and we drank them, then he went away, quite pleased that I had telephoned to him to come and have a drink.

from *The Towers of Trebizond* by Rose Macaulay

B 👥 **Discuss these questions:**

- Have you had any similar experiences with English or other foreign languages?
- How much of your language does a tourist in your country need to know?
- Which parts of the passage did you find amusing?
- What do you think happened next in the story?

C 👥 One of you should look at Activity 4, the other at 16. These Activities contain the next paragraphs of the story. Find out what happened when Mr Yorum was called down to the hotel lobby yet again. Then tell your partner about it in your own words.

6.3 **The future** **GRAMMAR REVIEW**

A 👥 **Discuss the differences in meaning, if any, between these sentences:**

1 I think I'm going to scream.   I think I'll scream.
2 It's still raining in Scotland.   It's still going to rain in Scotland.
   It will still be raining in Scotland.   It still rains in Scotland.
3 I'll phone him after work.   I'm phoning him after work.
   I'm going to phone him after work.   I'll be phoning him after work.
4 When are we having lunch?   When do we have lunch?
   When are we going to have lunch?   When shall we have lunch?
5 What time shall I get to your house?   What time will I get to your house?
6 I'll work hard tonight.   I'll be working hard tonight.
7 Will you be going shopping today?   Are you going to go shopping today?
   Are you going shopping today?   Will you go shopping today?
   Do you go shopping today?

B **Fill the gaps in these sentences, which all refer to the future, with suitable words. In some cases various answers are possible.**

1 I think I .... sneeze. .... you give me a tissue, please?
2 .... able to make people understand when you .... Turkey?
3 Have you decided how to get there? .... by car or .... a bus?
4 Supposing your car .... on the way there, what .... do?
5 Our flight is due .... at 9.30, but I'm afraid it .... delayed.
6 By the time the plane .... , we .... waiting for four hours.
7 No one knows for sure what the future .... us.
8 In the next century, tourism .... more and more highly developed.
9 While you .... holiday, I .... in the office. I hope you .... a postcard.
10 I've no idea when I .... finished my work.
11 As soon as I .... the results, I .... a ring to let you know.
12 It's time we .... what we .... this weekend.
13 I hope nobody .... me at 8 o'clock because I .... still .... dinner then.
14 What .... happen at the frontier if I .... my passport at home?
15 I'm looking forward .... the book, when you .... finished with it.

C 1 👥👥 **Discuss these questions about the future:**

- What are the most interesting things you're going to do during the coming month? Which are you looking forward to most?
- Looking ahead ten years or so: how will your life then be different from now?
- How will the world be different ten years from now?

2 ✏️ Write two paragraphs summarising the main points of your discussion.

6.4 One word – different meanings

Homonyms are words which are written the same but have different meanings:

This is a good book.   Can I book two tickets for the concert?
Do you understand this sentence?   His sentence was life imprisonment.
What do you mean?   Don't be so mean!
It's rude to point.   What is the main point?
The point of the knife was blunt.
When do you start work?   This pen doesn't work.
A work of art.

A **Fill each gap with a word that makes sense in the sentence:**

1 From here to the coast is a two-hour ....
   They avoid the beach in summer because the crowds .... them mad.

2 Turn .... at the next junction.
   Are there any biscuits .... in the tin?

3 Did you enjoy the .... ?
   Can you .... me how to work this gadget?

4 Please do not leave any .... of value in your room.
   Is 'the' the definite or the indefinite .... ?
   I read a fascinating .... in today's paper.

5 Could you wait a .... , please?
   This is the .... time this has happened.

6 I always .... at the sight of blood.
   This photocopy is so .... that I can hardly read it.

7 I didn't expect the bull to .... us.
   There is no .... for this service.

8 Don't you feel .... after eating so many cakes?
   Comedians make their living by being .... in public.

B **Think of ONE WORD which can be used appropriately in all three sentences, and write it in the box in CAPITAL LETTERS.**

1 If I had a .... for every time he apologised, I'd be a millionaire.
   200 grams is about half a .... in the USA.
   There was no answer so he began to .... on the door.

   `1 [        ]`

2 Thank you, I really .... what you've done for me.
   The value of a flat will .... over the years.
   You don't .... how much time and effort I've put into this.

   `2 [        ]`

3 There is plenty of .... evidence linking smoking with cancer.
   It's healthier to sleep on a .... mattress than a soft one.
   Jones and Son are a family .... established in 1977.

   `3 [        ]`

4 It may rain while we're out, in which .... we can expect to get wet.
   Don't forget to put a label on your ....
   The police are investigating the .... of the missing luggage.

   `4 [        ]`

5 When the .... was read they discovered they had been left a fortune.
   Where there's a .... there's a way.
   Do come to the party! Please say you .... !

   `5 [        ]`

6 Put a .... on the pan to keep the flies off.
   Don't worry about the rail fare, we'll .... your expenses.
   In a thunderstorm, don't take .... under a tree.

   `6 [        ]`

Preparation

Before the next lesson, read the passage in **6.5 B** and do the tasks in **C** and **D**.

6.5 The friendly skies

A 👥👥 **Discuss these questions:**
- Do you enjoy flying or are you afraid of flying? Give your reasons.
- What would you say to a friend who refuses to travel by plane?

B In this passage the writer, Jonathan Raban, is waiting at an airport somewhere in the USA for his flight to Seattle. First read the passage – and enjoy it.

I spend a lot of time anxiously listening to the announcements over the loudspeaker system. In almost all respects, these summonses and bulletins are enunciated with extreme clarity by women speaking in the painfully slow and fulsomely stressed tones of infant teachers in a school for special-need children. It is only when they reach the flight number of the plane concerned or the name of the passenger who must immediately report to the United Airlines information desk that their voices go into misty soft focus. I keep on hearing that I am urgently wanted, but sit tight, fearing paranoia. They don't want me. They can't want me. They want Josephine Rubin, or John A.T. Horobin, or Sean O'Riordain, or Jennifer Raymond, or Jonah the Rabbi, or Rogers and Braybourne.

When I first arrived here, I fed some coins into a newspaper-dispenser and took out a copy of the local broadsheet – the *Post-Dispatch*, the *Courant*, the *Plain Dealer*, the *Tribune*, the *Herald*, or whatever it was. It was an unhappy diversion. It spoke too eloquently of the world one had left behind by coming here – that interesting world of School Board Split, City Cop on Take, Teamsters Boss To Quit, Highways Commission Probe – Official. It made me feel homesick for reality: the only news that interested me now was the depressing stuff on the V.D.U.s. *Cancelled. Delayed*. Did the controllers ever get to write *Crashed, Missing, Hijacked* on these screens?

What puzzles me is that I seem to be entirely alone in my frustration and distress. Almost every flight is going out late, and there must be several thousand people in this airport, switching their departure gates, phoning home, putting another Scotch-and-soda down on their tab in the cocktail lounge. The men's neckties are loosened, their vests unbuttoned. They sit with open briefcases, papers spread in front of them as if this place was a comfortable home-from-home. I watch one man near me. He's got a can of beer, a basket of popcorn, and he's two thirds of the way through a sci-fi thriller by Arthur C. Clarke. The bastard hasn't got a care in the world. His eyes never drift up to the V.D.U.; he never cocks his head anxiously when Teacher starts talking through the overhead speakers. He's on a domestic flight. He's a domestic flier.

An hour and a half later it is still raining, but we're getting somewhere here – at least I thought so 50 minutes ago when I buckled in to seat 38F and began looking out through the lozenge of scratched plastic at the men in earmuffs and storm-gear on the ground below. Since then we haven't budged. We've suffered faint, pastiche imitations of Scott Joplin, Count Basie and Glen Miller on the muzak system. My neighbour in 38E, who is careless of the usual rules of body space, has worked her way slowly through four pages of the *National Enquirer*, moving her lips as she reads. In the seats ahead, there has been a good deal of folding and refolding of copies of *Business Week* and the *Wall Street Journal*. Still no-one seems much disconcerted except me. The inside of the plane is hot and getting hotter. The stewards, flirting routinely among themselves, are proof against any damn-fool questions from me.

The muzak clicks off. A voice clicks on.

"Hi!" – and that seems to be it for a good long time. Then, "I'm, uh, Billy Whitman, and I'm going to be your pilot on this flight here to ... " I think I can hear Mr Whitman consulting his clipboard. " ... uh, Seattle this morning. Well – it was meant to be morning, but it looks to me now to be getting pretty damn close to afternoon ... "

He's putting on the entire cowlicked, gum-shifting country boy performance.

"I guess some of you folks back there may be getting a little antsy 'bout this delay we're having now in getting airborne ... Well, we did run into a bit of a glitch with Control up there, getting our flight-plan sorted ... "

We haven't got a flight-plan? Is Mr Whitman waiting for someone to bring him a *map*?

"But they got that fixed pretty good now, and in, uh, oh, a couple or three minutes, we should be closing the doors, and I'm planning on getting up into the sky round about ten minutes after that. So if you all sit tight now, we'll be getting this show right on the road.

1

2

3

4

5

6

7

8

9

10

Looks pretty nice up there today ... no weather problems that I can see so far ... at least, once we get atop this little local overcast ... and I'm looking for a real easy trip today. Have a good one, now, and I'll be right back to you just as soon as we go past something worth looking out the window for. Okay?"

Click.

After the video and the stewards' dumbshow about what to do in "the unlikely event" of our landing on water (where? the Mississippi?), Captain Whitman takes us on a slow ramble round the perimeter of the airport. We appear to be returning to the main terminal again when the jet takes a sudden deep breath, lets out a bull roar, and charges down the runway, its huge frame shuddering fit to bust. Its wings are actually flapping now, trying to tear themselves out at their roots in the effort to achieve lift-off. It bumps and grinds. The plastic bulkheads are shivering like gongs. Rain streams past the window, in shreds, at 200 miles an hour.

This is the bit I hate. We're not going fast enough. We're far too heavy to bring off this trick. We're breaking up. To take this flight was tempting fate one time too many. We're definitely goners this time.

But the domestic fliers remain stupidly oblivious to our date with death. They go on reading. They're lost in the stock market prices. They're learning that Elvis Presley never died and has been living as a recluse in Dayton, Ohio. These things engage them. These guys are – bored. The fact, clear enough to me, that they are at this moment rocketing into eternity is an insufficiently diverting one to make them even raise their eyes from their columns of idiot print.

Somehow (and this Captain Whitman must know a thing or two) we manage to unpeel ourselves from the obstinate earth, which suddenly begins to tilt upwards in the glass. An industrial outskirt of the city shows as an exposed tangle of plumbing; there's a gridlock of cars on a freeway interchange, their headlamps shining feebly through the drizzle. The airport beneath us is marked out like a schoolbook geometrical puzzle. Then, suddenly, we're into a viewless infernal region of thick smoke, with the plane skidding and wobbling on the bumpy air. It's rattling like an old bus on a dirt road. In 38E we're deep in the miracle of Oprah Winfrey's diet. In 38F we're beginning to suspect that we might conceivably survive.

My ears are popping badly. The noise of the engines changes from a racetrack snarl to the even threshing sound of a spin-dryer. On an even keel now, we plough up steadily through the last drifts and rags of storm cloud and the whole cabin fills with sudden brilliant sunshine. We're in the clear and in the blue; aloft, at long last, over America.

from *Hunting Mr Heartbreak* by Jonathan Raban

C   👤 → 👤 **Choose the best answer to these questions. Then justify your answers to each other.**

1 The writer hears the announcer calling ...
    A children's names   **C** his name
    B other people's names   **D** people with names that sound like his

2 The other people at the airport seem to be ...
    A frustrated   **C** anxious
    B distressed   **D** indifferent

3 The word *disconcerted* in ¶4 means ...
    A terrified   **C** uncomfortable
    B anxious   **D** squashed

4 The flight attendants are ... to answer the writer's questions.
    A willing   **C** unable
    B too busy   **D** happy

5 The pilot's announcement ...
    A inspires confidence   **C** doesn't make the writer feel less nervous
    B is not informative   **D** makes the writer panic

6 The person sitting next to the writer is reading ...
    A a business newspaper   **C** a news magazine
    B a scandal sheet   **D** a TV guide

7 The writer was the only person on the plane who ...
    A thought they would die   **C** was amused by the pilot's announcement
    B read the safety instructions   **D** had nothing to read

D Highlight the vocabulary in the passage that you want to remember. But that doesn't mean every word you didn't know. For example, you probably didn't know the American slang words in red below, but you can probably guess their meanings from the context:

"... some of you folks back there may be getting a little antsy 'bout this delay we're having now in getting airborne ... Well, we did run into a bit of a glitch with Control up there, getting our flight-plan sorted ... "

E 👥 Highlight THREE parts of the passage that amused you. Point them out to a partner, and compare each other's reactions. Look again at the discussion questions in A – what would be the writer's OWN answers to the questions, do you think?

6.6 Repetition

WRITING SKILLS

A **1** Read these extracts from a Canadian tourist brochure. Highlight the places where the same words or the same grammatical structures are repeated in each extract. (Reasons 5 to 9 are: 5. The Wildlife; 6. The Country Life; 7. The City Life; 8. The History; 9. The Events.)

10 Great Reasons to Visit Saskatchewan

Saskatchewan is a big province that constantly surprises. With its vast and changing landscapes, its colourful events and its rich heritage, it has a lot to offer. Covering it in a few words and photos is no easy task.

In the next 20 pages we present 10 great reasons why you should travel to our province. Why Saskatchewan is special. Why it's a place where you belong.

We have thousands of reasons for you to see Saskatchewan – we're limited to 10 here. We're confident you'll find them reasons enough to visit. And that you'll find more reasons to return.

1 The Prairies

When people think Saskatchewan, they think prairies. They think fields of gold that stretch up against the horizon. They think bold, blue sky. They think vistas that seem flawlessly flat and that from the air resemble a patchwork quilt.

Prairie scenery can be breathtaking. Brilliant mustard and canola waving in the wind. Grain elevators standing like sentinels, signalling the approach of new towns. Sunsets offering their light shows of purple, orange and red.

The prairies are also rolling hills where you'd least expect them. Valleys full of wild flowers, prairie lilies and saskatoons. Plus plains and bush alive with prairie dogs, meadowlarks and white-tailed deer.

This year stop and smell the clover. See the images that have graced a thousand postcards. Visit the prairies.

2 The Parks

Hike a leafy aspen trail. Zip down a monster waterslide. Join a "wolf howl" under clear moonlight. Whatever your interests you can likely satisfy them in Saskatchewan's parks.

With nearly five million acres of Saskatchewan parkland, Mother Nature has plenty of places in which to work her spell on you. At our parks you can sink that championship putt, watch deer and elk by the roadside, relax at a four-season resort, or pitch your tent near a back country gurgling stream.

Waskesiu. Grasslands. Moose Mountain. Cypress Hills. Our parks are destinations, summer and winter. They put you in touch with a simpler, gentler world – a world where the sun shines bright and the deadlines and pressures of ordinary life are far, far away.

3 The Lakes

Get out your swimming trunks, unfurl those sails, dust off your water-skis, take the canoe and tackle box out of storage and book that cabin or resort. Saskatchewan's 100,000 – that's right 100,000! – lakes await you.

4 The Fishing

Picture a lazy day on a crystal clear lake. Morning mist comes off the water. An evergreen shoreline frames your horizon. A bald eagle circles overhead. Then suddenly your line tenses, and everything changes. Your battle with a monster of the deep has begun.

10 The People

If there are 10 great reasons to visit Saskatchewan, then there are a million reasons to come back. Our people. Superhearted. Lively. Famous for their hospitality.

With a mosaic of cultures, Saskatchewan is truly the world in one place. Native Indians and people with British, French and east-European roots. People who celebrate their uniqueness at annual celebrations like Vesna and Folkfest in Sasktatoon, or Mosaic in Regina. Where the food, fun and music of the homelands trail long into the night.

When all is said and done, it's the people you meet who make a vacation unforgettable. We invite you to meet ours. Through them discover the place where you belong.

2 👥👥 Compare what you've both highlighted and discuss what the effect of the repetition is in each case.

B **1** 👥👥 Make a list of TEN GREAT REASONS why tourists should visit your country, region or city. Then decide what you would write to justify ONE of the attractions.

2 🖋 Write around 100 words describing the attraction you've picked, in the same style as the Canadian brochure.

3 👥👥 Compare what you've both written. Then write another 100 words about another attraction of your country, region or city.

6.7 Revision and exam practice   ADVANCED GRAMMAR

Complete the second sentence so that it has a similar meaning to the first sentence using the word given. DO NOT CHANGE THE WORD GIVEN. Use between three and eight words, including the word given.

1 Why on earth didn't you tell me before?

ever   Why ....*ever didn't you*.......... tell me before?

2 We went on waiting until midnight for the plane to take off.

still   We .... for the plane to take off.

3 Someone told me my flight was cancelled when I got to the airport.

arriving   .... that my flight had been cancelled.

4 I had never flown before which was why I was very nervous.

having   Never .... I was very nervous.

5 I only want to spend the rest of my life with you.

thing   The .... the rest of my life with you.

6 They go on holiday in the winter and in the summer too.

only   Not .... in the winter but also in the summer.

7 We didn't realise that our hotel was right beside the airport.

did   Little .... our hotel was right beside the airport.

8 I propose that we send him a letter explaining the situation.

be   I propose .... explaining the situation.

9 She always gets the right answers.

never   She .... right answers.

10 We had to write several letters before we got our money back.

manage   Only after writing several letters .... our money back.

When doing this kind of exercise in Part 4 of the Use of English Paper, first identify the structure that is required, then rewrite the sentence. Concentrate on conveying the meaning as well as getting the grammar right. Don't change more than you have to.

6.8 / **The impact of tourism**   **LISTENING AND COMPOSITION**

A   **You'll hear an interview about tourism in the Maldives. Answer the questions by filling the boxes with a word or short phrase.**

1 How many inhabited islands are there in the Maldives? [**1**]

2 How many resort islands are there in the Maldives? [**2**]

3 Resort islands are [**3**] to ordinary Maldivians.

4 Most of the tourists who go to the Maldives are from [**4**] .

5 According to the Tourism Master Plan, what are the two major attractions of the Maldives?
[**5a**] and [**5b**] .

6 Most of what the tourists need has to be [**6**] .

7 The regulation of tourism on the Maldives has been [**7**] .

8 It's hard for many staff on a tourist island to [**8**] .

9 One result of *El Niño* is to make the coral less [**9**] .

10 The long-term problem facing the Maldives is [**10**] .

B **Discuss these questions:**

- What are your views on the way tourism is managed in the Maldives?
- What harm can tourism cause? What are the benefits of tourism?
- Should poorer countries segregate tourists in hotel zones to 'protect' the local people from them? Or should they discourage tourism altogether?
- What are the problems that face the tourist industry in your country?
- What are the most popular destinations for tourists from your country?
- How are foreign tourists treated in your country? How do they behave there?
- What has been the impact of tourism on your region, or elsewhere in your country?

C ✐ **Write a newspaper article describing the impact of tourism on a place in your country, or in another country you know (300–350 words). Make notes first.**

6.9 *come* **and** *go*   **VERBS AND IDIOMS**

A **Find synonyms for the phrases in red, or explain their meaning. Use a dictionary if necessary.**

1 She was very upset at first, but she came to terms with it eventually.
2 I expected my arrangements to go off without a hitch, but they came to nothing.
3 His early success went to his head and he did no more work the rest of the year.
4 'How is your work coming along?' 'If you come along with me, I'll show you.'
5 It's no good, I've gone off the idea. I can't go through with it.
6 Let's go through this point again, in case it comes up in the exam.
7 Go ahead, you can take my Swiss army knife with you – it may come in useful.
8 She kept teasing the dog, so it wasn't surprising that it went for her.
9 'She's decided to go it alone and start her own business.'
 'I only hope it comes to something and doesn't turn out to be a disaster.'
 'Don't worry, she's gone into all the financial forecasts very thoroughly.'
10 Her presentation at the conference went down very well.

B **Fill the gaps in these sentences with suitable phrases from the list below. You may need to change the form of the verbs.**

1 They .... the brilliant idea of taking in overnight guests.
2 When is her new book .... ?
3 'I see that bus fares have .... again.' 'Well, they never .... , do they?'
4 I've just been reading that fascinating old guidebook.
 Where did you .... it?
5 She .... him until he gave in and agreed to .... the competition.
6 The day before their holiday, they both .... flu.
7 He stays on the beach, while she .... water-skiing and skin-diving.
8 She took a lot of persuading but eventually she .... to our point of view.
9 I'll wait till the matter .... naturally in the course of the conversation.
10 My suitcase is practically brand new but it .... on the luggage carousel.

come across   come apart   come out   come round
come up   come up with
go down   go down with   go in for
go off   go on at   go up

7 Spending your money

7.1 | **Shop till you drop!**   TOPIC VOCABULARY AND LISTENING

A   **Discuss these questions:**

- Which of the places shown above do you enjoy shopping at? Give your reasons.
- Think of the area you live in. Which is your favourite place locally to get:
    magazines   stationery   books   clothes   CDs   electrical goods
- Do you enjoy going shopping? Give your reasons.

B   In these sentences, THREE of the alternatives are correct and the rest are wrong. Decide which are correct and why the wrong alternatives seem incorrect.

1   Believe it or not, there really are .... of soft drink called *Calpis, Pocari Sweat, Pschitt, Sic* and *Dribly*!
    brands ✓   categories   commodities   makes ✓   species   styles   varieties ✓

2   The .... was thronged with shoppers on the Saturday before Christmas.
    boutique   business   kiosk   mall   shopping centre   precinct

3   They stock a wide range of .... in most department stores.
    articles   goods   materials   merchandise   objects   supplies

4   The goods they have on offer in the market are certainly ....
    a bargain   good value   invaluable   value for money   valued   worthy

5   Complaints about goods should be made to the retailer, not the ....
    author   creator   inventor   manufacturer   supplier   wholesaler

6   Consumer protection laws must be observed by every ....
    end user   patron   purchaser   retailer   trader   vendor

7   An electronic cash register keeps a record of every ....
    bargain   contract   deal   negotiation   purchase   sale   transaction

8   If you want a shop to keep something for you until later, you may have to ....
    give a discount   give a refund   make a down payment   open an account   pay a bribe
    pay cash down   pay a deposit   pay a ransom

9   You can get something repaired free of charge if it's still under ....
    assurance   certificate   guarantee   twelve months old   warranty

10   I enjoy going to that shop because the staff are so ....
    courteous   helpful   humble   knowledgeable   lenient   obsequious   subservient

C **1** 🔊 You'll hear an interview with Amanda Hooper, who is a manager in a department store.

Note down your answers to these questions:

1 What does Amanda enjoy about her job?
2 What are her responsibilities?
3 What are the disadvantages of working in a department store?
4 What are her ambitions?

2 👥 Compare your answers with a partner. Then discuss what YOU would enjoy and not enjoy about doing Amanda's job – and the job of a sales assistant.

D 👥👥 Student A should look at Activity 3, student B at 10, C at 26 (and D at 29) for ideas to share. You'll each have some ideas on how to handle customers.

Decide which of the ideas seem most useful – not only for sales assistants, but also, more generally, when dealing with people in other situations too.

7.2 **Prepositions – 1** **GRAMMAR REVIEW**

Fill each gap in this newspaper article with a suitable preposition.

Money fit to launder

Great inventions rarely work first time. ____¹ 1990 the Reserve Bank of Australia, the country's central bank, shipped an order ____² commemorative banknotes, ____³ the first to be made ____⁴ plastic film rather than paper, ____⁵ Western Samoa. The Pacific islanders' excitement ____⁶ their new two-tala notes soon turned ____⁷ anger. Ink rubbed off the surface and smudged the portrait ____⁸ Malietoa Tanumafali, the revered head of state, ____⁹ whose honour the notes had been issued. ____¹⁰ their early days, plastic banknotes shed ink, jammed ____¹¹ note-counting machines and often refused to be refolded. But the Reserve Bank, which pioneered the technology, claims to have eradicated the sort of glitches that produced red (and smudged) faces ____¹² Western Samoa. Australia issued its own plastic tender ____¹³ the first time in 1992. ____¹⁴ 1996, the country had taken the last ____¹⁵ its paper money ____¹⁶ circulation. Now it is persuading other countries to follow its example.

The Australians say plastic cash has two main advantages ____¹⁷ the paper variety. First, it is hard to forge. As well as fancy inks and watermarks, it has a transparent window that makes life difficult ____¹⁸ counterfeiters. The second advantage is economic. Plastic notes are hard to rip and even survive washing machines. Although each note costs ____¹⁹ twice as much as a paper one to make, it lasts up to four times as long. The advantage is even greater ____²⁰ humid climates, where paper notes can survive as little as four months.

Armed ____²¹ these selling points, the Reserve Bank's printing division is running a healthy export business. It makes plastic notes ____²² several countries, including Thailand, Brunei and a forgiving Western Samoa. DuraNote, an American company ____²³ a plastic product, claims to be talking to central banks ____²⁴ twenty-four countries. "Until recently plastic cash was considered a novelty," says Al McKay ____²⁵ DuraNote. "Now the central banks have become more cost-conscious they are taking it very seriously."

Such scrimping ____²⁶ costs even extends ____²⁷ recycling, it seems. Australia plans to turn worn-out plastic notes ____²⁸ wheelbarrows, compost bins and plumbing fittings. There may be money ____²⁹ such products, ____³⁰ more ways than one.

from *The Economist*

Preparation Before the next lesson, read the article in 7.3 on the next page and do the task in **A1**.

A 1 ✎ Read this article and MAKE NOTES on which aspects of West Edmonton Mall would appeal to you, and which would not.

2 👥 Compare your notes with a partner, and discuss your reactions to the article.

Canada's palace of kitsch convenience

Dave Hill

1 FIRST IMPRESSIONS of the West Edmonton Mall are numbingly familiar, especially if you enter by the east wing. Outside, the sleet may be whipping across the flatlands of Alberta, but the processed ambience swiftly renders your senses supine in a manner well known to any visitor to Gateshead's Metro Centre or London's Brent Cross.

2 There is antiseptic Muzak and the glare of fluorescent lights. The concourse is decorated with indoor plants and "anchored" – to use the parlance of this most fanatical of service industries – at each end by a major department store.

3 Wander for a day among its glass and plastic halls and discover a complex so vast that its length is three times the height of the Empire State Building. The pursuit of aimless leisure here approaches the surreal. It is not the kind of place you drop in to for a bag of jelly babies and a packet of cigarettes. When you visit West Edmonton Mall and its avalanche of attractions, there is only one thing to do – hand in your coat at the cloakroom and submit.

4 You could go both barmy and bankrupt in this place and it wouldn't hurt a bit. For as well as the consumer seductions of IKEA, Sears, Athletes' World and 800 other shops, a thematic mock-up of New Orleans' Bourbon Street containing several of the Mall's 110 eating establishments, plus a chapel, a nightclub and a bingo hall, West Edmonton Mall offers far more.

5 There is Fantasyland, a full-scale children's funfair complete with dodgems, miniature railway and stomach-churning repertoire of plunges, slides and spins; the World Waterpark, whose main pool features the Blue Thunder wave machine and a labyrinth of spiralling, high-velocity tunnel rides; the Deep Sea Adventure, an artificial oceanscape containing a replica of Christopher Columbus's ship, the Santa Maria, six mini-submarines for sub-aquatic sightseeing, a school of dolphins and an entire community of undersea life;

a competition-standard skating rink, the Ice Palace; an 18-hole miniature golf course; a 19-studio cineplex and, of course, 15 banks and other financial service outlets.

When the Mall's public relations person reaches for comparisons, she does not trouble with the obvious competitors but talks about Disneyland. "We've created a 365-day-a-year summer environment which provides entertainment for people. We have something for everyone. Disney has set the standard, and I like to think we match it."

Mickey Mouse himself would have to admit she has a point. West Edmonton Mall is not so much a shopping city as a fully integrated consumer fantasy that succeeds in being mindless, utterly ridiculous and absolutely out of this world. My girlfriend and I, and our two young children, meandered among the fountains and plastic mouldings in a condition of ever-increasing gormlessness, simultaneously stunned and seduced by the diabolically manufactured mechanism for parting you from your critical faculties and your cash.

Everything is scrupulously designed to prolong your visit and, in the end, everything is welcome. For example, is there a Western parent alive who, in the middle of a frantic day, would not welcome the oasis of a children's facility like Fantasyland?

An hour of such blissful respite, followed by coffee and a sandwich at some glitzy pre-fab café, and we were ready once again to disappear into our consumer daze, blithely coughing up a few more dollars for a tiepin, a woolly hat or baseball pennant, pausing to peer down at the sharks which glide through the depths of the Deep Sea Adventure or to gawp swivel-eyed at the Ice Palace skaters. In its idiotic way, it's all too wonderful for words. I like malls, partly because they usually fulfill their promise to be clean, safe and efficient, but mostly because they emit such a stupefying sensory cocktail of obsession, ostentation and overkill. At West Edmonton Mall – the world's biggest, according to the Guinness Book of Records – these characteristics reach absurd heights.

¹⁰ Mall-building is a precise science and this indoor panorama is nothing if not state-of-the-art. It is not that the shopping itself is so very thrilling; as ever with such malls, the stores are plentiful but ultimately banal. Rather, the pleasure is in being part of a quietly lunatic alternative universe where the thin line that divides shopping from entertainment becomes almost totally erased.

¹¹ Entirely the product of private capital, West Edmonton Mall is owned by the Triple Five Corporation, the company of the Ghermazin family (three brothers and their father), who came from Iran to New York as rug traders, moved to Montreal and later made good with the discovery of Albertan oil. West Edmonton Mall has been built with the proceeds, a financial investment well over the $1 billion mark.

¹² As well as the World Waterpark, the Ice Palace and Fantasyland, it includes a hotel – the Fantasyland Hotel, naturally – as final confirmation, perhaps, that the Mall is not just a place to pass through, but a modern day pleasure dome.

¹³ Can you imagine spending your holiday in a glorified shopping precinct? Well, plenty of people do, booking in to any of half-a-dozen themed Fantasyland Hotel quarters with names like "Hollywood", "Polynesian" and "Truck". Others simply take in the Mall as part of bigger package tours. Of the annual 20 million visitors, around nine million are tourists, including a growing proportion of Japanese for whom no North American itinerary is complete without dropping in on Disneyland, Disney World and the Mall.

¹⁴ With pilgrims descending on it from all corners of the globe, the Mall enjoys a status approaching that of a sacred monument where worshippers pay homage with their credit cards. As a way to spend your time, West Edmonton Mall is as gratifyingly mind-rotting an experience as you could wish, positive proof that everyone should become a consumer zombie at least once in their lives.

B **1** **Highlight** the following words in the article and work out their meanings from the context. The paragraph numbers (¶) are given.

¶2	*parlance*	¶3 *avalanche*	¶4 *barmy*	*mock-up*
¶7	*meandered* *critical faculties*	¶8 *oasis*	¶9 *blithely*	*coughing up*
¶10	*state-of-the-art* *banal*	¶11 *proceeds*	¶12 *pleasure dome*	
¶13	*glorified*	¶14 *gratifyingly*		

Match their meanings to the words below.

ability to judge objectively   agreeably   crazy   in a carefree manner   jargon
palace of delights   plethora   profits   refuge   repetitious and dull   replica
seeming more important than in reality   spending   ultra-modern   wandered

2 Now fill the gaps in these sentences with suitable forms of the words in italics above:

1 It was a four-day camel ride before we reached the ....
2 They donated the .... of the jumble sale to charity.
3 They were .... complimentary about my essay, but I thought it was rather .... Maybe their .... are not very sharp!
4 The stream .... across the plain and then flowed into the river.
5 We had to .... £25 when we lost our car park ticket.
6 A shop is a 'retail outlet' in commercial ....
7 They received an .... of replies to the advertisement for 'senior administrator' – but I think they're just looking for a .... office boy.
8 The architect constructed a .... of the new mall to show to her clients.
9 This hi-fi system contains all the latest .... features.
10 He .... strolled into the interview room an hour late – he must be .... !

C Write your answers to these questions:

1 What did the writer and his family buy at the Mall?
2 The builders of the Mall gained their wealth from ....
3 The tourists who visit the Mall are likened to .... visiting a ....
4 How would you describe the tone of the article?
5 To sum up, what is the writer's attitude to the Mall? .... and ....
6 What would appeal to you and not appeal to you about the Mall? Write a summary of your reactions (50–70 words).

7.4 / Past and present   GRAMMAR REVIEW

A 👥 **Discuss any differences in meaning between these sentences:**

1 I didn't have time to read the paper   I haven't had time to read the paper
   this morning.   this morning.
2 I had tea when Pam came in.   I was having tea when Pam came in.
3 By the time we had had lunch it was 2.30.   By the time we had lunch it was 2.30.
4 Where has Steve gone for his holiday?   Where does Steve go for his holiday?
   Where is Steve going for his holiday?   Where did Steve go for his holiday?
   Where has Steve been going for his holiday?
5 I had hoped you would invite me.   I was hoping you would invite me.
   I did hope you would invite me.   I hoped you would invite me.
6 What are you doing?   What do you do?
   What have you done?   What have you been doing?

B **Fill each of the blanks with a suitable word or phrase.**

1 I *haven't seen* Ruth for ages. I believe I last *saw her at* Christmas.
2 Where .... that nice new jumper? The colour really .... you!
3 Come quickly! There .... accident – I think someone .... hurt.
4 Even though .... just .... rain, we .... to go out for a walk, thinking that it
   .... last long – and sure enough the sun soon ....
5 The back door .... just .... painted. If you .... it, you .... paint on
   your hands.
6 It's high time Bill .... to the hairdresser's – he .... his hair cut ....
   Christmas.
7 Here you are at last! We .... waiting for you .... 7.30 – where .... ? Why
   .... you tell us that you .... late? You .... phoned us before we ....
   home, then we .... the beginning of the show.
8 When I .... a child I .... spend all my money on sweets, but now I ....

C 1 👥👥 **Look at these photos and discuss the questions below. MAKE NOTES on your discussion.**

   • How have shops and stores changed over the past 10 or 20 years?
   • How has your local shopping area changed recently? What new shops have opened up?
     Which shops have closed down or gone out of business? Why?
   • How has the awareness (and power) of consumers changed over the years?
   • Describe your own shopping habits – past and present.

2 ✏ **Write a couple of paragraphs about your group's discussion, summarising the main ideas.**

7.5 Enhancing customers' lives — LISTENING

A Decide which of these factors are most important when buying the products below:

QUALITY   PRICE   SERVICE   PARKING   CONVENIENCE   FRIENDLY ADVICE
food   clothes   books   electrical goods   CDs   videos or DVDs   souvenirs

B You'll hear a broadcast about Japanese department stores. As you listen for the first time, choose the word or phrase which best completes each sentence:

1 The first Mitsukoshi store opened in ....
   a 1637   **b** 1673   **c** 1736   **d** 1763
2 Mitsukoshi-mae means '................. Mitsukoshi'.
   a beneath   **c** in front of
   b beside   **d** inside
3 At opening time, the sales staff are all ....
   a standing at the main entrance
   b ready to greet you as you enter their department
   c waiting at their tills
   d handing out brochures
4 The 'Ladies Club' provides ....
   a companionship   **c** free lunches
   b discounts   **d** courses
5 The facilities offered at other Japanese department stores are .... to Mitsukoshi's.
   a identical   **b** inferior   **c** dissimilar   **d** comparable
6 English is spoken by .... of the sales staff.
   a all   **b** most   **c** none   **d** some
7 Japanese department stores are open ....
   a every day of the week   **c** every day except Sunday
   b every day except national holidays   **d** six days a week
8 At one store the sales staff wear badges showing their hobbies so that ....
   a they don't need to wear a uniform   **c** you can discuss hobbies with them
   b customers can relate to them as people   **d** they seem more interesting

When you're doing a listening task in the exam, you'll hear the recording twice. During the first listening, just answer the easier questions.

C Listen to the broadcast again. Fill each blank with one or two words:

1 A ticket for a lunchtime performance at the theatre includes a .... containing *sushi*.
2 There is a crèche called a '................. room for resting babies'.
3 In the food department there are hundreds of .... selling everything from .... to ....
4 On the upper floors you can find many small ....
5 In summer, you can go up to the roof garden where you can sit in a .... and enjoy the .... and the ....
6 Summer in Japan officially begins on .... and ends on ....
7 At the main entrance you can get a .... and brochure in English.
8 As you enter the lift the operator will .... to you and .... you.
9 Department stores in Japan are open from .... to ....
10 Some department stores are owned by .... companies. There you can take the lift down to the .... where your .... is waiting.
11 Japanese department stores compete in terms of .... , how much of a .... it is to go there, and the .... of goods on offer.
12 At Mitsukoshi in London, helping Japanese tourists encourages ....

Then on the second listening, concentrate on the questions you missed. If you still can't get some answers, don't leave a blank – trust to luck and make a guess!

D Discuss your reactions to the broadcast:

- How do Japanese stores compare with department stores in your country?
- Which of their facilities and services seem most attractive?
- If you were going to open a shop, what would you sell? What facilities and services would you offer to your customers?

7.6 **Dear Sir, ...**   COMPOSITION

A Imagine that six months ago you bought a new hi-fi system from a department store. After four weeks the CD player went wrong, and you waited three weeks for the store to replace the hi-fi with a new one. Four weeks later the cassette player went wrong and you had to wait six weeks while the store repaired it. Now something else has gone wrong with it ...

👥 Role-play a conversation between the customer and the department manager.

B 🖊 Imagine that you're now living in a different part of the country, so you can't take the hi-fi back to the shop in person and you've been unable to get through on the phone. Write a letter, fax or e-mail to the store (300–350 words).

7.7 **Further uses of -ing**   ADVANCED GRAMMAR

A Fill the gaps in the sentences in this revision exercise. (If you have any problems look again at 4.4.)

1 When .... a complaint, I prefer to be friendly and polite, instead of ....
  aggressive or rude.
2 I found out what ingredients the product contained by .... the label. On ....
  that it contained artificial flavouring, I decided against .... it.
3 It's no use .... him, he won't take any notice of you.
4 There's no point in .... the book in translation if it's available in English.
5 It's impossible to sneeze without .... your eyes.
6 In addition to .... this course, she spends a lot of time at home .... things like
  .... novels in English and .... with friends by .... letters.
7 I've heard so much about you, I've really been looking forward .... you.
8 I felt depressed because I'm not used .... alone.

B Study these examples before filling the gaps in the exercise below:

> The possessive (*their, everyone's, her,* etc.) in these examples seems more formal than a straightforward pronoun or noun (*them, everyone, Janet*).
> I very much appreciated their/them coming to see me.
> We were puzzled about everyone's/everyone feeling ill after the meal.
> Janet/Her/Janet's arriving on time for a change was quite a surprise.
>
> A possessive is NOT normally used when several words are involved:
> I very much appreciated Janet and Maurice coming to see me.
>
> A possessive can't be used after verbs like *see, hear, feel, notice, watch* and *smell*:
> I didn't hear you calling me. ✓
> I didn't hear your calling me. ✗
> Can you smell something burning?

1 Their father doesn't approve of .... home late or .... television either. In fact, he
  insists on .... home before 11 and says that .... books will improve their minds.
2 We were all delighted to hear about Bill .... so well in the interview. His success is due
  to .... such a good impression on the interviewer.
3 They both smoke like chimneys, and I can't get used to .... during meals and
  .... me for a light is particularly irritating.
4 I'll never forget that time we went for a walk with Tony and Jane. Do you remember
  .... into the river and then .... to save him?

C Finish the incomplete sentences so that each means the same as the sentence before it.

1 I don't advise you to travel to London to do your shopping.   It isn't worth ....
2 We were upset that he forgot to inform us.   We were upset about his ....
3 It might be a better idea to save your money, not spend it.   Instead of ....
4 She is a champion athlete and speaks four languages fluently.   Besides ....
5 He has a job in an office and works in a shop at weekends.   As well as ....
6 You won't find out if they're open if you don't phone them.   Without ....
7 He has been in love with her from the moment he first saw her.   Ever since ....
8 It was inconsiderate of you not to consult me beforehand.   Your ....

7.8 **Compound nouns**   VOCABULARY DEVELOPMENT

A Read these notes. Then look again at the article about West Edmonton Mall in 7.3 and <u>underline</u> the compound nouns in paragraphs 1–6.

There are three types of compound nouns:

1 Noun + noun:
service industry   *department store*   *pleasure dome*   *credit card*   *bar code*   *charity shop*

2 Adjective + noun:
central heating   *public relations*   *open air*   *indoor plants*   *yellow pages*

– These aren't the same as 'normal adjectives', which modify a noun:
efficient heating = the heating is efficient   *yellow trousers = the trousers are yellow*

3 Longer phrases:
cost of living   *rule of thumb*   *do-it-yourself*   *value added tax*

Most compound nouns consist of two separate words. But some are hyphenated, and some are single words. There are no hard-and-fast rules about this:
dry-cleaning   *nightclub*   *sunglasses*   *back-seat driver*   *cover-up*

B Form compound nouns from the words in red and blue:

air	burglar	common	driving	estate	agent	alarm	attack	benefit
fancy	generation	greenhouse	hay		breakdown	business	clip	conditioning
heart	hire	income	junk	mail	crossing	dress	effect	fever	food
mother	nervous	package	paper		forecast	gap	licence	mall	meter
parking	pedestrian	pocket	shopping		money	order	purchase	sense
show	unemployment	weather	window		shopping	tax	tongue	tour

C Here are the first words of some common two-word compound nouns. What are the second words? In some cases there may be several possibilities.

inverted *commas*	mineral *water*	general *knowledge/election/public*	
one-parent	current	stainless	traveller's ....
compact	exclamation	swimming	skating ....
delivery	chain	clearance	travel ....
wastepaper			

D Fill the gaps with suitable compound nouns from A, B and C:

1 People in a .... often spend more time .... than actually buying things.
2 I didn't have enough money in my .... to cover a cheque, so I used my ....
3 You can pick up some good bargains at a .... or a ....
4 If you buy something from a .... catalogue, there's a .... to be added on.
5 Those black stripes on the back cover of this book are its ....
6 If you want to buy a house go to an ...., but to book a holiday go to a ....
7 I inadvertently threw my invitation to the .... party into the ....
8 Going on holiday? Don't forget to take your .... and ....

Preparation   Before the next lesson, collect some advertisements from magazines or newspapers. Include at least one that you DISLIKE or disapprove of, as well as ones you do like.

7.9   Advertising: sequencing your ideas

A   Paragraphs a–g are in the wrong order. Rearrange
them and number them in the correct order.

Benetton 'tasteless' ads in court

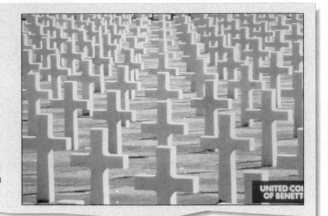

1   THE first of a series of lawsuits connected with a world-wide advertising campaign by the clothing giant Benetton opened yesterday, in which the company is accused of causing a sales slump through "tasteless" publicity.

a   "Many things come into play, not least a person's business sense. Many of our German branches are doing very well."

b   Benetton in turn is suing Mr Hartwich for withholding payments to the fashion chain and yesterday succeeded in postponing the court case until next month, saying it had no inclination to reach an amicable settlement in view of the publicity surrounding Mr Hartwich that had caused sales to drop by up to 60pc. A group of 70 Benetton retailers from four European countries met in Mainz on Sunday to coordinate their rebellion against the Italian company.

c   Heinz Hartwich, from Kassel, became the first of a group of retailers in Germany to sue the company for an undisclosed sum in respect of sales losses which they claim are a result of customer boycotts.

d   Mr Hartwich alleged that parents had told him that their children would be picked on by friends if they wore Benetton clothes and that shops had received anonymous threats complaining about the advertisements.

e   Religious and political circles in Germany have long protested against the advertisements, intended to focus on social issues, which included pictures of the bloodied uniform of a dead Croatian soldier and a baby attached by an umbilical cord.

f   Several similar cases of Benetton being sued in France have been settled out of court, but a company lawyer said the "media circus" generated by the complaints in Germany have led the company to fight the issue in court. A spokesman for Benetton said that blaming advertising for poor sales was absurd.

g   Some of the more commonly seen ads on hoardings and in magazines included oil-soaked birds and Aids sufferers.

9   Mr Ulfert Engels, a lawyer for Mr Hartwich, said that 150 of Benetton's 650 franchises in Germany have had to close. One third of the remaining 500 have survived only with financial support from the main company.

Robin Gedye

B   Explain who or what is referred to by the words highlighted in these quotations from
the article:

¶a ... our German branches ...
¶b ... payments to the fashion chain ...   ... saying it had no inclination ...
¶c ... to sue the company ...   ... which they claim ...
¶d ... if they wore ...
¶e ... protested against the advertisements ...
¶f Several similar cases ...

In a composition, the sequence in which points are made change the impact on your reader. Some points need to be arranged in a logical order with related ideas grouped together. Some points can be arranged in different ways to provide different kinds of emphasis.

The first point often 'sets the scene' for the rest of the text, while the final point is usually perceived as the conclusion.

C **Look at the advertisement on the right together with the ones you've brought to class. Discuss these questions:**

- How effective is each ad?
- Which do you like best and why?
- Which do you disapprove of and why?

While other people are reading their morning paper at Heathrow können Sie die Zeitung in Hamburg lesen.

British Airways news for businessmen is that we have more early flights each day to more European cities than any other airline.

D 1 Look at the notes below and decide which of the points you would include in an essay on the following topic. Bear in mind that the points must all be relevant, and that you can't make every single point in 300–350 words.

Write an essay outlining the harmful and the beneficial effects of advertising (300–350 words)

- Need created for totally unnecessary products (e.g. kitchen gadgets)
- Plethora of brands of goods, different only in name (e.g. detergents)
- Goods more expensive due to costly advertising budgets
- Young people may be harmed by certain advertisements (e.g. alcoholic drink)
- Ads stimulate envy among the less well-off; may lead to rise in crime rate (e.g. thefts of expensive cars)
- Commercials on TV interrupt programmes – very annoying
- Ads lead to dissatisfaction with one's standard of living – may lead to people trying to live beyond their means
- Ads create desire for more and more material possessions
- Many commercials on TV have insidious tunes that linger in the brain
- Many ads are amusing and informative – often more amusing than the programmes on TV or articles in a magazine
- Ads stimulate competition between companies, thus keeping prices down
- Ads create consumer awareness, giving information about a range of products
- Ads in newspapers and magazines keep their cost down – many couldn't survive without advertisements
- The world would be duller and drabber without amusing and colourful ads

2 Add any important further points you want to make to the notes above.

3 Decide on the best sequence of the points for your essay.

4 Write your essay, citing examples of particular advertisements that support your arguments.

8

Have I got news for you!

8.1 **The media**   **TOPIC VOCABULARY**

A **Discuss these questions:**

- What do you think has happened in the photos?
- How do you find out what's in the news?
- Which newspapers do you read regularly? Which do you prefer and why?
- What current affairs programmes do you watch or listen to on the TV or radio?
- If you go to websites for news, which do you prefer and why?
- Which English-language newspapers have you read? What were they like?
- Is there a local English language newspaper in your country? What's it like?
- Do you believe everything you read in the newspapers? Why/Why not?

B **Match the words and phrases in red to their synonyms in blue.**

article	circulation	editorial	issue		critic	the dailies	journalist	lead story
magazines	main story	newsreader			leader	monthlies & weeklies	newscaster
the papers	reporter	reviewer			number	number of copies sold	report

C **Here are some (genuine) newspaper headlines. Explain the double meaning or joke.**

1 POLICE FOUND DRUNK IN SHOP WINDOW

2 Butter battle spreads

3 Hospital guards stab victim

4 Dog rescues cat

5 Mine exploded on building site

6 The teacher from hell

7 Fish talks in Brussels

8 Women who smoke have lighter children

A   Discuss the differences in meaning (if any) between these sentences:

1. Could you finish the article?   Were you able to finish the article?
2. Can you carry this box?   Could you carry this box?
3. You can't leave yet.   You needn't leave yet.
4. I don't need to read the paper today.   I needn't read the paper today.
   I don't have to read the paper today.   I shouldn't read the paper today.
   I haven't read the paper today.   I haven't got to read the paper today.
5. There could be an election this year.   There has to be an election this year.
   There should be an election this year.   There will be an election this year.
6. That could be Tony at the door.   That must be Tony at the door.
   That will be Tony at the door.   That can't be Tony at the door.
   That might be Tony at the door.   That should be Tony at the door.

B   Write TWO reports of each sentence; one using a modal verb, and one using a longer phrase, as in the example:

1. 'You must do it now.'   He said that ....
   a   *He said that we had to do it.*
   b   *He said that we were obliged to do it / it was necessary for us to do it.*
2. 'Maybe we can help you.'   They said that ....
3. 'You can't use a dictionary in the exam.'   He told me that ....
4. 'Must you leave so soon?'   She asked me if ....
5. 'You mustn't believe everything you read in the newspapers.'   He told us that ....
6. 'I daren't dive into the swimming pool.'   She told us that ....
7. 'You need to book a table.'   He told us that ....
8. 'What time must I arrive there?'   She wondered ....

C   Rewrite each headline as a full sentence:

1. **'Non-swimmers on the up' says sports minister**
2. **Ban on smoking in cinemas**
3. **Seat belts to be worn in rear seats**
4. **70 mph speed limit to be lifted**
5. **1000s forced to flee after quake**
6. **RECESSION LOOMS AGAIN**
7. **Left set to win election**
8. **Rail strike stops commuters getting home**

D 1   Imagine that you're giving advice to a British person who is about to visit your country for the first time. What advice would you give about social customs, rules of behaviour and laws, using these modal verbs:

     can / can't   have to / don't have to
     need to / don't need to / needn't
     must / mustn't   should / shouldn't

2   Write a paragraph, giving the most important pieces of advice.

A Read this *Guardian* leader. It appeared the morning after the accident in which Diana, Princess of Wales, and Dodi Al Fayed were killed – and before the causes of the accident came to light.

Flying too close to the sun

1 SHE WAS 36. She leaves two young sons. She died at a moment when her personal life had brightened and her public life seemed to be making progress. "Unthinkable," people said when they heard of the news of Princess Diana's death, but few families altogether escape such tragedies. Though treated yesterday as barely more than a sideline, the death of Dodi Al Fayed is a tragedy too. So too is the death of their chauffeur, not even dignified in yesterday's reports with a name. Maybe he too was young; maybe he too leaves young children.

2 Yet the death of Diana was also spectacular, an event which reverberated across the world. She was probably the most famous woman, perhaps the most famous person, of her time. People will remember for years where and when they heard of her death, as they did with the death of John F Kennedy. As with Kennedy and with James Dean, John Lennon and Marilyn Monroe, she was a superstar who died young in violent circumstances, and as with them, it will guarantee her a mythological status.

3 In her time, and with her participation, the process accelerated which has made the British monarchy more and more a mix of fantasy with reality. Its role as the most dignified ingredient in our constitution, once apparently unassailable, is so badly eroded today that it looks beyond repair. The Queen herself commands a continuing respect, but for many people in Britain, the principal use of the Royal Family now is to keep us entertained and titillated and tantalised, to give us something new and spicy to discuss in the pub and the shops. More and more, their story has become a kind of rich psychological drama, more gripping even than any soap opera because its people really exist: a drama in whose cast list Diana had become not just the most alluring but perhaps the most influential player.

4 She came to all this hopelessly unprepared; sweet, shy, gauche, somewhat untutored, plucked from nowhere at 19 to be the bride of the heir to the throne, in the sort of transformation one doesn't expect outside bedtime stories. Even had things gone well, this would have been a brutally tough assignment. As it was, they began to go wrong chillingly soon – as we later learned, within a few months of the marriage. The truth about the marriage, at first shadowy and elusive, seeped gradually into the light: the shade of Camilla; her own uncertain temperament; the post-natal depression; the bulimia; the desperate alienation. Her very misfortunes increased the fascination she held for the Press and the public: not just a romantic figure, but a tragic figure too.

5 As things came apart, she had several options. One – which she briefly chose, but soon abandoned – was to pull out of public life and go into hiding; a second, simply to carry on with the life she wanted and do her best to survive the constant, unrelenting exposure; the third, to turn that exposure to positive use by enlisting it to promote her favourite causes. This last she did to huge beneficial effect.

6 She didn't just meet victims of Aids, she embraced them, in defiance of a tabloid press which taught that they were unclean. Her campaign to ban landmines, from which government agents made public and private attempts to dissuade her, took a cause long and obscurely argued by others without her magnetism, and put it on front pages across the world.

7 In doing this, in exploiting her hybrid role, part royal and part non-royal, she laid herself open to the charge of manipulation. It was hard to escape the impression that while claiming to hate the unsleeping eye of the media, she also craved it: not least because a quiet retreat to obscurity would be bowing her knee to the will of an Establishment which had wronged and damaged her and now wanted her out of the way. The result was to put her even more on the nation's centre stage. Increasingly, the story of the Royal Family's troubles came to resemble a script where the scriptwriters had excelled themselves in piling one twist on another. No scriptwriter, in this sense, could have contrived a more symbolic dénouement than that which occurred in the midnight streets of Paris this weekend.

8 And now the princess takes her place in the long and melancholy record of queens and princesses who led sad lives and met still sadder deaths. She will enter into legend, where it may come to be said of her that she met the fate which so often awaits those who fly too near to the sun.

B Highlight the following words and phrases in the article. Match their meanings in this context to the definitions below.

¶1 sideline   dignified
¶2 reverberated   mythological status
¶3 accelerated   unassailable   eroded   titillated and tantalised   spicy   alluring
¶4 gauche   chillingly   elusive   alienation
¶5 unrelenting   causes
¶7 hybrid   craved   Establishment   dénouement

attractive   awkward   charities   continuous   couldn't live without   damaged   echoed
ending   excited and fascinated   exciting   feeling of isolation   frighteningly   invulnerable
legendary position   mixed   mysterious   ruling classes   shown respect   went faster
unimportant event

C   Discuss these questions:

- Do you remember where you were when you heard about Princess Diana's death? How did the news affect you?
- What points are made in the article which praise Princess Diana?
- What points are more critical of her and of the Royal Family?
- How would you feel if photographers took photos of YOU everywhere?
- Who is most to blame for invading the privacy of famous people: the photographers or the people who buy newspapers and magazines?
- Does the press have too much power? What should be done to control the press?

8.4   '. . . that is part of the job'   LISTENING

A   Jayne Evans is a news journalist. Complete the sentences with a word or short phrase.

1 When you're a news journalist, you're never really [1   ] .

2 A news anchor reads from an autocue but must be ready to [2a   ] those words if instructed, and remain [2b   ] .

3 Shocking stories are very [3   ] but she must report them calmly.

4 It's almost impossible to remain detached when reporting disasters, but that is [4   ] .

5 In her career she has to enjoy the [5   ] .

6 The funniest situation she has been in was when [6   ] .

7 Being a news journalist is almost like being another [7   ] service.

8 Although your adrenalin is pumping, your report must be [8   ] .

B 👥👥 Discuss your reactions to the interview:

- What kind of personality and skills do you need to be a news journalist?
- What would it be like to have Jayne's job? Do you envy her? Why (not)?
- What difference does it make to see a TV on-the-spot report, rather than hear a news anchor person give the same information?
- How can reporters manage to give unbiased versions of events?

8.5 Cream and punishment

READING

A Six paragraphs/sentences have been removed from this article. Choose the most suitable paragraph/sentence from the list A–F for each gap (1–6) in the article.

Cream and punishment

"WATCH this bit carefully," says Noël Godin, fast-forwarding the video to the right place. "Bill Gates is walking towards the government building, slowly, slowly, his security guards all around him. Meanwhile, 30 pie-throwers, who have been standing in groups of three, suddenly come together, and, in a whirlwind of cakes, they strike their target. Gloup. Gloup. Gloup."

With a contented chuckle, Godin leans back in the black-leather sofa in his Brussels flat. On the screen, his victim is wiping cream pie from his face. "See, he is trying to suppress a small smile," says Godin, delightedly. Suppressing it very successfully, it appears. Gates looks completely stunned.

1 _____

The first few seconds after an attack reveal the true character of the target, believes Godin. Jean Luc Godard, the film director, showed 'real stature'. "He smiled, pulled off his bespattered jacket, lit a cigar and said: 'It tastes rather good.'"

Godin, who also acts under the pseudonym *Georges le Gloupier*, shakes his head sorrowfully. "After nearly 30 years of attacks, Godard is the only one who turned the situation to his advantage. I was very pleased with his reaction and I will never attack him again." Sylvie says that he is exhausted after all the excitement surrounding the Bill Gates coup.

2 _____

Godin prides himself on the rigorous selection of his targets, mostly those who have an inflated sense of their own importance and little sense of humour. But he also targets those who, in his opinion, abuse their power or simply get in the way of the total freedom he thinks should be every person's right. Any politician is fair game, although he is wary about attacking them individually as he does not want to give them 'free publicity'.

3 _____

His list of potential targets in England is growing. "Mr Virgin [Richard Branson] would be a good idea and Rupert Murdoch is also on the list." When she comes here, perhaps later this year, priority number one will be Lady Thatcher. "We will not leave her in peace just because she no longer has power. She is a symbolic target and we will go on a safari mission after her." After that, he is not sure.

4 □

So, during the Gates attack, he stood in a side street, waiting to intervene with back-up cream pies if needed. Sylvie, who has long feared that he will get himself shot by an over-alert bodyguard, is pleased, but Godin says that he will still deliver the pie to some of his victims, just to keep his hand in.

5 □

He works on a very low budget, with cream pies donated by local pâtissiers and part-time gloupiers drawn from friends, would-be actors and students.
"I am very careful about who I target. For example, I have been offered lots of money to do Sharon Stone and Catherine Deneuve. But I like them both. I'm not a cream-cake mercenary. I will accept sponsorship, but only for targets I think are worthy."

6 □

Ideally, he would like more people to follow his example. "Unlike Bill Gates, I don't feel I have a monopoly on my trade. Quite the reverse. If everyone attacked big bosses and pompous people, the message might start getting through. Custard pies are a sort of esperanto: a universal language."

▬▬▬▬▬▬▬ **Helena de Bertodano**

A   Bill Gates, as "a symbol of the new merchant arrogance", has been Number One on his hit list for some time. Now Bill Clinton and the Pope have replaced Gates as top targets, with Margaret Thatcher and Tony Blair running close behind.

B   Godin, 52, loves watching re-runs of his attacks and if Sylvie, his partner, were not here to restrain him, he would probably have rewound the tape and started again. Last month's attack on Bill Gates was his most high-profile yet and has earned him a new fan club in the United States, with an Internet site and lengthy articles about him appearing in papers such as The Wall Street Journal.

C   I ask him if it has ever occurred to him that he might be a little mad. "Of course. Like Falstaff. The world needs a bit of madness."

D   Inevitably, he has become a target of his own joke. Once, on a talk show, the presenter planted a cream pie in his face. How did he react? "I went and sat on the knee of the most important guest and wiped myself all over him." Does he ever get angry when he is flanned? "I laugh every time. If not I would be a perfect imbecile."

E   These days Godin himself reluctantly stands back from the front line of attack. He is so well-known in Belgium that his presence would be a giveaway. "When I go to the theatre, even in a private capacity, there is instant panic around me."

F   Usually he only carries out one or two attacks a year. Each *entartement*, or flanning, is meticulously planned and he agrees that it is a form of terrorism. "It is a burlesque terrorism. We do not wound our victims, they are only wounded in their *amour propre*." Sylvie points out that they were very careful not to ram Bill Gates' glasses too hard against his nose.

B   👥👥 **Discuss these questions:**
- Do you approve or disapprove of Noël Godin's philosophy and tactics? Why?
- Which famous people would you like to attack with a cream pie? Why?

C   🖊 **Summarise Noël Godin's attitude to famous people (50–70 words).**

1 👥 **Before writing, first make notes and discuss them with a partner.**

2 **When you've written your summary, compare it with a partner's.**

8.6 Prefixes

All the prefixes in this section are 'ACTIVE' prefixes – they can be used to form new words or phrases.

A Study the examples and then add the words below to the appropriate lists:

anti-	(= opposed to)	anti-nuclear anti-government anti-war	
pro-	(= supporting)	pro-environment pro-nationalist pro-strike	
pre-	(= before)	pre-recorded pre-Christmas pre-prepared	
super-	(= larger/greater than usual)	superglue super-rich superpower	
half-	half-finished half-empty half-full half-frozen		

*American   asleep   brother   cooked   democracy   expect   federal   feminist
intelligent   monarchy   packed   star   store   test   time   truth   union   way*

B Study the examples and then add the words below to the appropriate lists:

re	(= again)	re-elect rewritten recycled
un	(= reverse action)	unbutton undress untie
over	(= too much)	over-react overcooked overindulge
under	(= too little)	underfunded underdeveloped
out	(= more than)	outlive outrun outsell

*appear   block   build   capture   estimate   fasten   fillable   grow
load   number   print   simplify   united   usable   value   vote   work*

C Study the examples and then add the words below to the appropriate lists:

self-	(= by or for itself/oneself)	self-adjusting self-catering self-contained
co-	(= together)	co-author co-educational
counter-	(= against)	counter-attack counter-productive counter-intuitive
ex-	(= former)	ex-colleague ex-boyfriend ex-boss
semi-	(= half)	semi-professional semi-final semi-precious
sub-	(= below)	sub-zero sub-committee

*automatic   circular   defeating   director   educated   employed   exist
explanatory   governing   heading   measure   official   owner   policeman
preservation   president   productive   standard   sufficient   title*

The examples in A, B and C show which prefixes generally take hyphens. When pronunciation might be difficult, a hyphen is generally used: *re-election* (not *reelection*) and *super-rich* (not *superrich*). If in doubt, use a hyphen.

D Fill each gap using a prefix with a suitable form of the words in red:

1 It's an .... to say that a change of leader will solve all our problems.	simple
2 The minister was accused of .... the numbers of unemployed.	estimate
3 The .... members were .... by the moderate union members.	strike vote
4 It may be .... to force them into making a decision, and if you upset	produce
them they're quite likely to	react
5 Foreign-language films may be dubbed or shown with	title
6 Magazines devoting page after page to reports on the lives of the	rich
and .... usually .... more serious magazines.	star sell
7 You needn't refer to the manual: the use of the camera is	explain
8 He .... his .... to turn up at the wedding ceremony.	expect wife
9 The .... began after the troops received a .... signal.	attack arrange
10 He went out into the snow and .... later looking	appear frozen

A **1** Rephrase each sentence, using *there* … :

1 Someone is waiting to see you. *There's someone waiting to see you.*
2 Most political problems have no easy answers.
3 It's pointless trying to explain the problem to them.
4 Some papers give more coverage to sport than others.
5 Luckily for us a telephone box was nearby.
6 It's unnecessary to shout, I can hear you perfectly well.
7 Mitsukoshi has 14 branches in Japan and 14 associate stores.
8 Come quickly! An accident has happened! Someone may have been hurt.
9 He stood in the doorway with a sheepish grin on his face.
10 I was waiting in the lecture hall with fourteen other students.

> Verbs that describe actions (rather than states) can't be used with *there*:
>
> There fell an apple off the tree. ✗

2 Discuss the difference in emphasis when *there* is used in each sentence.

B Fill the gaps in these examples with suitable words:

1 We expect there .... difficulties ahead.
2 There .... misunderstanding about this: you have to arrive at 7.15 sharp.
3 There .... a time when everyone has to face up to their responsibilities.
4 There .... nonsense talked about politics by people who ought to know better.
5 There .... more question I'd like to ask.
6 There's no .... that some newspapers distort the truth.
7 We were surprised/amazed/shocked at there .... so many people present.
8 There .... to be something wrong with my back, doctor.

> Yesterday there came my friend to see me. ✗
>
> There arrived the train on time. ✗

C Explain the meaning of each headline in a full sentence, using *there*:

1	**'Fewer than 5,000 attend peace demo'**	The police say …
2	More sunshine next week	The forecasters say …
3	**'NO DOUBT ABOUT A VICTORY'**	The England soccer manager says …
4	**'Too many cars cause pollution and accidents'**	Environmentalists say …
5	General election possible this year	According to the newspaper …
6	**Peace moves in teachers' dispute**	There …
7	Road accidents down this year	There …
8	**None killed in ferry sinking**	There …

D Student A should look at Activity 8, student B at 17 and C at 27. There's a short news item for you to read and then retell to your partners in your own words, using *There* …

8.8 ## Hitting the headlines **LISTENING AND SPEAKING**

A 🔊 You'll hear a radio programme. Indicate where the events in 1–8 happened by writing the appropriate letter in each box.

In each box write:

    I   if it happened in Italy
or   **J**   if it happened on the way to Japan
or   **USA**   if it happened in the USA

1 One can of beer every evening.
2 Police knew the licence number of the car.
3 Roller-skating champion.
4 Accurate throwing caused deaths.
5 Shortage of fresh water.
6 Video camera stolen, but not videotape.
7 Waving to relatives was dangerous.
8 Workmates were very kind to their colleague.

1	
2	
3	
4	
5	
6	
7	
8	

B Which places in the world are in the news this week? What headline news has come from each of the continents during the past month?

C **1** Before the next lesson, listen to the news on the radio or TV (or read the news on the Internet) and make notes on the main points of TWO interesting stories.

2 Then, back in class, tell your partners about your stories.

8.9 Freedom

SPEAKING

A Read this poem and then discuss the questions below.

EPITAPH ON A TYRANT

Perfection, of a kind, was what he was after,
And the poetry he invented was easy to understand;
He knew human folly like the back of his hand,
And was greatly interested in armies and fleets;
When he laughed, respectable senators burst with laughter,
And when he cried the little children died in the streets.

W.H. Auden (1938)

- Which tyrants and dictators spring to mind when you read the poem?
- Why is it that tyrants and dictators succeed in politics – and on a smaller scale in business and family life too?
- What can the individual (i.e. you and I) do to stop them from succeeding?
- How important is it for a country to have a strong, charismatic leader?

B Which of these quotations do you agree with, and which do you disagree with? Which do you agree with up to a point? Give your reasons.

'All men are created equal.'   – Thomas Jefferson (1743–1826)

'The ballot is stronger than the bullet.'   – Abraham Lincoln (1809–1865)

'No one can be perfectly free till all are free; no one can
be perfectly happy till all are happy.'   – Herbert Spencer (1820–1903)

'Nationalism is an infantile disease. It is the measles of mankind.' – Albert Einstein (1879–1955)

'Unhappy the land that is in need of heroes.'   – Bertolt Brecht (1898–1956)

'Politics is too serious a matter to be left to the politicians.'   – General de Gaulle (1890–1970)

'Political power grows out of the barrel of a gun.'   – Mao Zedong (1893–1976)

'Ask not what your country can do for you; ask
what you can do for your country.'   – John F. Kennedy (1917–1963)

'All animals are equal, but some animals are more equal   – *Animal Farm* by George Orwell
than others.'   (1903–1950)

'There is no such thing as a free lunch.'   – anon

C Take turns to talk for about two minutes WITHOUT INTERRUPTION on ONE of the topics below. Then the others should react to your talk by answering these questions:

- Is there anything you'd like to add?
- Is there anything you don't agree with?

Should individuals be free to decide whether or not to do the following things – or should there be laws to control them?

drink alcohol at any age	drive at any speed
take drugs	have an abortion
do military service	immigrate into your country
wear seat belts in cars	own a gun

In Part 3 of the Speaking Paper you'll have to speak for two minutes about a topic you are given. You don't have time to prepare a talk, so this is quite hard to do. You have to express your opinions and develop the topic. This is something you can practise on your own at home, preferably using a cassette recorder with a microphone.

After both candidates have spoken and answered follow-up questions, the interlocutor leads a general discussion on a related topic.

8.10 Long and short sentences WRITING SKILLS

A Read this magazine article and then discuss the questions below:

These are bad times for talking. According to a recent study, dinnertime conversation is disappearing, with people now preferring to eat meals in front of the television. "Social conversation will soon be a thing of the past," said one researcher. It already is in Australia, where one couple haven't spoken to each other for 43 years. Doris and Ivan Weeds stopped communicating in 1954, shortly after their marriage. "We talked incessantly when we were courting," recalled Mrs Weeds, "and I guess we just said everything we had to." They've since lived in near total silence, chattering away happily to friends, but saying nothing whatsoever to each other. Early in the Seventies Mr Weeds did break his silence to ask his wife if she wanted to go to Thailand, and she broke hers to say no, but otherwise all has been mutual muteness, a fact which, insists Mrs Weeds, in no way affects their love for each other. "There are many ways of saying, 'I love you' without actually saying it," she explained, "like blowing kisses, and tap dancing together."

Paul Sussman

1 Which is the shortest sentence? What is the effect of this?
2 Which is the longest sentence? How many different ideas and clauses are there in that sentence? What is the effect of this?
3 How much is direct speech used? (How would the effect be different if reported speech had been used instead?)

B Re-read the first TWO paragraphs of *Flying too close to the sun* on page 86 and *Cream and punishment* on page 88.
Then discuss the same questions.

C 1 ✎ Rewrite these notes, using a suitable mixture of long and short sentences, and direct or reported speech.

Possibly worst day in history of crime – Miami thief Natron Fubble, 35 – 'World's Most Inept Robber'

Early morning raid on delicatessen – shop owner hit Mr Fubble with giant salami – broke his nose

Attempted bank robbery – met mother in same bank – sent to do shopping for her

Climax: late in afternoon – another failed hold-up – pursued by irate customers – hid in boot of empty car – car was police surveillance vehicle – owners returned from cup of coffee – drove 5 days across America tailing lorry

Whimpers eventually heard near Seattle – removed at gunpoint, arrested

Sentenced to two years – despite claim: 'On top-secret undercover mission for FBI'

2 👥 Read each other's stories. What are the best features of each?

3 ✎ Write a final version, combining the best features of the versions you've read.

Shorter sentences tend to be easier to understand (and easier to write) than long ones, but lots and lots of very short sentences may look silly. 'A good balance' of long and short sentences is preferable.

Put yourself in your reader's position as you write and bear in mind these questions:

'Would I like to be reading this?'   'Have I made my meaning clear?'

8.11 Points of view

SPEAKING AND COMPOSITION

A 1 👥 The class is divided into an even number of pairs (or groups of three). Half the pairs should work out together how they would tell the story of what happened in the photos from the point of view of the person on the LEFT of each photo – the other half from the point of view of the person on the RIGHT of each photo.

2 👥 → 👥 Then each 'left-hand' pair joins a 'right-hand' pair to tell their stories.

B **1** Find an interesting news story in a newspaper – it can be in your own language, not in English – preferably one involving more than one person. Alternatively, you may prefer to use a photograph instead.

2 Make notes on the events that occurred. Don't attempt to translate the article into English but use your own words.

3 Write a report to the police on what happened, from the point of view of one of the protagonists (300–350 words). Use section headings in your report.

8.12 *bring* and *get*

VERBS AND IDIOMS

A Explain the phrases in red, or find synonyms. Use a dictionary if necessary.

1 Talking to her really brought it home to me how important it is to bring children up in the right way. They shouldn't be allowed to get away with bad behaviour.
2 Whatever brought this problem about, we must get round it somehow.
3 They hope to get over their difficulties by bringing in a management consultant.
4 Her attitude brings out the worst in me, I'm afraid. I just can't get on with her. The whole situation's really getting me down.
5 He told an anecdote which brought the house down. But I didn't get the joke.
6 He gets terribly upset when he thinks people are getting at him, but he usually gets over it fairly quickly.
7 I've been cheated and I want to get my own back. How can I get even with them?
8 Time's getting on, I think we'd better get the meeting over with.
9 It was hard to get it across to them that they had to work harder.
10 What did he mean? I really didn't understand what he was getting at.
11 He's terribly gauche and shy with strangers, he needs someone to bring him out.
12 'I had a terrible night: I didn't manage to get off to sleep till 3 a.m. I was so worried about getting behind with my work.'
'You should have got up and got on with some reading. You could have got through quite a lot during that time.'

B Fill the gaps with suitable phrases from the list below. You may need to change the form of the verbs.

1 She's a very gregarious person and seems to .... everyone.
2 I promised to go food shopping for them and now I can't .... it.
3 Was it because they pleaded guilty that they .... a fine, instead of a jail sentence? Or was it because the judge had been .... ?
4 There's no point in having good ideas if you don't .... them .... in writing.
5 The UN intervention .... a peaceful settlement of the conflict.
6 If you want to .... in politics you have to have the right connections and .... the people who matter.
7 I'm sorry to .... the subject of politics, I know it's a sore point with you.
8 I know how to handle him, so leave it to me – I'll be able to .... him.
9 I haven't done the work yet and I don't know when I'll .... it.
10 I have to be at work early tomorrow, can you .... me .... at 5.30?
11 I'm sorry to .... this .... – I know it's embarrassing.
12 What have the children been .... while I've been away?

bring about   bring up
get at   get down   get in with
get off with   get on   get on to
get on with   get out of   get round
get round to   get up   get up to

9

A learning curve

9.1 Happy days?

LISTENING AND TOPIC VOCABULARY

A 🔊 **You'll hear three people remembering their schooldays. Fill the gaps in these notes:**

1 **Ruth**, at her comprehensive school in Wales, hated .... lessons because the teacher, Mr James, seemed to .... She didn't like .... because at 14 she didn't appreciate the .... of science.

2 **Sarah**'s favourite subject at her school in England was .... The teacher not only had a passion for her .... but also ....

3 **Christine** describes four phases in the way the girls viewed the boys at her school in Scotland:
   a From the ages of 5 to 10 she thought the boys were ....
   b From 10½ to 14 the girls thought the boys were ....
   c At 14 or 15 they admired the older boys but their contemporaries were ....
   d In the sixth form the boys and girls formed lovely ....

4 **Christine** remembers Miss Rae, who was a .... Pupils who made spelling mistakes were .... Anne Black was punished because she was .... and she spelt words in the way she .... them. Since that time Christine has always .... of teachers intimidating pupils.

B 👥 **Compare your reactions to the interviews:**

- Did you have any similar experiences at school?
- What is the point of going to school? What should the aims of education be?
- Is it better to specialise or to have a broad education?
- What should be the balance between a theoretical, academic approach and a more practical, vocational education?

C 👥 **Discuss which of these words and phrases have similar meanings, or are used in similar situations. In some cases there are various ways of linking them. Underline one word in each list which seems to be the odd one out and is NOT connected with education or training.**

1 award   grant   loan   prize   <u>reward</u>   scholarship
   award → grant → scholarship   grant → loan   prize → award
   <u>reward</u> isn't connected with education, unless discussing its rewards or pleasures

2 certificate   degree   diploma   doctorate   licence   recommendation
   reference   testimonial

3 article   assignment   composition   dissertation   essay   paper   report   thesis

4 comprehensive school   grammar school   gymnasium   junior school   kindergarten
   law school   medical school   nursery school   primary school   secondary school

5 BA   bachelor   BSc   doctorate   first degree   MA   master's   MSc   PhD

6 credits   grades   marks   numbers   scores

7 continuous assessment   evaluation   examination   questionnaire   study   test

8 class   conference   lecture   seminar   study group

9 apprentice   contestant   freshman   graduate
   participant   post-graduate   pupil   schoolchild
   student   trainee   undergraduate

10 academic year   financial year   half-term   holiday
    semester   term   vacation

11 correspondence course   degree course   distance learning course
    evening course   part-time course   race course   sandwich course

12 associate professor   business associate   coach   don   instructor
    lecturer   professor   teacher   trainer   tutor

D Look at the photos and discuss these questions:

- What are the pros and cons of the kinds of schools shown?
- What do you remember most fondly about being in primary school?
- Describe your favourite primary school teacher.
- What did/do you enjoy most at secondary school? What did you dislike most?
- Which were/are your favourite subjects? Why?
- Describe a typical school day for a secondary school pupil in your country.
- How much do you think on-line learning is replacing classrooms?

9.2 Writing an application

COMPOSITION

A Imagine that you are attending an interview for a job or for a place on a higher education course. Describe your own education to your partner, concentrating on your achievements and the qualifications you have attained. Take it in turns to be the interviewer.

B **1** Imagine that you are keen to apply for the scholarship in this advertisement. Note down some reasons why YOU would benefit from learning Japanese.

2 Compare your notes with a partner.

(If you *are* Japanese, write an application for a similar scholarship, offered by the same organisation, to learn another language, such as Spanish or German, but not English.)

SAKURA SCHOLARSHIP SCHEME

Learn Japanese in Japan

Sakura Scholarships offer students the opportunity of taking part in a three-month Japanese language course in the historic city of Kyoto. The Scholarship covers free accommodation, meals and tuition. Return air fares between their country of residence and Osaka are paid, and $1000 pocket money is also provided.

To apply for one of these Scholarships, you should write 300–350 words describing your own education so far, and giving reasons why you think you would benefit from participation in the Sakura Scholarship Scheme.

The closing date for applications is February 1. Applicants who have been selected for the short list will be notified by March 31. The final selection will be made on the basis of interviews held during May.

Applications are open to all students, regardless of age, sex or nationality, and are also welcome from people who are not currently full-time students.

Please send your application to Ms Kyoko Matsumoto, Sakura Scholarship Scheme, Sakura Trading Co, 200 East Avenue, London E9 7PS

3 Write an appropriately dazzling application for the scholarship (300–350 words).

(A) **1** **Read this article, then look at the questions below and decide on your answers.**

My lessons in the classroom

"You must be mad!" was the general comment of family, friends and colleagues. "Giving up a teaching post now, when there isn't much chance of finding another one, ever!

"And what about all that lovely money you're earning, and all those long holidays!"

But I had already come to my lonely decision, after months of concealed suffering. I knew I could no longer continue in the teaching profession. To wake in the morning with a fear of the day ahead, to force a hasty breakfast down an unwilling throat, and then set off for work with pounding heart and frozen face had become habitual, and I had turned to tranquillizers to help me along.

It had not always been as bad as this. Ten years ago I managed well enough, and the holidays for rest and recuperation used to come round just in time.

But I, in common with most other teachers, am enormously self-critical, and I knew now that I was no longer "managing". My classes were noisy, the children were not learning very much, my attempts to cope with changing teaching methods were patchy, I had run out of enjoyment and enthusiasm. It was time to stop.

But was it all my own failure? In fairness to myself, I don't think it was. I had plenty of ideas, I loved my subject, and, by and large, I liked children.

I had been idealistic. But the reality I faced was bored children, over-stimulated by video-watching the night before and tired out by a late bedtime. They were children who were given the wrong food at the wrong time, who came breakfast-less to school and then stuffed themselves with gum, crisps and sweets bought on the way; who were "high" with hunger in the lesson before lunchtime and giggled restlessly as the smell of chips from the school kitchen came wafting to all floors.

There were children who absorbed all the smutty side of sex before they were 10, and were constantly teasing and titillating each other; bright, hard-working little girls who changed, under the pressures of peer group and advertising, into assertive, screeching empty-heads, with make-up in their pencil cases and a magazine concealed on their desks.

Then there were the ones from difficult homes, such as Simon, whose parents had split up after many years together and who was not wanted by either – his tired eyes flickered all round when I tried to remonstrate with him privately, and his pale face never stopped twitching. But he could bring chaos to my lessons with his sniggerings and mutterings.

The rudeness I had to put up with, and the bad language, appalled me. I had no redress, as the only form of punishment available was a detention, which meant keeping myself in too.

Sometimes parents could be contacted, and their help sought, but frequently they were as bewildered and incapacitated as we ourselves.

A frequent image came before me, as I lay in bed after an early wakening – the maths room, after a "wet break", chairs turned over, books and orange peel on the floor.

The tenth year are due for their English lesson, so I come in and attempt to assert myself and restore order. Jeremy is telling jokes. Donna is cackling. Andrew is standing on a desk and yelling out of the window.

At one time my very presence in the doorway would have been enough to ensure a partial silence. Now they give a vague "Hello, Miss", and carry on.

I distribute the work sheets, expensively photocopied, and we try to start, but two slow girls are making noises: "Miss, I can't understand this!" And James is quietly reading his football magazine, Jeremy continues to tell jokes, more quietly now, and Michele bares her gum-filled teeth and urges Paul to shut his face.

I have been trying to create the basic conditions in which teaching becomes possible, but I have failed, and no longer have the stomach for the job. And that is why I'm giving up.

Anne Bonsall

1
2
3
4
5
6
7
8
9
10
11
12
13
14
15
16

2 **Highlight** the relevant information in the passage. Make notes on your answers to these questions:

1 Why were the writer's friends and family taken by surprise?
2 Why was the writer's heart pounding as she set off for work?
3 How well had she managed to adapt to new methods during her ten years' teaching?
4 Why did the hard-working little girls change?

5 Why was the writer unwilling to punish pupils who misbehaved?
6 Who are referred to as *we ourselves* in ¶11?
7 How do the tenth year English class react to the writer's entry into the room?
8 What is meant by *the stomach for the job* in the last line?

3 👤→👤 **Write down your answers to the questions. Compare your answers.**

B **Find words or phrases in the passage that mean the same as these:**

beating loudly   incomplete   hungry   tell off   laughing disrespectfully
way of putting things right   unable to take action   exercise control   laughing shrilly

C ✐ **Why doesn't the writer blame her lack of success as a teacher on her own shortcomings? Summarise the reasons in 50–70 words.**

MAKE NOTES on the reasons. Compare your notes with another pair, and make sure you have only noted down the relevant information. Then write your summary.

In Part 5 of the Use of English Paper, when writing a summary, remember that you should try to use your own words and not quote directly from the passage. Make sure that you only select the required information – you'll lose marks if you write more than 70 words.

9.4 'It's just the most wonderful thing'   LISTENING

A 🔊 **You'll hear interviews with Sarah Wilson, a teacher at St Mary's School in Cambridge, and Claudine Kouzel, a sixth-former. Tick the boxes in Question 1 and write a word or short phrase in the boxes for Questions 2 to 8.**

1 Sarah explains why she enjoys being a teacher. Tick the things she mentions:

the long holidays ☐   helping students to manage their work ☐
a good lesson ☐   working with people ☐
helping students to pass exams ☐   making a contribution to students' lives ☐
the funny things that happen ☐   finding quick solutions to students' problems ☐
communicating her love of English literature ☐

2 She says she needs the holidays to [____2____] who she is.

3 She doesn't like having to balance the needs of the [____3a____] with the needs of the [____3b____].

4 She recommends teaching as a profession to someone who not only loves their [____4a____] but also likes [____4b____].

5 Claudine is hoping to study [____5a____] at university, but she doesn't know if she'll do a [____5b____] before starting university.

6 Claudine enjoys school because she has her [____6a____] around, and she has the [____6b____] of her teachers.

7 It's hard for her to balance [____7a____] activities with her heavy [____7b____].

8 She prefers a single-sex school because there are fewer [____8a____], which helps her to [____8b____] on her work.

B 👥 **Discuss these ideas:**
- Would you like to be a teacher? Why (not)?
- What are the differences between St Mary's School and Anne Bonsall's school in 9.3?
- Is it usual for students to do a 'gap year' in your country? Why (not)?
- What are the qualities of a 'good student' or a 'good pupil'?

9.5 Question tags and negative questions GRAMMAR REVIEW

A 👥 **Discuss the differences in meaning or emphasis (if any) between the sentences.**

1 He didn't use to play squash, did he?   Didn't he use to play squash?
   He used to play squash, didn't he?   Did he use to play squash?
   He used to play squash, did he?

2 Isn't this a great party!   This is a great party, isn't it?
   This is a great party!   What a great party!

3 So you enjoyed my talk, did you?   So didn't you enjoy my talk?
   So you didn't enjoy my talk?   So did you enjoy my talk?

4 Isn't it strange that everyone thinks they are experts on education?
   It's strange that everyone thinks they are experts on education.

5 Didn't she do well in her exam!   Didn't she do well in her exam?
   She did very well in her exam.   Did she do well in her exam?
   How did she do in her exam?

B **Add question tags to these sentences. Then rewrite the first four sentences as negative questions.**

Apart from rhetorical questions, question tags and negative questions are rare in writing, except in personal letters.

1 We'd better stop work soon, ... ?
2 I'm right about this, ... ?
3 You'd rather stay in bed than get up early, ... ?
4 Anyone can apply for the scholarship, ... ?
5 If we don't get a move on, there won't be much time left, ... ?
6 Let's have a rest, ... ?
7 Nobody anticipated what would happen, ... ?
8 Do try to relax, ... ?
9 He never used to study so hard, ... ?
10 They ought to work much harder, ... ?

C 🔊 **Listen to the recording and decide whether the speakers sound SURE or UNSURE about the information they're giving. You'll hear these examples first:**

This is a great **par**ty, **isn't** it! ↘   = I'm sure – but I want you to agree

He used to play **squash, didn't** he? ↗   = I'm unsure – but I think you know

sure or unsure?		sure or unsure?	
1		6	
2		7	
3		8	
4		9	
5		10	

D 1 **Rewrite each sentence so that its meaning remains unchanged, using a question tag at the end, as in the example. The passive is required in each one.**

1 Experts are finding new ways of using computers all the time.   New uses ....
   New uses for computers are being found all the time, aren't they?

2 One day robots and computers will do all our work for us.   All our work ....

3 I don't think that computers could be installed in every
   classroom.   Computers ....

4 No one has yet invented a robot teacher.   No robot teachers ....

5 The government should pay teachers on results.   Teachers ....

6 Students' parents often support them.   Students ....

7 The government might raise the school-leaving age to 19.   The school-leaving ....

8 Schools would have to employ more teachers in that case.   More ....

2 **Rewrite each of your passive sentences as negative questions.**

Aren't new uses for computers being found all the time?

9.6 Abstract nouns

VOCABULARY DEVELOPMENT

A 1 Look at the examples. What is the equivalent verb for each of the abstract nouns?

-ation	evaluation *evaluate*	recuperation *recuperate*	cooperation	administration
-ion	detention *detain*	destruction	satisfaction	suspicion
-ment	accomplishment	astonishment	enjoyment	punishment

2 Form abstract nouns from these verbs, adding them to the appropriate list above.

apply   achieve   acknowledge   amuse   concentrate
contribute   describe   embarrass   encourage   explain
invent   isolate   justify   manage   negotiate   object
oppose   pronounce   receive   recommend   represent   vary

B 1 Look at the examples. What is the equivalent adjective or noun for each of the abstract nouns?

-ty	anxiety *anxious*	reality *real*	humility	seniority
-ance	brilliance *brilliant*	insignificance	intolerance	
-ence	absence	presence	intelligence	reference
-ism	realism	absenteeism	nationalism	optimism
-ness	clumsiness	fairness	happiness	rudeness
-ship	apprenticeship	relationship	scholarship	sponsorship

2 Form abstract nouns from these adjectives and nouns, adding them to the appropriate list above.

authentic   available   careless   companion   creative   diffident   equal
extravagant   familiar   favourite   friend   generous   half-hearted
honest   incompetent   inconvenient   independent   insolent   leader
loyal   mischievous   narrow-minded   productive   professional
relevant   reliable   self-confident   selfish   stable   symbolic

C Add two more nouns to each group in A and B, then compare your ideas with another pair.

D What adjective is each of these nouns associated with, or derived from?

-dom	wisdom *wise*	boredom	freedom					
-th	breadth	filth	health	length	stealth	strength	warmth	wealth width
-cy	democracy	bureaucracy	delicacy	efficiency	fluency	frequency		
	inadequacy	inefficiency	redundancy	urgency				
and ...	delight *delighted*	enthusiasm	hysteria	hunger	pride	sarcasm	success	

E Fill the gaps in these sentences with suitable nouns from A, B and D:

1 They apologized for the .... we had been caused.
2 We were sceptical about the .... of the statistics he had quoted.
3 She was full of .... for her job and her talk included a fascinating .... of a typical day's work.
4 Contending with .... in government offices leads to .... and delays.
5 Teachers should not show .... to individual pupils – their motto should be .... to each child and they should encourage .... among their pupils.
6 I didn't quite see the .... of the answer he gave and I asked him to give us some .... for it. His .... was totally convincing.
7 I have all the right .... for the job but I don't know what the salary will be, because the advertisement says that it's 'subject to ....'.
8 They want me to supply them with three character .... , as they are particularly interested in my qualities of ....
9 Two things I disapprove of are .... and ....
10 Two qualities I appreciate in a person are .... and ....

A Read this article and then answer the multiple-choice questions opposite:

Managing your study time

1 I was in a student coffee bar during my first week at university soaking in the atmosphere when a lad from Oldham, of conspicuously cool and languid manner, announced calmly that he intended to get a first in classics. He would work 25 hours a week, study five hours a day on weekdays and leave the weekends free. That would be sufficient.

2 I was vaguely committed to endless hours of work. I imagined that at some point I would spend weeks of intensive study. The vice-chancellor had told us in his address to freshers to look at the person on either side and note that in all probability one of us would not be around the following year. The message struck home: I would turn myself into a paragon of academic virtue. I could see that the classicist in the coffee bar had got it all wrong, or was bluffing.

3 Three years later he sailed to his first whilst other friends struggled to very modest achievements. As I discovered when sharing his lodgings, he worked more or less to the plan he had outlined. He slept late in the mornings, only stirring himself if there was a lecture to attend. He played cards with the rest of us after lunch. Then he moved to his desk and stayed there till around seven. The evenings he spent more wildly than most – hence the late mornings. Nevertheless, when I came to look back I realised he had studied more than anyone else I knew. Through sticking assiduously to a modest but well-defined, realistic plan, he had achieved a great deal. He had enjoyed work much more, too. He argued that it was not possible to work productively at intensive intellectual tasks for more than a few hours at a time. I aimed to do much more. But I was easily distracted. By the time it was apparent that stretches of a day had slipped away, I felt so guilty that I blotted studies out of my mind, comforting myself with the thought of all the days which lay ahead.

4 I was too inexperienced at looking after my own affairs to realise I was already failing one of the major tests of studenthood, the organisation of time. I thought that success in studying was to do with how brilliantly clever and original you were; I had yet to discover that one of the central challenges of adult life is time management.

5 At school the work timetable was defined for us and teachers made sure we fitted all that was required into the school year. At university I was at sea. Time came in great undifferentiated swathes. What to do with it all? With 168 hours in a week — or 105, allowing nine a day for sleeping and eating — how many was it reasonable to spend on study? Individuals vary and different subjects make different demands. Nevertheless with a target you can plan your studies, not just stumble ahead in hope. The sketchiest of weekly timetables, setting aside 40 hours to cover all study, is an invaluable aid in defining time. Then you can divide it into segments and use it strategically, rather than let it dribble away.

6 Defining what to do is harder. Take the booklists. How many books are students expected to read? How long should a book take? It took me so long to read just a few pages that I felt defeated when I looked ahead. Should I take notes? How many? What would I need them for?

7 I would sit in the library for a whole day, dipping into one book after another, often with glazed over eyes. What was my purpose? How would I know when I had achieved it? By comparison I went to lectures gratefully – at least I knew when they started and finished. Although my lecture notes weren't up to much, I could tell myself I had accomplished something, which would bring down my anxiety level.

8 Much later I discovered I could learn a great deal from a close reading of selected sections; that taking notes could sometimes be very satisfying and at other times was not necessary. The trick was to take control; to decide what I wanted to find out – something specific – and then work at it until I had taken in enough to think about for the time being.

9 Dividing big jobs into smaller sub-tasks helps to bring work under control, allows you to set targets and check your progress. There is so much pressure to be ambitious – to go for the long dissertation, to read the huge tomes. Yet achievement arises out of quite modest activities undertaken on a small scale. The trouble with the big tasks is that you keep putting them off. Their scope and shape is unclear and we all flee from uncertainty. The more you can define your work as small, discrete, concrete tasks, the more control you have over it.

10 Organising tasks into the time available can itself be divided into strategy and application. It is useful to think of yourself as "investing" time. Some tasks require intense concentration and need to be done at a prime time of day, when you are at your best and have time to spare. Others can be fitted in when you are tired, or as "warm-up" activities at the start of a session. Some, such as essay writing, may best be spread over several days. Some need to be done straight away.

11 There are few reliable guidelines. Essentially you have to keep circling round a self-monitoring loop: plan an approach to a task, try it out, reflect afterwards on your success in achieving what you intended and then revise your strategy.

12 Once you start to think strategically, you begin to take control of your studies rather than letting them swamp you.

Andrew Northedge

Choose the word or phrase which best completes each sentence:

1 The vice-chancellor's speech .... the writer.
   a amused   **b** failed to convince   **c** frightened   **d** terrified

2 The lad from Oldham's time at university was .... than the writer's.
   a less successful   **b** more fun   **c** more intellectual   **d** more strenuous

3 While he was in the university library the writer ....
   a couldn't concentrate   **c** read books from cover to cover
   b dozed off   **d** worked hard

4 Towards the end of his time at university the writer ....
   a gave up hope   **c** worked harder
   b organised himself better   **d** wrote a long dissertation

5 The writer recommends ....
   a studying for a short time every day   **c** finishing one task before starting another
   b studying only when you are alert   **d** deciding when each kind of task is best done

6 *Circling round a self-monitoring loop* (¶11) means ....
   a approaching studies in a circuitous way   **c** continuing to study for a long time
   b planning your study methods   **d** evaluating the success of your study methods

B **Highlight** these words and phrases in the passage, and use a dictionary to look up the meanings of any you are unsure of. Make sure you look at the examples given as well as the definitions. Then look again at the words in context.

bluffing (¶2)   assiduously (¶3)   blotted out (¶3)   at sea (¶5)   segments (¶5)   strategically (¶5)
dribble away (¶5)   dipping into (¶7)   glazed over (¶7)   prime (¶10)   swamp (¶12)

C **Highlight** FOUR phrases in the passage which you consider to be key phrases. Then compare your ideas with another pair and discuss these questions:

- Which of the advice given in the passage do you agree with?
- Which do you already follow? Which ought you to follow?
- How does a British university, as described in the passage, differ from a university in your country?

9.8   Reporting – 2   **ADVANCED GRAMMAR**

A Each of the statements on the left is reported in two different ways. What is the difference in emphasis between the two reports on the right?

1 "I'll be arriving tomorrow."
   He told me that he would be arriving tomorrow.
   He told me that he would be arriving the next day.

2 "You should spend more time reading."
   She advised me to spend more time reading.
   She urged me to spend more time reading.

3 "I don't think your plan will work."
   He dismissed my plan as unrealistic.
   He had doubts about the effectiveness of my plan.

4 "I'll phone them soon."
   He promised to make the call soon.
   He said that he was going to make the call soon.

5 "You're absolutely right."
   She agreed.
   She assured me that I was right.

B **1** You'll hear the same words spoken in five different ways, each conveying a different attitude or mood. Select ONE adjective to describe each attitude:

1	
2	
3	
4	
5	

amazed   angry   depressed

diffident   disappointed   impressed

half-hearted   heart-broken

hysterical   sarcastic   shocked

2 Write four sentences SUMMARISING what Speakers 2 to 5 said, imagining that you were the person addressed. For example:

   1 The first speaker complained that my work hadn't improved and compared it unfavourably with everyone else's.

C 👤→👤 **Use these verbs to report what the people said in as few words as possible. Then compare your sentences with a partner's.**

assure   claim   congratulate   disagree   deny✓   insist   promise   remind   regret   reproach
suggest   warn

1 "No, it wasn't me. I didn't borrow your bike."   *She denied borrowing my bike.*
2 "I'll let you know as soon as they get here. OK?"
3 "Don't forget: you've got to hand in your work this evening."
4 "It's a shame you couldn't make it to the party last night."
5 "Well done! I always thought you'd pass."
6 "Don't worry, as long as you keep your head, you'll manage all right."
7 "You really must come and visit us next weekend!"
8 "I don't really think that what you said makes sense."
9 "If you park on this double yellow line, you'll get a ticket."
10 "You shouldn't have behaved like that. You should be ashamed of yourself."
11 "If I had more time, I'd help you with your work."
12 "Might it be a good idea if we all organised our time more efficiently?"

9.9 Progressive v. traditional methods

LISTENING AND COMPOSITION

A 1 👥 **Read this description of Summerhill School, then discuss these questions:**

• What might you like and dislike about attending Summerhill?
• What do you think the drawbacks of Neill's approach might be?

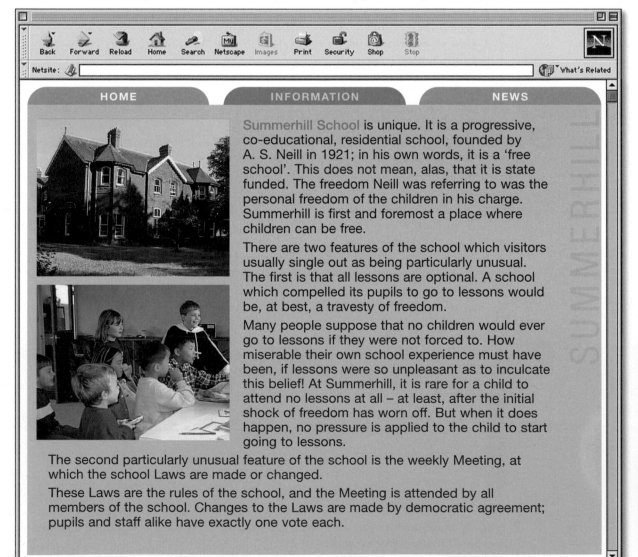

Back   Forward   Reload   Home   Search   Netscape   Images   Print   Security   Shop   Stop

Netsite: [   ]   What's Related

HOME   INFORMATION   NEWS

Summerhill School is unique. It is a progressive, co-educational, residential school, founded by A. S. Neill in 1921; in his own words, it is a 'free school'. This does not mean, alas, that it is state funded. The freedom Neill was referring to was the personal freedom of the children in his charge. Summerhill is first and foremost a place where children can be free.

There are two features of the school which visitors usually single out as being particularly unusual. The first is that all lessons are optional. A school which compelled its pupils to go to lessons would be, at best, a travesty of freedom.

Many people suppose that no children would ever go to lessons if they were not forced to. How miserable their own school experience must have been, if lessons were so unpleasant as to inculcate this belief! At Summerhill, it is rare for a child to attend no lessons at all – at least, after the initial shock of freedom has worn off. But when it does happen, no pressure is applied to the child to start going to lessons.

The second particularly unusual feature of the school is the weekly Meeting, at which the school Laws are made or changed.

These Laws are the rules of the school, and the Meeting is attended by all members of the school. Changes to the Laws are made by democratic agreement; pupils and staff alike have exactly one vote each.

Internet zone

2 🔊 **Beth Titchener is a pupil at Summerhill, Michael Newman is a teacher there. Listen to the interviews and choose the best answer for each of the questions.**

Beth Titchener

1 Beth enjoys being a pupil at Summerhill because she can
  a skip lessons   **b** make her own decisions   **c** speak at the Meetings

> [ ] 1

2 She left her previous school because it
  a was boring   **b** didn't give her enough freedom   **c** made her unhappy

> [ ] 2

3 She attended all the Japanese lessons because
  a she wanted to understand her Japanese friends   **b** the lessons were interesting
  c she thought Japanese lessons would be fun

> [ ] 3

4 Because pupils at Summerhill come from many different countries
  a British pupils are outnumbered   **b** not everyone can speak English well
  c everyone is valued as an individual

> [ ] 4

Michael Newman

5 Michael enjoys teaching at Summerhill because
  a it's easy to control the classes   **b** the teachers and kids are friends
  c everyone gets on really well with each other

> [ ] 5

6 To an outside observer his English lessons would
  a seem chaotic   **b** appear disorganised   **c** not seem unusual

> [ ] 6

7 Michael's previous job was teaching English
  a to Italians   **b** in an English grammar school   **c** in a community school

> [ ] 7

8 At the Meetings, Summerhill pupils learn how to
  a speak in public   **b** value the opinions of younger pupils
  c make decisions about moral issues

> [ ] 8

3 👥👥 **Discuss these questions:**

- What are your views on Summerhill and similar schools?
- Would you send your children to such a school? Give your reasons.
- What features of Summerhill ought to be a part of mainstream schools?
- What are your views on progressive v. traditional teaching methods?
- What are your views on comprehensive v. selective schools?

B **In this section we'll concentrate on making and using notes when writing a composition with the clock running. Keep a record of how long each of the following steps takes you:**

1 MAKE NOTES **for an essay on this topic:**

Give your views on progressive versus traditional methods of education (300–350 words).

2 EDIT **your notes: eliminate the irrelevant points and the less important points. Decide on the best sequence of points.**

3 🖊 **Write your essay, timing yourself to see how long the whole process takes.**

In the exam you'll have two hours to write two compositions, but this includes the time you need to decide which topics to choose, and time to check your work through for mistakes afterwards. Ideally, though, planning (including writing your notes) and actually writing each composition should take no longer than 50 minutes. It's not wise to allow a full hour for both.

*"I had all the right answers, but
I had them in the wrong order."*

10 Mother nature

A 1 **Discuss these questions:**

- What are your reactions to the two pictures? What are the implied attitudes to animals, nature and the countryside?
- Do you have any pets at home – or do any of your relatives have them?
- To what extent would you describe yourself as an animal-lover or a nature-lover?
- In what ways do you try to be 'environmentally friendly'?

2 Note down TEN vocabulary items connected with the topic of this unit.

B 1 **Choose one word that best completes each of the sentences:**

1 Many species of animals and plants today are ....
  dangerous   endangered   precarious   risked   risky

2 Modern farm animals and crops are the result of centuries of selective ....
  breeding   cultivation   education   mating   reproduction

3 It took a long time for the theory of evolution to be ....
  absorbed   accepted   acknowledged   tolerated

4 My friend is a keen amateur ....
  natural historian   naturist   naturalist   nationalist

5 He gets very .... about experiments being carried out on live animals.
  worked down   worked out   worked over   worked up

6 One of the effects of acid rain is that it causes plants to ....
  contract   flourish   shrink   thrive   wither

7 Waste paper can be .... instead of being burnt.
  decomposed   incinerated   recycled   revamped

8 There are over 850,000 named .... of insects on this planet.
  colonies   families   species   styles   varieties

9 Rabbits and mice are ....
  amphibians   carnivores   marsupials   rodents

10 Crocodiles and alligators are ....
  crustaceans   herbivores   mammals   reptiles

11 The lioness lay in wait for her ....
  game   lunch   prey   target   victim

12 Cattle and chickens are .... animals.
  domestic   domesticated   house-trained   obedient   tame   wild

13 Rats, mice and cockroaches are usually considered to be ....

    pets   cuddly   mischievous   vermin   weeds

14 Your cat has scratched me with its ....

    claws   fangs   hoofs   nails   paws   pincers   whiskers

15 We all admired the parrot's beautiful ....

    coat   bark   fleece   fur   hide   plumage

16 Many insects, such as wasps and ants, use their .... to touch objects.

    aerials   antlers   feelers   horns   whiskers

17 We saw a huge .... of birds through our binoculars.

    crowd   flock   herd   pack   shoal   swarm

18 Squirrels and rabbits are .... little creatures.

    amiable   courteous   delicious   elegant   endearing   extravagant   fierce   tasty

2 Look again at the words that you DIDN'T use in the gaps. Why is each wrong in the context? Highlight any of them that you want to remember.

10.2 'Our cousins in the ocean'

LISTENING

A 👥 You'll hear an interview with Ray Gamble, an expert on whales. Before you hear it, discuss with your partner what you already know about whales.

B **1** 🔊 In the first part of the interview you'll hear about different people's attitudes to 'saving the whales'. Answer these multiple-choice questions.

1 The Inuit peoples (Eskimos) of the Arctic ...
  a hunt whales together for enjoyment
  b would die out if they didn't hunt whales
  c depend on whale meat and products for their survival
  d don't actually like the taste of whale meat

2 When Ray watched Eskimos hunting whales he found the experience ...
  a sickening **b** fascinating **c** shocking **d** unsettling

3 To Western people today the whale represents the idea of
  a beauty **b** freedom **c** pleasure **d** food

4 For Western people, the whale is no longer thought of as a source of ...
  a meat **b** oil **c** raw materials **d** wonder

5 Nowadays Western people view commercial whale hunters as ...
  a brutal **b** primitive **c** distasteful **d** profitable

2 🔊 In the second part of the interview, Ray talks about why he thinks whales are exciting animals. Put a tick beside the reasons he gives.

he feels an inexplicable affinity with them	☐	their brains are large	☐
they have feelings like human beings	☐	all whales are enormous	☐
they can move in spectacular ways	☐	they can perform tricks	☐
they can communicate with each other	☐	they may be on the verge of extinction	☐
some whales are impressively large	☐	they are perfectly suited to living in the sea	☐

C 👥👥 Discuss your reactions to the recording.

• What other species do you know about which are endangered?
• Why is it important that endangered animals and plants don't become extinct?
• How can endangered species be protected?

10.3 The Third Chimpanzee

A 1 Read this text and then answer the questions opposite:

It is obvious that humans are unlike all animals. It is also obvious that we are a species of big mammal, down to the minutest details of our anatomy and our molecules. That contradiction is the most fascinating feature of the human species. It is familiar, but we still have difficulty grasping how it came to be and what it means.

On the one hand, between ourselves and all other species lies a seemingly unbridgeable gulf that we acknowledge by defining a category called 'animals'. It implies that we consider centipedes, chimpanzees and clams to share decisive features with each other but not with us, and to lack features restricted to us. Among these characteristics unique to us are the abilities to talk, write, and build complex machines. We depend completely on tools, not just on our bare hands, to make a living. Most of us wear clothes and enjoy art, and many of us believe in a religion. We are distributed over the whole Earth, command much of its energy and production, and are beginning to expand into the ocean depths and into space. We are also unique in darker attributes, including genocide, delight in torture, addictions to toxic drugs, and extermination of other species by the thousands. While a few animal species have one or two of these attributes in rudimentary form (like tool use), we still far eclipse animals even in those respects.

Thus, for practical and legal purposes, humans are not animals. When Darwin intimated in 1859 that we had evolved from apes, it is no wonder that most people initially regarded his theory as absurd and continued to insist that we had been separately created by God. Many people, including a quarter of all American college graduates, still hold to that belief today.

On the other hand, we obviously are animals, with the usual animal body parts, molecules and genes. It is even clear what particular type of animal we are. Externally, we are so similar to chimpanzees that eighteenth-century anatomists who believed in divine creation could already recognize our affinities. Just imagine taking some normal people, stripping off their clothes, taking away all their other possessions, depriving them of the power of speech, and reducing them to grunting, without changing their anatomy at all. Put them in a cage in the zoo next to the chimp cages, and let the rest of us clothed and talking people visit the zoo. Those speechless caged people would be seen for what we all really are: a chimp that has little hair and walks upright. A zoologist from outer space would immediately classify us as just a third species of chimpanzee, along with the pygmy chimp of Zaire and the common chimp of the rest of tropical Africa.

Molecular genetic studies over the last half-a-dozen years have shown that we continue to share over ninety-eight per cent of our genes with the other two chimps. The overall genetic distance between us and chimps is even smaller than the distance between such closely related bird species as red-eyed and white-eyed vireos, or willow warblers and chiffchaffs. So we still carry most of our old biological baggage with us. Since Darwin's time, fossilized bones of hundreds of creatures variously intermediate between apes and modern humans have been discovered, making it impossible for a reasonable person to deny the overwhelming evidence. What once seemed absurd – our evolution from apes – actually happened.

Yet the discoveries of many missing links have only made the problem more fascinating, without fully solving it. The few bits of new baggage we acquired – the two per cent of our genes that differ from those of chimps – must have been responsible for all of our seemingly unique properties. We underwent some small changes with big consequences rather quickly and recently in our evolutionary history. In fact, as recently as a hundred thousand years ago that zoologist from outer space would have viewed us as just one more species of big mammal. Granted, we had a couple of curious behavioural habits, notably our control of fire and our dependence on tools, but those habits would have seemed no more curious to the extraterrestrial visitor than would the habits of beavers and bowerbirds. Somehow, within a few tens of thousands of years – a time that is almost infinitely long when measured against one person's memory but is only a tiny fraction of our species' separate history – we had begun to demonstrate the qualities that make us unique and fragile.

What were those few key ingredients that made us human? Since our unique properties appeared so recently and involved so few changes, those properties or at least their precursors must already be present in animals. What are those animal precursors of art and language, of genocide and drug abuse?

Our unique qualities have been responsible for our present biological success as a species. No other large animal is native to all the continents, or breeds in all habitats from deserts and the Arctic to tropical rainforests. No large wild animal rivals us in numbers. But among our unique qualities are two that now jeopardize our existence: our propensities to kill each other and to destroy our environment. Of course, both propensities occur in other species: lions and many other animals kill their own kind, while elephants and others damage their environment. However, these propensities are much more threatening in us than in other animals because of our technological power and exploding numbers.

from The Rise and Fall of the Third Chimpanzee – Jared Diamond

Write your answers to these questions:

1 What are the other two species of chimpanzee?
2 How is the human use of tools different from the way other animals use them?
3 Which other creatures can be found in every continent?
4 Which other creatures kill members of the same species?
5 Which other creatures do harm to their environment?

6 Summarise the reasons why a zoologist from outer space would classify humans as a third species of chimpanzee (50–70 words).

2 👥 **Compare your answers.**

B Find words in the passage with similar meanings to these words and phrases and highlight them in context:

¶1   very smallest
¶2   difference   more evil   characteristics   primitive   outdo
¶3   suggested   at first
¶4   resemblances   making incoherent sounds
¶5 & 6   influences
¶7   properties which existed before
¶8   tendencies

In the exam you can't use a dictionary – and there's no time to ponder over words you don't understand. So, when there are unfamiliar words in a text, you have to guess what they mean – and hope for the best. But only bother do do this if the words are relevant to a particular question.

10.4 Conditionals – 1   GRAMMAR REVIEW

A 👥 **Discuss any differences in meaning or emphasis between these sentences:**

1 I feel upset when I think about the destruction of the rainforests.
I'd feel upset when I thought about people destroying the rainforests.
I'd feel upset if I thought about the rainforests being destroyed.
I feel upset if I think about the destruction of tropical rainforests.
I felt upset when I thought about jungles being destroyed.

2 If you don't leave now, you'll be late.
If you leave now, you won't be late.
If you left now, you wouldn't be late.
If you didn't leave now, you'd be late.
Unless you leave now, you'll be late.

3 If you're interested I'll tell you about my dream.
If you were interested I'd tell you about my dream.

4 When I have time, I'll feed the cat.
If I have time, I'll feed the goldfish.
If I had time, I'd feed the ducks.
If I had time, I'd have fed the birds.
When I had time, I'd feed the rabbits.
If I'd had time, I'd have fed the dog.

B Rewrite each sentence, beginning each new sentence with *If...*, keeping the meaning as close as possible to the original sentence.

1 Don't go too close to that dog in case it bites you.   If ...
2 I couldn't give you a hand because I didn't realise that you needed help.   If ...
3 The amount of carbon dioxide in the atmosphere must be reduced,
   otherwise the ozone layer will be permanently damaged.   If ...
4 Forests once covered most of Europe, before they were cut down.   If ...
5 Pollution is caused by ignorance about its effects on the environment.   If ...
6 Animals can't speak in their own defence, so we must speak up for them.   If ...
7 Everyone should drive more slowly so that there is less pollution.   If ...
8 Without acid rain these lakes would still have fish in them.   If ...

C Complete each sentence with your own ideas, as in the example.

1 Would you feel sick if *you had to eat raw fish?*
2 If he hadn't been so generous, ...
3 If you aren't careful, ...
4 If she doesn't phone me by Friday, ...
5 If everyone cared more about the environment, ...
6 If any species becomes extinct, ...
7 If human beings became extinct, ...
8 Unless the governments of the world cooperate, ...

D 1 Discuss these questions:

• What might happen if global warming continues?
• What might happen if everyone voted for the Green Party?
• What might happen if everyone stopped eating meat and fish?
• What might have happened if recycling hadn't become popular?

2 Write a paragraph summarising your discussion. Compare your summary with another group.

10.5 Showing your attitude   WRITING SKILLS

A The writer of this passage, a zoologist and zoo owner, wants to convince the reader of his views on zoos and safari parks.

Look at the highlighted examples, then decide which alternatives below fit best in gaps 1–8.

I must agree with you (if you are anti-zoo), that not all zoos are perfect. Of the 500 or so zoological collections in the world, a few are excellent, some are inferior and the rest are
¹ . Given the premises that zoos can and should be of value scientifically, educationally and from a conservation point of view (thus serving both us and other animal life), then I ²
that one should strive to make them better. I have had, ironically enough, a great many ³
opponents of zoos tell me that they would like all zoos closed down, yet the same people accept with equanimity the proliferation of safari parks, where, by and large, animals are ⁴ worse off than in the average zoo. An animal can be ⁵ unhappy, ⁶ ill-treated, in a vast area as in a small one, but the rolling vistas, the ⁷ trees, ⁸ criticism, for this is the only thing that these critics think the animals want.

1 appalling · bad   3 rabid · strong   5 equally · just as   7 ancient · old
2 believe · feel very strongly 4 far · much   6 as · just as   8 obliterate · prevent

B Highlight the words and phrases in the rest of the passage which show the writer's feelings, attitude and passionately held opinions.

It is odd how comforted people feel by seeing an animal in a large field. Safari parks were invented purely to make money. No thought of science or conservation sullied their primary conception. Like a rather unpleasant fungus, they have spread now throughout the world. In the main, their treatment of animals is disgraceful and the casualties (generally carefully concealed) appalling. I will not mention the motives, or the qualifications of the men who created them, for they are sufficiently obvious, but I would like to stress that I know it to be totally impossible to run these vast concerns with a knowledgeable and experienced staff, since that number of knowledgeable and experienced staff does not exist. I know, because I am always on the look-out for such rare beasts myself.

I am not against the conception of safari parks. I am against the way that they are at present run. In their present form, they represent a bigger hazard and a bigger drain on wild stocks of animals than any zoo ever has done. Safari parks, properly controlled and scientifically run, could be of immense conservation value for such things as antelope, deer and the larger carnivores. But they have a long way to go before they can be considered anything other than animal abattoirs in a sylvan setting.

I feel, therefore, that one should strive to make zoos and safari parks better, not simply clamour for their dissolution. If Florence Nightingale's sole contribution, when she discovered the appalling conditions in the hospitals of the last century, had been to advocate that they should all be closed down, few people in later years would have praised her for her acumen and far-sightedness.

My plan, then, is that all of us, zoo opponents and zoo lovers alike, should endeavour to make them perfect; should make sure that they are a help to animal species and not an additional burden on creatures already too hard pressed by our unbeatable competition. This can be done by being much more critical of zoos and other animal collections, thus making them more critical of themselves, so that even the few good ones will strive to be better.

from The Stationary Ark by Gerald Durrell

C **1** Here are more examples of words and phrases which show a writer's attitude. **Highlight** the ones that you would like to remember.

1 It is ... that animals are kept in captivity.
appalling   disgraceful   dreadful   frightful   shocking   terrible   absurd
incomprehensible   odd   ridiculous   strange   ironic

2 Some zoos are ... but most of them are ... .
admirable   excellent   fine   praiseworthy   appalling   atrocious   disgraceful   dreadful
frightful   shocking

3 ... something must be done as soon as possible.
Clearly   Obviously   Quite frankly   There is no doubt that   Undoubtedly
You must agree that   Without a shadow of doubt   As far as I'm concerned
I feel very strongly that   My view is that   I would like to stress that   It seems to me that
Personally I believe that   It is generally agreed that

4 ..., there is a straightforward solution to this problem.
Ironically enough   Strangely enough   Oddly enough   Actually   In fact   In spite of this
Mind you   Nevertheless   Still

5 I ... good zoos but I ... bad ones.
am all in favour of   advocate   applaud   approve of   favour   support   am against
condemn   strongly disapprove of   object to   reject the idea of

2 Fill these gaps with words or phrases you highlighted in C1 above:

1 It is .... that most safari parks are simply money-making enterprises.
2 .... there are some zoos which are run to make a profit, but not all.
3 ...., some zoos are absolutely ....
4 I .... zoos as such – .... I enjoy a day at the zoo.
5 .... hunting animals is a(n) .... leisure activity.
6 .... there is nothing wrong with people having pets, ... keeping a large dog in a city apartment is ....

D ✎ Write a couple of paragraphs, giving your own views on ONE of these topics you feel strongly about:

Using animals in laboratories for testing cosmetics   Killing animals for 'sport'
Keeping large, fierce dogs as 'pets'   The destruction of the rainforests
Training animals to perform in circuses   Eating meat

10.6 Uses of the past   ADVANCED GRAMMAR

A 👥 Discuss the differences in meaning (if any) between these sentences:

1 I wish that dog would stop barking.   I wish that dog had stopped barking.
  I wish that dog didn't bark.   I want that dog to stop barking.
2 It's time for you to do the washing-up.   It's time you did the washing-up.
3 If only it were Friday!   If it were only Friday ...
  Only if it was Friday ...   If it's only Friday ...
4 Would you rather I didn't help you?   Would you rather not help me?
  Would you prefer it if I didn't help you? Would you prefer me not to help you?
5 I was going to phone her tonight.   I intended to phone her tonight.
  I am to phone her tonight.   I was to have phoned her tonight.
6 I wish I knew the answer.   I wish to know the answer.

B Fill each gap with suitable words or phrases:

1 I do wish you .... me when I'm trying to study.
2 It's high time something .... industry from polluting the environment.
3 You're very late! I'd prefer .... a little earlier next time.
4 If only people .... the dangers of global warming 20 years ago!
5 I wish .... ride a horse.
6 I wish there .... to save the whales.
7 We .... and see you on Sunday but there wasn't enough time.
8 What a noise you're making! I'd rather .... a bit more quietly.
9 Well, it's 9.30, do you think it's .... yet?
10 Isn't it time the cat ....? It looks very hungry.

10.7 **Biological diversity**   READING

A Read this passage and then answer the questions on the next page.

So much to save

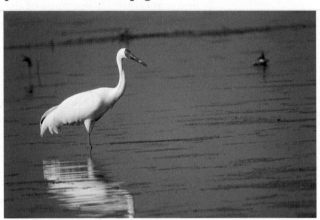

1 THE idea of preserving biological diversity gives most people a warm feeling inside. But what, exactly, is diversity? And which kind is most worth preserving? It may be anathema to save-the-lot environmentalists who hate setting such priorities, but academics are starting to cook up answers.

2 Andrew Solow, a mathematician at the Woods Hole Oceanographic Institution, and his colleagues argue that in the eyes of conservation, all species should not be equal. Even more controversially, they suggest that preserving the rarest is not always the best approach. Their measure of diversity is the amount of evolutionary distance between species. They reckon that if choices must be made, then the number of times that cousins are removed from one another should be one of the criteria.

3 This makes sense from both a practical and an aesthetic point of view. Close relatives have many genes in common. If those genes might be medically or agriculturally valuable, saving one is nearly as good as saving both. And different forms are more interesting to admire and study than lots of things that look the same.

4 Dr Solow's group illustrates its thesis with an example. Six species of crane are at some risk of extinction. Breeding in captivity might save them. But suppose there were only enough money to protect three. Which ones should be picked?

5 The genetic distances between 14 species of cranes, including the six at risk, have already been established using a technique known as DNA hybridisation. The group estimated how likely it was that each of these 14 species would become extinct in the next 50 years. Unendangered species were assigned a 10% chance of meeting the Darwinian reaper-man; the most vulnerable, a 90% chance. Captive breeding was assumed to reduce an otherwise-endangered species' risk to the 10% level of the safest. Dr Solow's computer permed all possible combinations of three from six and came to the conclusion that protecting the Siberian, white-naped and black-necked cranes gave the smallest likely loss of biological diversity over the next five decades. The other three had close relatives in little need of protection. Even if they became extinct, most of their genes would be saved.

6 Building on the work of this group, Martin Weitzman, of Harvard University, argues that conservation policy needs to take account not only of some firm measure of the genetic relationships of species to each other and their likelihood of survival, but also the costs of preserving them. Where species are equally important in genetic terms, and – an important and improbable precondition – where the protection of one species can be assured at the expense of another, he argues for making safe species safer, rather than endangered species less endangered.

7 In practice, it is difficult to choose between species. Most of those at risk – especially plants, the group most likely to yield useful medicines – are under threat because their habitats are in trouble, not because they are being shot, or plucked, to extinction. Nor can conservationists choose among the millions of species that theory predicts must exist, but that have not yet been classified by the biologists assigned to that tedious task.

8 This is not necessarily cause for despair. At the moment, the usual way to save the genes in these creatures is to find the bits of the world with the largest number of species and try to protect them from the bulldozers. What economists require from biologists are more sophisticated ways to estimate the diversity of groups of organisms that happen to live together, as well as those which are related to each other. With clearer goals established, economic theory can then tell environmentalists where to go.

from The Economist

Answer these multiple-choice questions about the article:

1 Dr Solow believes that ....
  a all species should be saved   **c** very rare species can't be saved
  b all very rare species should be saved   **d** only some species are worth saving

2 Dr Solow's work depended on ....
  a previous biological research   **c** the premise that not all species are the same
  b the cost of preserving cranes   **d** the premise that all cranes should be protected

3 Endangered species of cranes can be saved by ....
  a keeping them in zoos or wildlife parks   **c** stopping hunters from killing them
  b protecting their habitats   **d** encouraging them to mate with their cousins

4 Three of the six species of endangered cranes ....
  a were so rare they couldn't be saved   **c** were less interesting to admire than others
  b could be allowed to become extinct   **d** shouldn't be protected

5 Dr Weitzman's ideas ....
  a disregard Dr Solow's   **c** take Dr Solow's ideas one step further
  b contradict Dr Solow's   **d** confirm Dr Solow's

6 Dr Weitzman believes that if two species are equally important genetically we should
  protect ....
  a the rarer one   **c** them both
  b the less endangered one   **d** the one that is more attractive

7 Most species are endangered because ....
  a they are hunted or picked   **c** we don't care enough about them
  b biologists haven't classified them   **d** the places they live in are being destroyed

8 According to the writer what has to be done first is for ....
  a biologists to instruct economists   **c** economists to instruct biologists
  b developers to stop destroying habitats   **d** biologists to classify undiscovered species

---

When answering multiple-choice questions, it's sometimes easier to eliminate (and cross out) the wrong answers first, and *then* decide what the right answers might be. Be careful though: sometimes it's the least likely looking answer that is actually right – especially if the writer holds unconventional views, or If you're reading about an unfamiliar topic!

B   **Find words in the passage with similar meanings to these words and phrases and highlight them:**

¶1 an unacceptable idea   formulate   ¶2 assert   ¶4 theory   ¶5 death   calculate
¶7 produce

10.8 *put* and *set*   **VERBS AND IDIOMS**

A   **Which of the following would be preceded by *put* and which by *set*?**

  pressure on someone   a trap for someone   your teeth on edge   two and two together
  someone at their ease   a question to someone   a stop to something   a good example
  someone in the picture   fire to something   your watch   pen to paper   the scene

B   **Find synonyms for the phrases in red, or explain their meaning. Use a dictionary if necessary.**

1 I think I put my foot in it when I asked him what the matter was.
2 Having the car fixed set me back £250! That's put paid to my holiday plans.
3 Keep your options open: don't put all your eggs in one basket.
4 If you take a flash photo while he's playing the violin you may put him off.
5 Her bad performance in her flute exam can be put down to nerves. Let's
  hope it doesn't put her off playing altogether.
6 You've let her get away with being late too often: it's time you put your
  foot down.
7 The bad weather has set the building programme back by several weeks.
8 When they set up the scheme they set out to make it as innovative as possible.
9 You're always putting me down! Put yourself in my shoes and imagine what
  it feels like. Don't you realise that it puts both of us in a bad light?
10 I wouldn't put it past him to have made the whole story up. I'm sure he was
  putting me on!

C Fill the gaps in these sentences with suitable phrases from the list below.
You may need to change the form of the verbs.

1 It wasn't his idea – someone else must have .... him .... it.
2 They were going out together for five years before they .... home together.
3 He has tremendous ideas but he's not very good at .... them ....
4 I don't want to .... you .... but I've got nowhere to stay.
  Can you .... me .... for the night?
5 If you don't like the situation, you'll just have to .... it, I'm afraid.
6 I .... my order last month and I still haven't received the goods.
7 Holidays are expensive: you can save up by .... a little money each month.
8 In her book she .... to examine the wide variety of species in the world.
9 5,000 words! You must have .... a lot of hours on this work.
10 They won't turn on the central heating until the really cold weather ....

> put across/over   put aside/put away/set aside   put in   put in   put out
> put up   put up to   put up with   set in   set out   set up

---

10.9 Different styles

VOCABULARY DEVELOPMENT AND
WRITING SKILLS

A **1** How would you describe the style of each of these sentences: FORMAL, COLLOQUIAL, or
NEUTRAL (i.e. neither stiffly formal nor very colloquial)?

1 **a** Different forms are more interesting to admire and study than lots of things that look the
    same.
  b It's a lot more interesting to admire and study different forms than lots of things that look
    the same.
  c Different forms are more interesting to admire and study than a large number of similar
    looking species.

2 **a** I do like little kittens and puppies – they're ever so sweet, aren't they?
  b I consider young kittens and puppies to be the most endearing creatures.
  c Small kittens and puppies are delightful, I think.

2 Highlight some examples of NEUTRAL style in the first half of *So much to save* on page 112.

B Rewrite these colloquial sentences in a more neutral (i.e. more formal but not stiffly formal) style:

When writing a
composition in the
exam it's best to
aim for a fairly
neutral style, rather
than a style that is
over-colloquial or
stiffly formal.
However, a personal
letter should be
written in a friendly,
colloquial style.

1 It's a lot better to use renewable energy – not fossil fuels like coal, gas and oil.
  Renewable energy resources are preferable to fossil fuels, such as coal, gas and oil.
2 How's your dad? Is he OK again yet?
3 Well, she hit the roof when they broke it to her that she'd got the sack.
4 To grow organic fruit and vegetables they don't use artificial fertilisers,
  you know.
5 We were ever so scared when this huge great dog came bounding up to us.
6 For pity's sake, mind what you're doing with that knife!
7 There's no point in testing cosmetics on animals – and it's cruel too.
8 Why on earth didn't you turn the light off when you left the room?
9 Hey, it looks as if it's going to rain pretty soon.
10 Don't throw litter in the street – put it in a bin or something, for goodness sake.

C Rewrite these formal sentences in a more neutral, less formal style:

Contractions (*isn't,
it's,* etc.) are often
used in a neutral
style. In the exam
you wouldn't be
penalised for using
them, but it may be
safer to stick to full
forms. In academic
essays or job
applications
contractions should
not be used, though.

1 It is unwise to bathe here due to possible contamination of the water.
  It's not advisable to go swimming here because the water may be polluted.
2 Meteorologists maintain that the rate of increase in the global warming process is
  accelerating.
3 It is conceivable that a slight rise in temperature would have a dramatic effect on the ice in
  polar regions.
4 Discarding cans and bottles leads to excessive consumption of energy and materials. It is
  preferable to recycle them.
5 The serving of luncheon commences at noon.
6 Passengers are requested to exercise caution when alighting from the train.
7 We regret that the playing of musical instruments is not permitted on the premises.
8 Whilst all vegetarians eschew meat, vegans consume neither fish nor dairy products.

A First, read this through, just to get the gist before you look at the alternatives in B below:

It is not ___¹___ to ___²___ an unknown animal. Spend a day in the tropical forests of South America, turning over logs, looking beneath bark, sifting through the moist litter of leaves, followed by an evening ___³___ a mercury lamp on a white screen, and one way and another you will ___⁴___ hundreds of different kinds of small creatures. Moths, caterpillars, spiders, long-nosed bugs, luminous beetles, harmless butterflies ___⁵___ as wasps, wasps shaped like ants, sticks that walk, leaves that open wings and fly – the variety will be ___⁶___ and one of these ___⁷___ will almost certainly be undescribed by science. The difficulty will be to find ___⁸___ who know enough about the groups ___⁹___ to be able to single out the new one.

No one can say ___¹⁰___ how many species of animals there are in these greenhouse-humid dimly lit jungles. They contain the ___¹¹___ and the most varied assemblage of animal and plant life to be found anywhere on earth. Not only are there many categories of creatures – monkeys, rodents, spiders, hummingbirds, butterflies, but most of those types ___¹²___ in many different ___¹³___ . There are over forty different species of parrot, over seventy different monkeys, three hundred hummingbirds and tens of thousands of butterflies. If you are not ___¹⁴___ , you can even be ___¹⁵___ by a hundred different kinds of mosquito.

from *Life on Earth* by David Attenborough

B **1** 👥 **Decide which words are most suitable to fit in each of the numbered gaps above – some are grammatically or stylistically unsuitable.**

In Part I of the Use of English Paper there are no alternatives to help you. Bear in mind the context, the sense of the passage, and its style. In the exam some of the gaps require grammatical words: prepositions, articles, conjunctions, etc.

1 difficult ✓ hard ✓ problematic ✗ strenuous ✗ tricky ✗
2 come across discover find identify meet
3 lighting pointing reflecting shining
4 collect discover gather glimpse identify pick up
5 disguised dressed masquerading posing
6 ample big enormous huge immense
7 animals creatures insects things types
8 experts friends guys people specialists
9 characteristics concerned themselves there
10 almost exactly just nearly precisely quite sincerely
11 best biggest deepest richest strangest thickest wildest
12 are become exist happen remain survive
13 forms manners types ways zones
14 asleep awake careful cunning fortunate unlucky
15 attacked bitten poisoned stung threatened

2 **Where you ticked more than one answer, which is the one you feel is the best?**

A Look at the statistics, quotations and photos below and opposite and discuss your reactions.

According to the experts:

- Between 2000 and 2010 10% of the estimated 30 million species of plants and animals will be lost forever. By 2030 another 20% are likely to be lost. The extinction of one plant species can cause the loss of 30 dependent organisms.

- Half the world's rainforests have already been destroyed. Of the remaining half, two thirds will disappear by 2030.

- Between 2000 and 2010 the average temperature will rise by 1°C. By 2100 it will rise by 3° to 5°C. This will have unpredictable effects on local weather patterns. By 2100 the sea level is likely to rise between 10cm and 2m.

- There are 750 million motor vehicles in the world. By 2030 there will be 1,100 million.

- The total world population is over 6,000 million. By 2030 there may be 8,000 to 10,000 million mouths to feed and by 2100 11,000 to 14,000.

- Glaciers melting in Greenland are sending more and more icebergs into the North Atlantic and cooling the ocean. This may divert the Gulf Stream and bring much colder weather to Western Europe.

Greenpeace

'This is what you should do: love the Earth and sun and the animals, despise riches, give alms to everyone that asks, stand up for the stupid and crazy, devote your income and labour to others, hate tyrants, argue not concerning God, have patience and indulgence towards the people, take off your hat to nothing known or unknown or to any man or number of men . . . re-examine all you have been told at school or church or in any book, dismiss what insults your own soul, and your very flesh shall be a great poem.'

Walt Whitman

If the Earth
were a few feet in diameter,
floating a few feet above a field somewhere,
people would come from everywhere to marvel
at it. People would walk around it marvelling at its
big pools of water, its little pools and the water flowing
between. People would marvel at the bumps on it and the
holes in it. They would marvel at the very thin layer of gas
surrounding it and the water suspended in the gas. The people
would marvel at all the creatures walking around the surface of
the ball and at the creatures in the water. The people would
declare it as sacred because it was the only one, and they would
protect it so that it would not be hurt. The ball would be the
greatest wonder known, and people would come to pray to
it, to be healed, to gain knowledge, to know beauty and to
wonder how it could be. People would love it and defend
it with their lives because they would somehow
know that their lives could be nothing
without it. If the Earth were
a few feet in diameter.

Joe Miller

B ✏ Write an article for a magazine explaining your views for and/or against ONE of the following points of view (300–350 words).

> The future of the planet looks bleak, but there's nothing I can do about it.

> What happens in poor countries on the other side of the world doesn't concern me.

> There's no point in worrying about things that will only affect our grandchildren.

> The world will be a better place for our children and grandchildren.

11 Another world

11.1 Enjoying reading   LISTENING AND TOPIC VOCABULARY

A **You'll hear Christine, Jonathan, Karen and William talking about reading. Indicate which of the speakers expresses each of these opinions by writing** C, J, K **or** W **in each box. If more than one person expresses the same opinion, write more than one letter in the box.**

1 I forget the real world when I'm reading a book.   `1`

2 I can experience the world through another person's eyes.   `2`

3 I learn about history from the books I read.   `3`

4 I like the feel of a book in my hands.   `4`

5 I love stories where you want to know what will happen in the end.   `5`

6 I love to re-read passages I have enjoyed.   `6`

7 I prefer books to films.   `7`

8 I prefer books to TV.   `8`

9 Reading a book can remind you of other places.   `9`

10 Reading a book can take you to another world.   `10`

B **Discuss these questions:**

• Which of the people interviewed do you identify with most?
• What enjoyment do you get from reading for pleasure?
• What kinds of books and magazines would you like to read if you had more time?
• Name one fiction or non-fiction book you've enjoyed. What did you enjoy about it?
• 60% of people read a book at least once a month (but 40% don't)! How many books do you read in a year? How many are in your own language, and how many in English?

C In these sentences THREE of the alternatives are correct and the rest are wrong. Tick the correct words.

1 As I prefer fiction to non-fiction I often read ....
   best-sellers   biographies   memoirs   thrillers   whodunits

2 Before buying a book it's a good idea to read the ....
   bibliography   blurb   contents   dustjacket   sleeve

3 The opening page of a book often has a(n) ....
   appendix   dedication   foreword   index   preface

4 I've just read the reviews of a newly-published .... of poetry.
   album   anthology   book   collection   gathering

5 The plot of a popular romantic novel is not usually very ....
   complex   intricate   involved   mixed   multiple

6 It was a very long book and it took me ages to .... through it.
   flip   get   struggle   thumb   wade

7 The contents page of a book usually gives the titles of all the .... in it.
   chapters   excerpts   extracts   passages   sections   units

8 The language she uses can be interpreted literally or ....
   descriptively   figuratively   illustratively   metaphorically   symbolically

9 Although the book has a serious .... , it is very accessible and witty.
   author   message   plot   purpose   satire   side

10 His books not only have exciting plots but are also very ....
   gripping   readable   thought-provoking   thrilling   well-written

D These abbreviations are found in non-fiction books and footnotes, as well as in reports and articles. Rewrite each one as a complete word or phrase.

e.g. *for example* **etc.** *and so on/and so forth /et cetera*
i.e. **cf.** **ff.** **pp.** **ibid.** **viz.** **N.B.** **sic** © ¶

11.2 'My last novel is the best work I can do' LISTENING

A You'll hear an interview with the novelist William Boyd. First, discuss how he might answer these questions:

- Do you have regular working hours?
- How do you invent your characters?
- What do you really enjoy about what you do?
- Do you write on a computer?
- Which of your novels is your favourite?

B 🔊 Listen to the interview and fill each box with a word or short phrase.

1 William Boyd's first writing job was as a [____ **1**] critic.

2 At the moment his working hours are [____ **2**].

3 His characters are not based on [____ **3**].

4 In order to write from a woman's perspective he forgets [____ **4a**] and focuses on [____ **4b**].

5 Tick the reasons he gives for enjoying what he does:
being autonomous ☐   being famous ☐   feeling free ☐
making money ☐   being self-sufficient ☐   solitude ☐

6 Writers who moan about how hard it is to write should [____ **6**].

7 He finds that he can write anywhere because, when he was younger, he worked in [____ **7**].

8 He writes the [____ **8**] of his novels in longhand.

9 He thinks that it's a mistake to [____ **9a**] what your 'ideal reader' wants to read. A writer should be [____ **9a**] to him/herself.

10 Which of his novels is his favourite? [____ **10**].

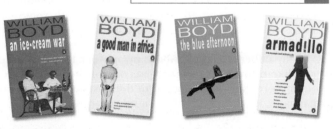

C 👥👥 Discuss these questions:

- What do you think you might enjoy / not enjoy about William Boyd's novels?
- Who is the most famous living writer in your country? What do you know about him/her?
- What is the most famous classic book written in your language? Describe it.
- Who are your favourite British and American writers? What do you like about their works?

11.3 **Setting the scene...** READING AND SPEAKING

Here are the opening paragraphs of three bestselling British novels. Read each extract carefully, then discuss the questions below:

 A Read the beginning of *Brazzaville Beach* (1990) by William Boyd and answer the questions below:

I live on Brazzaville Beach. Brazzaville Beach on the edge of Africa. This is where I have washed up, you might say, deposited myself like a spar of driftwood, lodged and fixed in the warm sand for a while, just above the high tide mark.

The beach never had a name until last April. Then they christened it in honour of the famous *Conferença dos Quadros* that was held a few years ago in Congo Brazzaville in 1964. No one can explain why but, one day, over the laterite road that leads down to the shore, some workmen erected this sign: 'Brazzaville Beach', and written below that, *Conferença dos Quadros, Brazzaville, 1964.*

It is an indication, some people say, that the government is becoming more moderate, trying to heal the wounds of our own civil war by acknowledging a historic moment in another country's liberation struggle. Who can say? Who ever knows the answers to these questions? But I like the name, and so does everyone else who lives around here. Within a week we were all using it unselfconsciously. Where do you live? On Brazzaville Beach. It seemed entirely natural.

I live on the beach in a refurbished beach house. I have a large cool sitting-room with a front wall of sliding meshed doors that give on directly to a wide sun-deck. There is also a bedroom, a generous bathroom with bath and shower, and a tiny dim kitchen, built on to the back. Behind the house is my garden: sandy, patchy grass, some prosaic shrubs, a vegetable plot and a hibiscus hedge, thick with brilliant flowers.

2 How many other characters are mentioned? What is the effect of this?
3 What do we find out about the place and time that are described?
4 How many times is the word *beach* used? What is the effect of this?
5 How is each paragraph different in content and style?

B Read the beginning of *A Dark-Adapted Eye* (1986) by Barbara Vine and answer the questions below:

1

On the morning Vera died I woke up very early. The birds had started, more of them and singing more loudly in our leafy suburb than in the country. They never sang like that outside Vera's windows in the Vale of Dedham. I lay there listening to something repeating itself monotonously. A thrush, it must have been, doing what Browning said it did and singing each song twice over. It was a Thursday in August, a hundred years ago. Not much more than a third of that, of course. It only feels so long.

In these circumstances alone one knows when someone is going to die. All other deaths can be predicted, conjectured, even anticipated with some certainty, but not to the hour, the minute, with no room for hope. Vera would die at eight o'clock and that was that. I began to feel sick. I lay there exaggeratedly still, listening for some sound from the next room. If I was awake my father would be. About my mother I was less sure. She had never made a secret of her dislike of both his sisters. It was one of the things which had made a rift between them, though there they were together in the next room, in the same bed still. People did not break a marriage, leave each other, so lightly in those days.

I thought of getting up but first I wanted to make sure where my father was. There was something terrible in the idea of encountering him in the passage, both of us dressing-gowned, thick-eyed with sleeplessness, each seeking the bathroom and each politely giving way to the other.

1 What do we find out about Vera? Why is she going to die?
2 How many times is the word *die* or *death* used? What is the effect of this?
3 What do we find out about the narrator?
4 What do we find out about the place and time that are described?

C   **Read the beginning of *Nice Work* (1988) by David Lodge and answer the questions below:**

Monday January 13th, 1986. Victor Wilcox lies awake, in the dark bedroom, waiting for his quartz alarm clock to bleep. It is set to do this at 6.45. How long he has to wait he doesn't know. He could easily find out by groping for the clock, lifting it to his line of vision, and pressing the button that illuminates the digital display. But he would rather not know. Supposing it is only six o'clock? Or even five? It could be five. Whatever it is, he won't be able to get to sleep again. This has become a regular occurrence lately: lying awake in the dark, waiting for the alarm to bleep, worrying

Worries streak towards him like enemy spaceships in one of Gary's video games. He flinches, dodges, zaps them with instant solutions, but the assault is endless: the Avco account, the Rawlinson account, the price of pig-iron, the value of the pound, the competition from Foundrax, the incompetence of his Marketing Director, the persistent breakdowns of the core blowers, the vandalising of the toilets in the fettling shop, the pressure from his divisional boss, last month's accounts, the quarterly forecast, the annual review ...

In an effort to escape this bombardment, perhaps even to doze awhile, he twists onto his side, burrows into the warm plump body of his wife, and throws an arm round her waist. Startled, but still asleep, drugged with Valium, Marjorie swivels to face him. Their noses and foreheads bump against each other; there is a sudden flurry of limbs, an absurd pantomime struggle. Marjorie puts up her fists like a boxer, groans and pushes him away. An object slides off the bed on her side and falls to the floor with a thump. Vic knows what it is: a book which one of Marjorie's friends at the Weight Watchers' club has lent her, and which she has been reading in bed, without much show of conviction, and falling asleep over, for the past week or two.

1 What do we find out about Victor Wilcox?
2 What do we find out about Marjorie?
3 What do we find out about the place and time that are described?
4 How many of Victor's worries are listed in the second paragraph? What is the effect of this?
5 How is each paragraph different in content and style?

D   **Discuss these questions:**

* What do you think is going to happen in each of the stories?
* Which of the three novels would you like to read more of, and why?
* Which seems to have the most readable or attractive style?

11.4   **Describing a book**   SPEAKING AND COMPOSITION

A   **Discuss these questions about reading in general:**

* How much reading do you do? How much time do you spend each week reading books, and how much time reading newspapers or magazines? How much do you read in English, rather than in your own language?
* What kinds of books do you enjoy reading? Do you choose different sorts of books for different occasions (journeys, holidays, reading in bed, etc.)?
* If you could choose between reading a book or seeing the same story as a film, on video or on TV, which would you prefer? Why?
* Who are your favourite authors? Describe the kinds of books they write.
* Describe one book you have particularly enjoyed reading recently. What did you like about it? What were its faults?
* Are there any books you'd like to re-read one day (or is there one that you have re-read)? What are the qualities of such a book?
* Is there any particular book you'd recommend to your partners? What do you think they'd enjoy about it?

"They're books, dad needs them for reading."

In the exam, if one of your compositions is too short you'll lose marks.

If one of your compositions is too long, not only will it probably contain more mistakes but writing all those extra words will take up more of your time.

B   ✎ **Write a composition on ONE of these topics (300–350 words):**

Either: Write a review for a student magazine of a book you have particularly enjoyed reading, making it sound as appealing as possible to potential readers.

or: Write an essay explaining what you find particularly striking or moving about the prescribed book you are reading.

Make notes before you start writing. Try to cover the following aspects of the book:

Theme   Plot   Characters   Style   Message   Relevance to your life

Do you know how many lines of your handwriting are equivalent to 100 words? And how many lines are equivalent to 350 words?

To check how long a composition is: count the words in 10 lines, divide by 10 (to get the average number of words per line) and then multiply the answer by the total number of lines.

11.5   Conjunctions and connectors – 1   GRAMMAR REVIEW

A 1 Study these examples and highlight the conjunctions and connectors you want to remember:

Explaining results and reasons
because   and so   since   as   the reason why   consequently   therefore
as a result of this

Contrasts, unexpected results
but   although   nevertheless   all the same   however   though   even though
and yet   still   on the other hand

Mentioning exceptions
but not   apart from   except   with the exception of

Reservations, qualifications
anyway   at least   at any rate   in any case

Making further points
and also   moreover   what is more   yet   besides   furthermore
not only ... but also

Emphasising
especially   in particular   above all   particularly   chiefly   primarily

Clarifying
i.e.   in other words   that is to say   which means that

Giving examples
e.g.   for example   such as   for instance   like

Not mentioning further examples
etc.   and so forth   and so on   as well as other similar things/books

2 Rewrite these sentences using conjunctions and connectors you highlighted above:

1   She likes reading but she doesn't have much time for it.
    She doesn't have much time for reading even though she enjoys it a lot.
2   Many blockbusters, e.g. James Mitchener's *Alaska*, are over 1,000 pages long.
3   He enjoys reading biographies – especially ones about politicians.
4   Science fiction is an acquired taste – anyway that's what sci-fi fans say.
5   She prefers reading non-fiction books, i.e. biographies, history books, etc.
6   The book contained a lot of explicit sex and violence and so it was a best-seller.
7   He reads thrillers but he doesn't read much else.
8   Reading is an inexpensive hobby and it is enjoyable.

B Fill each gap with a suitable conjunction or connector – without using *and* or *but*.

1 All of E.M. Forster's novels, ... *A Passage to India*, are set in Europe.
2 Jane Austen's novels were popular in her day, ... they are still widely read.
3 Katherine Mansfield's short stories are brilliant examples of the genre; .... I'd recommend the ones she wrote later in her life.
4 I've never appreciated D. H. Lawrence's work .... he's supposed to be a great English writer – .... I think he's rather overrated.
5 Charles Dickens' novels, ... *Oliver Twist*, were published monthly as serials; .... each new instalment was eagerly awaited by readers.
6 Mary Ann Evans was an independent, free-thinking woman; .... all her novels were written under a male pseudonym: George Eliot.
7 Kingsley Amis' *Lucky Jim* is his best work – .... that's what I think.
8 Anne, Charlotte and Emily Brontë all wrote novels which are well worth reading – .... Emily's *Wuthering Heights* and Charlotte's *Jane Eyre*.

11.6 Collocations: idioms VOCABULARY DEVELOPMENT

A In some fixed, idiomatic phrases, words go together like *salt and pepper*, *fish and chips*, *sweet and sour*, or *Marks and Spencer*. Fill the gaps in these sentences with suitable expressions from the list below:

1 Can we discuss the .... of your proposals later on?
2 Can you show me the .... to support your argument?
3 They get on quite well together, even though they have their little ....
4 You gain some things and you lose others: it's a case of ....
5 The police are responsible for maintaining ....
6 It was .... whether the rescuers would get there in time.
7 They've shared a lot of experiences: they've been through .... together.
8 You can't claim on insurance for .... , only for damage.
9 I need another £100 .... the amount I've already saved up.
10 Nuclear physicists who are also bestselling writers are ....
11 He makes a little money out of writing but teaching is his ....
12 After all their adventures, they reached home ....

bread and butter	facts and figures	few and far between	law and order	over and above
pros and cons	safe and sound	swings and roundabouts	thick and thin	touch and go
ups and downs	wear and tear			

B Look at these examples and then match the words in the lists below together:

a **swarm** of bees   a **bag** of flour   a **box** of matches   a **tank** of petrol
a **pair** of scissors   a **pair** of binoculars   a **pair** of sunglasses   a **pair** of tights

a/an   basket   bucket   bunch   carafe   **of**   beans   bother   bread   cake
cup   flight   flock   gust   herd   cards   cattle   equipment   flowers
item   jug   loaf   pack   pair   fruit   helpers   hills   honey
piece   pot   puff   range   sack   luggage   milk   potatoes   sheep
school   slice   spoonful   spot   smoke   socks   stairs   sugar   tea
team   tin or can   tube   tights   toothpaste   tweezers   water
                                              wind   wine or water   whales

C Fill these gaps with suitable expressions from B:

1 In the distance we could see .... and beyond that a snow-capped mountain.
2 If you give your hostess .... , she'll be very pleased.
3 How many .... are you allowed to check in for this flight?
4 If you've got .... , we can play poker.
5 There was a sudden .... and her umbrella blew inside out.
6 We want .... to help us to redecorate our flat.
7 I'm having .... with my work, could you help me?
8 Don't be so silly! There's no need to be scared of ....
9 I went down .... and came to a locked door.
10 I've got a splinter in my finger, have you got .... I can borrow?

D Match the two halves of these idiomatic expressions:

muscular:	He's as strong as …	toast
short-sighted:	She's as blind as …	a horse/an ox
not rough:	The sea was as calm as …	a fiddle
without obligations:	She's as free as …	the hills
unemotional:	He's as cool as …	a sheet
tough:	She's as hard as …	a mouse
self-effacing:	He's as quiet as …	nails
healthy:	She's as fit as …	a picture
pale:	He looked as white as …	a cucumber
ancient, traditional:	That story is as old as …	the air
attractive:	She looked as pretty as …	a millpond
well-behaved:	The children were as good as …	a feather
not heavy:	She's as light as …	gold
cosy:	We were as warm as …	a bat

11.7 A good beginning   WRITING SKILLS

A 👥 Read this article about first lines and first novels and then compare your reactions to it.

Sifting the nodders from the shakers

"I WAS gazing out beyond Beachy Head contemplating the ruins of my life." This, in the jargon of book publishing, is a shaker, a complete no-no as an opening line. Unless the author performs some miracle in the next couple of paragraphs, the publishing company's reader will flick to the next chapter and, if there's more of the same, cast the manuscript aside.

A similar fate awaits books that begin: "The day after my husband died"; "Picking up the pieces was never going to be easy" or, what one publisher describes as the Enid Blyton* opener: "Peter and Bob decided to go to the market in Leeds that day". These are all shakers (as in head-shakers) of the first order.

On the other hand, the first line of Tolstoy's *Anna Karenina* – "All happy families resemble one another, but each unhappy family is unhappy in its own way" – is what another publisher describes as a nodder, in the sense that it makes you think Yes, there's something I recognise in that. For the unpublished author, the first line or paragraph is all-important.

Mass literacy and the premise that "everyone has a book in them" causes thousands of unsolicited manuscripts to thud on to the doormats of publishers and literary agents every week. Nearly all are rejected. One agency calculated that all but 0.001 percent are sent back.

Stephen Burgen

* Enid Blyton wrote in a very easy style. She wrote lots and lots of story books for boys and girls.

B 👥 → 👥 Look at the first lines of the passages in 11.3 on pages 120–1 and 11.9 on page 126 – and the passages in units 12 and 13. Choose five that are 'nodders', in your view – and any that you think are 'shakers'. Compare your findings with another pair.

C **1** Look at these first lines of some students' compositions on the topic 'The effect of tourism on a place in my country' (which you tackled in unit 6). Which of them make you want to read on?

a The first time I went to Venice it was rainy and quite chilly. I remember it was December and so there were not many tourists around. That's the very time you have to go there – in the middle of winter when it's freezing and foggy.

b Switzerland has been traditionally a very famous country for tourism. But having a huge number of tourists every year causes a lot of problems for a small country like mine.

c Gordes is a magically beautiful village in the south of France. Its medieval houses are perched on a cliff, looked down upon by a church. The view it offers over Provence is breathtaking: an endless landscape of lavender fields, vineyards and poplars, vanishing into the distance in a dim April haze.

d Venice has always been a tourist resort and probably tourism will be its main source of income for ever. Venice itself was conceived as a tourist destination and therefore it is impossible to imagine it otherwise.

e Tourism in the Canary Islands has had a great impact on the way of life of the local people and on the scenery of the islands. Before tourism became one of the main sources of income for the islands, most of the people lived from agriculture and fishing.

f The sun is burning. For three days now it has been extremely hot. The asphalt on the street seems to be melting away, trapping the cars that try to force their way to the beach.

2 How could you improve each one, particularly the very first sentence of each?

D **1** Look at the first lines of your own recent compositions. Which do you think are 'nodders' and which are 'shakers'? Write improved opening lines for the ones you're not satisfied with.

2 Show your improved versions, together with the original first lines, to a partner and ask for comments.

11.8 *It . . .* constructions   ADVANCED GRAMMAR

A Discuss the differences in emphasis between these sentences:

1 Did Jane Austen write *Emma*?
Was it Jane Austen who wrote *Emma*?
Was Jane Austen the author of *Emma*?
Was the author who wrote *Emma* Jane Austen?

Was *Emma* written by Jane Austen?
Was it *Emma* that Jane Austen wrote?
Was Jane Austen the author who wrote *Emma*?

2 What I enjoy reading is thrillers.
Thrillers are what I enjoy reading.

I enjoy reading thrillers.
It's thrillers that I enjoy reading.

3 It was me who borrowed your book.

I borrowed your book.

B Fill these gaps with suitable words or phrases:

1 It was .... that he managed to .... of the mountain so quickly.
2 Was it Hemingway or Steinbeck who .... *A Farewell to Arms*?
3 It's .... that you .... me about the danger.
4 It's not because he .... , it's because he .... that he can't make friends.
5 It wasn't .... before we .... what a big mistake ....
6 Why .... that my friends are so unpunctual and .... on time?
7 If you call the office I expect it .... John .... the phone.
8 It used .... my sister .... the great reader in our family, but now it .... the most books.

Verbs and adverbs of manner can't be used with *It's . . . that . . .*:

It's fall over that he did. ✗   It was fast that he ran. ✗   It was well that she did in the test. ✗

C Rewrite these sentences, using an *It . . .* construction to emphasise the words in red:

1 She finished reading the book only yesterday.   It ....
2 Do you enjoy the humour of her stories?   Is it ....
3 Did you read *Emma* or *Persuasion* recently?   Was it ....
4 I went to bed early because I was feeling worn out.   It was because ....
5 A strange noise woke me up in the early hours.   It ....
6 I heard the noise at half past four in the morning.   It ....
7 I realised what had happened when I looked out of the window.   It ....
8 Then I found I couldn't get back to sleep.   It ....
9 I finally did get to sleep at about eight o'clock.   It ....
10 I didn't wake up until lunchtime.   It wasn't ....

11.9 Three American novels

READING

 A These are the opening paragraphs of three well-known American novels. Read them through before you answer the questions below.

1 In the late summer of that year we lived in a house in a village that looked across the river and the plain to the mountains. In the bed of the river there were pebbles and boulders, dry and white in the sun, and the water was clear and swiftly moving and blue in the channels. Troops went by the house and down the road and the dust they raised powdered the leaves of the trees. The trunks of the trees too were dusty and the leaves fell early that year and we saw the troops marching along the road and the dust rising and leaves, stirred by the breeze, falling and the soldiers marching and afterwards the road bare and white except for the leaves.

The plain was rich with crops; there were many orchards of f~~...~~ ~~...~~beyond~~...~~
the m~~...~~

2 To the red country and part of the grey country of Oklahoma the last rains came gently, and they did not cut the scarred earth. The ploughs crossed and recrossed the rivulet marks. The last rains lifted the corn quickly and scattered weed colonies and grass along the sides of the roads so that the grey country and the dark red country began to disappear under a green cover. In the last part of May the sky grew pale and the clouds that had hung in high puffs for so long in the spring were dissipated. The sun flared down on the growing corn day after day until a line of brown spread along the edge of each green bayonet. The clouds appeared, and went away, and in a while they did not try any more. The weeds grew darker green to protect themselves, and they did not spread any more. The surface of the earth crusted, a thin hard crust, and as the sky became pale, so the earth became pale, pink in the red country and white in the grey country.

In the water-cut gullie~~...~~

3 We drove past Tiny Polski's mansion house to the main road, and then the five miles into Northampton, Father talking the whole way about savages and the awfulness of America, how it got turned into a dope-taking, door-locking, ulcerated danger-zone of rabid scavengers and criminal millionaires and moral sneaks. And look at the schools. And look at the politicians. And there wasn't a Harvard graduate who could change a flat tyre or do ten push-ups. And there were people in New York City who lived on pet food, who would kill you for a little loose change. Was that normal? If not, why did anyone put up with it?

'I don't know,' he said, replying to himself. 'I'm just thinking out loud.' Before leaving Hatfield, he had parked the pick-up truck on a rise in the road, and pointed south.

'Here come the savages,' he said, and up they came, tracking across the fields from a sickle of trees through the gummy drizzling heat-outlines of Polski's barns. They were dark and their clothes were rags and some had rags on their heads and others wide-brimmed hats. They were men and boys, a few no older than me, all of them carrying long knives.

Father's finger scared me more than th~~...~~

B **Refer back to the three extracts and discuss these questions:**

1 Which book on the right do you think each extract comes from?
2 Which extract conveys an impression of time passing?
3 Which conveys an impression of movement?
4 Which conveys an impression of a degenerating, violent world?
5 How are these impressions conveyed? What stylistic devices are used to create the impressions?
6 Which uses the fewest modifying adjectives?
7 Which uses the simplest grammatical structures?
8 Which uses the style of spoken conversational English?
9 Which uses repetition to achieve its effect?
10 What do you think might be the THEME of the book each extract comes from? What might come next in the story?

11.10 The future of reading? SPEAKING AND COMPOSITION 11

ANOTHER WORLD

A 👥 Read about the Rocket eBook and then discuss the questions below:

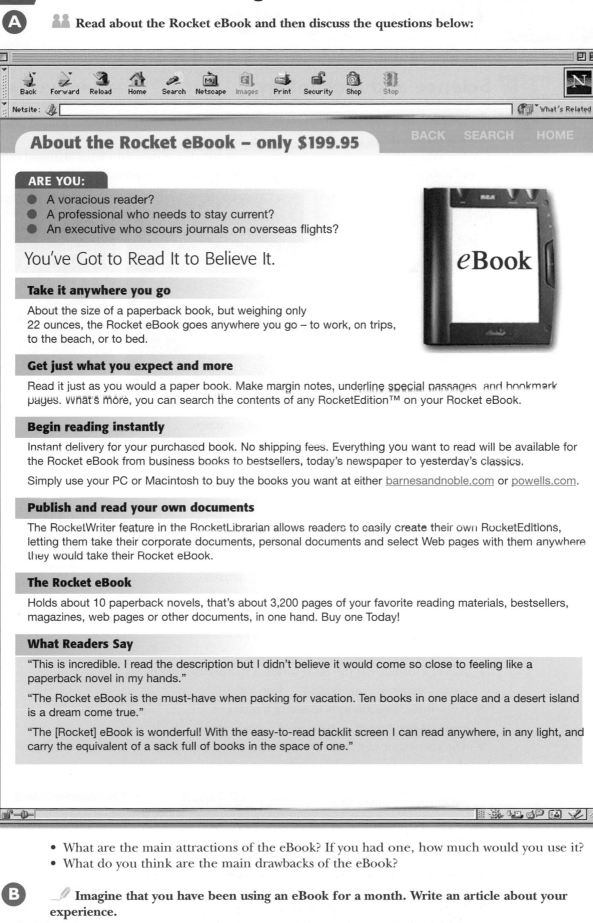

About the Rocket eBook – only $199.95

BACK   SEARCH   HOME

ARE YOU:
- A voracious reader?
- A professional who needs to stay current?
- An executive who scours journals on overseas flights?

You've Got to Read It to Believe It.

Take it anywhere you go

About the size of a paperback book, but weighing only
22 ounces, the Rocket eBook goes anywhere you go – to work, on trips,
to the beach, or to bed.

Get just what you expect and more

Read it just as you would a paper book. Make margin notes, underline special passages, and bookmark pages. What's more, you can search the contents of any RocketEdition™ on your Rocket eBook.

Begin reading instantly

Instant delivery for your purchased book. No shipping fees. Everything you want to read will be available for the Rocket eBook from business books to bestsellers, today's newspaper to yesterday's classics.

Simply use your PC or Macintosh to buy the books you want at either barnesandnoble.com or powells.com.

Publish and read your own documents

The RocketWriter feature in the RocketLibrarian allows readers to easily create their own RocketEditions, letting them take their corporate documents, personal documents and select Web pages with them anywhere they would take their Rocket eBook.

The Rocket eBook

Holds about 10 paperback novels, that's about 3,200 pages of your favorite reading materials, bestsellers, magazines, web pages or other documents, in one hand. Buy one Today!

What Readers Say

"This is incredible. I read the description but I didn't believe it would come so close to feeling like a paperback novel in my hands."

"The Rocket eBook is the must-have when packing for vacation. Ten books in one place and a desert island is a dream come true."

"The [Rocket] eBook is wonderful! With the easy-to-read backlit screen I can read anywhere, in any light, and carry the equivalent of a sack full of books in the space of one."

- What are the main attractions of the eBook? If you had one, how much would you use it?
- What do you think are the main drawbacks of the eBook?

B 🖋 Imagine that you have been using an eBook for a month. Write an article about your experience.

If you're doing a set book, it's worth searching the Internet for any study aids on the book you're reading. Your first port of call should be www.sparknotes.com, which provides free notes on a large number of books.

12 The cutting edge

12.1 Science and technology

TOPIC VOCABULARY

 Discuss these questions:

* What do you think each photograph shows?
* What other 20th century inventions or scientific breakthroughs have changed our lives as much as, or even more than, the inventions shown in the photos?

B **Choose ONE answer to complete each sentence.**

1 Technology deals with the .... of science.
   apparatus   application   empiricism   practicability

2 .... is one of the physical sciences.
   anatomy   botany   meteorology   sociology

3 .... is one of the life sciences.
   archaeology   astronomy   astrology   zoology

4 .... is one of the social sciences.
   anthropology   geology   chemistry   physics

5 IT (Information Technology) is the study of ....
   computers   libraries   laboratories   keyboards

6 If the warning light should come on, turn the red .... to off.
   button   dial   knob   lever

7 Albert Einstein was the most brilliant mathematician of his ....
   class   country   generation   year

8 A scientific hypothesis is tested in a series of .... experiments.
   controlled   limited   supervised   theoretical

9 The success of her research can be attributed to 10% .... and 90% hard work.
   common sense   greed   effort   inspiration

10 His ideas are invariably criticised as .... by fellow scientists.
   imaginative   impractical   ingenious   theoretical

11 A food processor has become an indispensable piece of .... in the home.
   contraption   device   equipment   gadget

12 The designer has applied for a .... for her new invention.
   copyright   patent   royalty   trade mark

13 It must have taken a genius to .... this complicated apparatus.
   think of   think out   think through   think up

14 This appliance has to be plugged into a(n) .... to make it work.
   cable   inlet   plug   socket

15 Many solutions to technical problems are discovered by ....
   experience   hit and miss   rule of thumb   trial and error

12.2 / The Freedom Ship

A   You'll hear part of a broadcast about the Freedom Ship. Write a word, number or short phrase to answer these questions about the project.

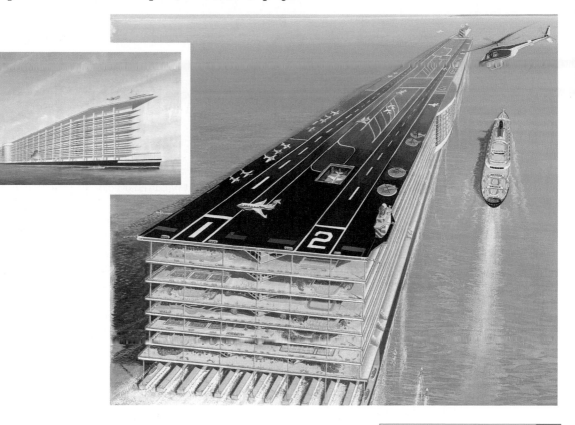

1   How many homes will there be on board?

2   How much is the cheapest home?

3   How much is the most expensive home?

4   How will people get to and from the port?

5   What proportion of the time will the ship be stationary?

6   How long will the ship be?

7   How wide will the ship be?

8   How long will it take to travel around the world?

9   What is the largest plane that will be able to land?

10   Why will there be a lot of open-air space and parks?

11   What educational facilities will there be?

12   How much tax will residents have to pay?

13   How will residents be encouraged to run businesses?

14   What will be done with non-recyclable waste?

15   What kind of fuel will the ship use?

16   How will the ship be affected by rough seas?

B 1   Discuss these questions:
- What would be the advantages and disadvantages of living on the Freedom Ship?
- Would you like to study in the Freedom Ship's university? Why (not)?
- Do you think this scheme will ever be realised? Give your reasons.

2   Design your own ideal city of the future. What facilities would it have? How would it be constructed? How large would it be?

3 Give a short presentation of your ideas to another group or to the whole class.

1 Read this article and highlight the parts that amuse you, or which strike a chord with you.

DESIGN FLAWS

I have a teenaged son who is a runner. He has, at a conservative estimate, 6,100 pairs of running shoes, and every one of them represents a greater investment of cumulative design effort than, say, Milton Keynes.

These shoes are amazing. I was just reading a review in one of his running magazines of the latest in 'sport utility sneakers', as they are called here, and it was full of passages like this: 'A dual-density EVA midsole with air units fore and aft provides stability while a gel heel-insert absorbs shock, but the shoe makes a narrow footprint, a characteristic that typically suits only the biomechanically efficient runner.' Alan Shepard went into space with less science at his disposal than that.

So here is my question. If my son can have his choice of a seemingly limitless range of scrupulously engineered, biomechanically efficient footwear, why does my computer keyboard suck? This is a serious enquiry.

My computer keyboard has 102 keys – almost double what my old manual typewriter had – which on the face of it seems awfully generous. Among other typographical luxuries, I can choose between three styles of bracket and two kinds of colon. I can dress my text with carets (^) and tildes (~). I can have slashes that fall to the left or to the right, and goodness knows what else.

I have so many keys, in fact, that over on the right-hand side of the keyboard there are whole communities of buttons of whose function I haven't the tiniest inkling. Occasionally I hit one by accident and subsequently discover that several paragraphs of my w9rk n+w look l*ke th?s, or that I have written the last page and a half in an interesting but unfortunately non-alphabetic font called Wingdings, but otherwise I haven't the faintest idea what those buttons are there for.

Never mind that many of these keys duplicate the functions of other keys, while others apparently do nothing at all (my favourite in this respect is one marked 'Pause', which when pressed does absolutely nothing, raising the interesting metaphysical question of whether it is therefore doing its job), or that several keys are arrayed in slightly imbecilic places. The delete key, for instance, is right beside the overprint key, so that often I discover, with a trill of gay laughter, that my most recent thoughts have been devouring, Pacman-like, everything I had previously written. Quite often, I somehow hit a combination of keys that summons a box which says, in effect, 'This Is a Pointless Box. Do You Want It?' which is followed by another that says, 'Are You Sure You Don't Want the Pointless Box?' Never mind all that. I have known for a long time that the computer is not my friend.

But here is what gets me. Out of all the 102 keys at my disposal, there is no key for the fraction ½. Typewriter keyboards always used to have a key for ½. Now, however, if I wish to write ½, I have to bring down the font menu and call up a directory called 'WP Characters', then hunt through a number of sub-directories until I remember or more often blunder on the particular one, 'Typographic Symbols', in which hides the furtive ½ sign. This is irksome and pointless and it doesn't seem right to me.

But then most things in the world don't seem right to me. On the dashboard of our family car is a shallow indentation about the size of a paperback book. If you are looking for somewhere to put your sunglasses or spare change, it is the obvious place, and it works extremely well, I must say, so long as the car is not actually moving. As soon as you put the car in motion, however, and particularly when you touch the brakes, turn a corner, or go up a gentle slope, everything slides off. There is, you see, no lip round this dashboard tray. It is just a flat space, with a dimpled bottom. It can hold nothing that has not been nailed to it.

So I ask you: what, then, is it for? Somebody had to design it. It didn't just appear spontaneously. Some person – perhaps, for all I know, a whole committee of people in the Dashboard Stowage Division – had to invest time and thought in incorporating into the design of this vehicle a storage tray that will actually hold nothing. That is really quite an achievement.

But it is nothing, of course, compared with the manifold design achievements of those responsible for the modern video recorder. Now I am not going to go on about how impossible it is to programme the typical video recorder because you know that already. Nor will I observe how irritating it is that you must cross the room and get down on your belly to confirm that it is actually recording. But I will just make one small passing observation. I recently bought a video recorder and one of the selling points – one of the things the manufacturer boasted about – was that it was capable of recording programmes up to twelve months in advance. Now think about this for a moment and tell me any circumstance – and I mean any circumstance at all – in which you can envision wanting to set a video machine to record a programme one year from now.

I don't want to sound like some old guy who is always moaning. I freely acknowledge that there are many excellent, well-engineered products that didn't exist when I was a boy – the pocket calculator and kettles that switch off automatically are two that fill me yet with gratitude and wonder – but it does seem to me that an awful lot of things out there have been designed by people who cannot possibly have stopped to think how they will be used.

Just think for a moment of all the everyday items you have to puzzle over – fax machines, photocopiers, central heating thermostats, airline tickets, television remote control units, hotel showers and alarm clocks, microwave ovens, almost any electrical product owned by someone other than you – because they are ill thought out.

And why are they so ill thought out? Because all the best designers are making running shoes. Either that, or they are just idiots. In either case, it really isn't fair.

Bill Bryson

2 Find words in the text which mean the same as the following:

¶3 *infinite*   ¶4 *decorate*   ¶5 *typeface*   ¶6 *idiotic*   ¶7 *discover by accident*   ¶8 *hollow area*
¶9 *without human intervention*   *numerous*   ¶10 *imagine*   ¶11 *complaining*

B   Choose the word or phrase which best completes each sentence:

1 The writer finds his computer keyboard ...
   a inefficient   **c** frustrating
   b confusing   **d** infuriating
2 *with a trill of gay laughter* (¶6) is an example of ...
   a heavy irony   **c** his cheerfulness in the face of adversity
   b gentle irony   **d** a paradox
3 What irritates the writer most about his computer is ...
   a the pointless boxes that appear   **c** the lack of a ½ key
   b how easy it is to delete accidentally   **d** the keys he never uses
4 The indentation on his car's dashboard works fine ...
   a when the car is driven slowly   **c** except when it is used for loose change
   b when the car is stationary   **d** except when the car is parked on a slope
5 The facility of being able to set a video recorder to record 12 months from now is ...
   a a useful feature   **c** pointless
   b a good marketing feature   **d** likely to make programming it harder
6 The problem with many products is that the designers ...
   a have concentrated on appearance   **c** are inadequately trained
   b haven't considered the users   **d** know how to use their own products

C   Write a SUMMARY of what the writer LIKES about modern design and technology (50–70 words).

D   Discuss these questions:
- What did you find funny about the article? Tell each other which parts struck a chord with you.
- Look again at paragraph 10. Is the writer just *an old guy who is always moaning*?
- Look again at paragraph 12. Which of the products have you had to puzzle over? Do you share the writer's feelings about them?

12.4 Verbs + prepositions

(A) Read each set of notes and then do the exercises below. Choose from among these prepositions:

about   against   at   by   for   from   in   on   out   of   to   with

1 Some verbs normally **HAVE TO BE** followed by a preposition:

Who does that white coat belong to?
You must be confusing me with someone else.
Where do you come from?

Fill in the missing prepositions in this list:

combine something	*engage*	*part* ....
compare something	*invest*	*reason* ....
contrast something	*lean*	*rely* ....
depend	*mistake it/them*	*separate something* ....

2 Some verbs **CAN** be used with a prepositional phrase (but they needn't be):

I think he applied last week.
Yes, but what did he apply for? Who did he apply to? When did he apply?
He applied to his father's company for a job.

Add the missing prepositions. The verbs in blue can be used with more than one preposition.

agree	*insist*	*smell* ....
apologise	*interfere*	*struggle* ....
approve	*intrude*	*succeed* ....
bargain	*negotiate*	*suffer* ....
care	*object*	*talk* ....
decide	*quarrel*	*vote* ....
experiment	*resign*	*watch* ....
hope	*retire*	*worry* ....

3 Some verbs normally followed by an object can **ALSO** be used with prepositional phrases:

She accused someone. Yes but what did she accuse them of?
He borrowed something. Yes, but who did he borrow it from?

Add the missing prepositions. The verbs in blue can be used with more than one preposition.

admire him	*deliver it*	*thank her* ....
blame her	*punish him*	*threaten them* ....
congratulate him	*rescue them*	*use it* ....
consult her	*respect her*	*warn him* ....
convince them	*take it*	

(B) Fill each gap with a suitable preposition.

Penguin power pushes
propellers aside

A ship that flaps its way ____[1] the water like a penguin is to be built ____[2] the United States after engineers realised that the bird is much better at moving ____[3] the water than a propeller-driven boat.

Boat builders have been using propellers ____[4] over 150 years but researchers have been uncomfortable at the knowledge that the aquatic world, ____[5] 150 million years ____[6] evolutionary experience, has ignored propellers as a means of moving ____[7] water.

After studying the fins ____[8] various fish, the researchers, ____[9] the Massachusetts Institute of Technology, realised that penguins slide ____[10] water at least 15 per cent more efficiently than boats.

From videos of swimming penguins, the researchers watched the birds' pectoral fins waft towards and away from each other. The sideways forces cancelled each other out and the resulting thrust was almost entirely forwards. Last month the engineers, led [   ]¹¹ Prof Michael Triantafyllou, demonstrated a 12ft computer-controlled boat [   ]¹² two "oscillating foils" based [   ]¹³ the same principles.

The foils [   ]¹⁴ the prototype boat look just like two ordinary rudders, but they work [   ]¹⁵ an entirely different way. Two large motors swivel the foils towards and away from each other [   ]¹⁶ a rudder-like movement. Two smaller motors also make the foils twist slightly.

[   ]¹⁷ ensuring that the foils work together to make an opening and closing motion, their sideways forces cancel each other out just as with a penguin.

The prototype boat's maiden voyage [   ]¹⁸ Charles River, Boston, was a success. Triantafyllou has now agreed [   ]¹⁹ a shipyard to build a 40ft wide, 150ft long version [   ]²⁰ the penguin-inspired ship. [   ]²¹ larger fins mounted underneath the stern the efficiency could be even better, he says. And the fish-like wake is difficult to detect, which could be an advantage [   ]²² military vessels.

The group's first attempt [   ]²³ fish-like propulsion led to Robotuna, a robot that swims like a tuna. The scientists say the penguin is a better bet [   ]²⁴ human transport because it holds its body still as it swims.

Aisling Irwin

12.5 **The passive – 2**   ADVANCED GRAMMAR

(A) **1** Study the following reasons and then decide which of them apply to sentences 1–10 below:

Why the passive is used

The passive may be used for a variety of reasons, including the following:

a to dissociate speakers or writers from an unpopular decision or announcement
b to give an impression of objectivity – especially in scientific or technical texts and in news reports
c to give the effect of formality
d to arouse sympathy for the victim
e to describe actions where the people responsible are unknown, unimportant or irrelevant – or obvious
f to avoid blaming anyone directly for what has happened
g for variety – to make a change from using the active
h when using the passive makes the sentence easier to read and the meaning easier to understand than a clumsy or inelegant active sentence – i.e. the passive is more concise
i to emphasise the people responsible (using *by* . . .)

1 Dictionaries may not be used in the examination.   ....
2 He was criticised by his father, but praised by his mother.   ....
3 He's been misunderstood and made to feel inadequate all his life.   ....
4 It has been decided to restrict parking by students in the college grounds. ....
5 Several people have been injured in accidents at this junction.   ....
6 The solution was heated to boiling point and then allowed to cool to 20°. ....
7 Although we arrived early, we were kept waiting for an hour.   ....
8 We arrived late because our flight was delayed.   ....
9 The documents are being photocopied at the moment.   ....
10 Some money has been taken from my room.   ....

2 Now rewrite each sentence in the active voice. How does the emphasis of each sentence change when it's rewritten?

(B) Rewrite each of these sentences using the passive, starting with the words on the right:

1 Everyone looks down on her and she's fed up with it.   She's fed up with ....
2 The children's grandparents looked after them.   The children ....
3 My assistant is dealing with this matter.   This matter ....
4 Customers must pay for any breakages.   All breakages ....
5 You can't rely on Tony to finish the work on time.   Tony can't ....

6 I'll get someone to see to the repairs right away. The repairs ....
7 Someone had broken into her apartment during the night. Her apartment ....
8 People often look on scientists as experts. Scientists ....
9 Someone pointed out to me that I was wearing odd socks. It ....
10 People might refer to him as 'technophobic'. He ....
11 Without permission for a new runway they can't expand the airport. Until permission ....
12 Electronics might intimidate some people, but not me. Some ....
13 I can't figure out how to dispose of all these old magazines. How can all ....
14 You'll have to get rid of all those old magazines. Those old magazines ....
15 They have accounted for all the survivors of the accident. All the ....

12.6 *give* and *take*   VERBS AND IDIOMS

A **Which of the following would you GIVE and which would you TAKE?**

> a liking to someone or something   a photograph   a pride in something   advice to someone
> an answer   an explanation   an interest in something   encouragement   evidence
> issue with someone   part in something   permission   pity on someone   someone a kiss
> someone a lift   someone a ring   someone a shock   someone some help
> your time over something

B **Find synonyms for the phrases in red, or explain their meaning. Use a dictionary if necessary.**

1 Don't take it for granted that everything's going to be easy: you should be prepared to take the rough with the smooth when you take up a new job.
2 When we criticised him I half expected him to take offence, but he took it in good part, and in the ensuing discussion he gave as good as he got.
3 She was quite taken aback when I took her up on her offer.
4 They were quite taken with each other on their first meeting.
5 He nearly took us in, but he gave himself away when he started giggling.
6 He took exception to the fact that she was starting to take him for granted.
7 I know you're annoyed but don't take it out on me – take it up with the people who were responsible.
8 Cheer up! Why don't you take him out for a meal, it may take you out of yourself.
9 She can take off her father's voice and mannerisms brilliantly – especially the way he takes off his glasses when his patience is about to give out.
10 There was so much information that I couldn't take it all in.

C **Fill the gaps in these sentences with suitable phrases from the list below. You may need to change the form of the verbs.**

1 The sight was so beautiful it .... her breath ....
2 I remember .... the message but I've forgotten where I put it.
3 About 75% of the land area of Britain is .... agriculture.
4 You really should .... insurance before you travel.
5 You've .... more work than you can manage and it seems to be .... it .... of you. Why don't you .... a few days .... ?
6 I used to go jogging but now I .... it .... Perhaps I'll .... swimming instead.
7 I'm feeling a bit tired of driving, would you mind .... for a while?
8 I apologise. I .... all those things I said about your new hairstyle.

> give over to   give up   take away   take back   take down
> take off   take on   take out   take out   take over   take up

A **Read these notes and then look at the pairs of nouns below:**

- How are the nouns different? What do they have in common – if anything?
- What abstract noun or verb is associated with each noun – or does a phrase have to be used instead?

These suffixes can be used to form nouns from verbs, or from abstract nouns:

-er	employer gangster examiner adviser reviewer office cleaner
	computer vacuum cleaner timer tranquilliser
-ee	employee trainee addressee absentee
-or	inventor supervisor operator juror perpetrator impersonator
-ist	scientist technologist terrorist environmentalist

astrologer • astronomer

Astronomers look through telescopes but astrologers work out horoscopes. Both an astronomer and an astrologer study the stars. The nouns are astrology and astronomy.

administrator • dictator	attacker • hijacker	bartender • moneylender
chauvinist • feminist	councillor • counsellor	demonstrator • spectator
employer • employee	fortune-teller • storyteller	landowner • loner
miner • minor	pawnbroker • stockbroker	payer • payee
persecutor • prosecutor	predecessor • successor	psychologist • psychiatrist
researcher • searcher	shareholder • householder	troubleshooter • troublemaker

B **Read these notes and then form verbs from the adjectives and nouns below, using *-ise/-ize* or *-en*:**

These suffixes can be used to form verbs from adjectives and nouns:

-en	dampen ripen harden
-ise/-ize	modernise advertise popularise

British English spelling: *-ise* or *-ize* (as you prefer)
American English spelling: *-ize*

context *contextualise* deaf emphasis familiar general glamour loose moist
national sharp straight strong subsidy summary sweet sympathy synthetic
thick tight victim visual wide

C 1 **Highlight** the words you'd like to remember – and any spellings you find troublesome. Use a dictionary, paying particular attention to the examples.

2 **Write a short exercise with gaps and give the sentences to another pair to do.**

e.g. *A person who is sent for to deal with problems is a .... (troubleshooter)*

(A) **1 Read the text through before looking at the questions below.**

Over the years I have fumbled my way through life, walking into doors, failing to figure out water faucets, incompetent at working the simple things of everyday life. "Just me," I would mumble. "Just mechanical ineptitude." But as I studied psychology and watched the behavior of other people, I began to realize that I was not alone. My difficulties were mirrored by the problems of others. And we all seemed to blame ourselves. Could the whole world be mechanically incompetent?

The truth emerged slowly. My research activities led me to the study of human error and industrial accidents. Humans, I discovered, do not always behave clumsily. Humans do not always err. But they do when the things they use are badly conceived and designed. Nonetheless, we still see human error blamed for all that befalls society. Does a commercial airliner crash? "Pilot error," say the reports. Does a Soviet nuclear power plant have a serious problem? "Human error," says the newspaper. Do two ships at sea collide? "Human error" is the official cause. But careful analysis of these kinds of incidents usually gives the lie to such a story. At the famous American nuclear power plant disaster at Three Mile Island, the blame was placed on plant operators who misdiagnosed the problems. But was it human error? Consider the phrase "operators who misdiagnosed the problems." The phrase reveals that first there were problems – in fact, a series of mechanical failures. Then why wasn't equipment failure the real cause? What about the misdiagnoses? Why didn't the operators correctly determine the cause? Well, how about the fact that the proper instruments were not available, that the plant operators acted in ways that in the past had always been reasonable and proper? How about the pressure relief valve that failed to close, even though the operator pushed the proper button and even though a light came on stating it was closed? Why was the operator blamed for not checking two more instruments (one on the rear of the control panel) and determining that the light was faulty? (Actually, the operator did check one of them.) Human error? To me it sounds like equipment failure coupled with serious design error.

And, yes, what about my inability to use the simple things of everyday life? I can use complicated things. I am quite expert at computers, and electronics, and complex laboratory equipment. Why do I have trouble with doors, light switches, and water faucets? How come I can work a multimillion-dollar computer installation, but not my home VCR? While we all blame ourselves, the real culprit – faulty design – goes undetected. And millions of people feel themselves to be mechanically inept. It is time for a change. ■

from the Preface to *The Psychology of Everyday Things* by Donald A. Norman

2 👥 **Go through the text and answer these questions:**

1 Highlight THREE sentences that seem to sum up the writer's message.
2 Look at the cases where he uses *I, me* or *my* and underline them – what is the effect of this?
3 How many times does the writer use *we* or *ourselves*?
4 How many times does he use *you* or *your*, addressing the reader directly?
5 How many times does he use imperatives, addressing the reader directly?
6 How many questions does the writer ask? What is the effect of this?
   Put a ring round all the question marks: (?) (?)
7 How many answers does he give?
   How many questions are unanswered?
8 How well does the writer succeed in involving the reader?
9 What kind of reader does the writer seem to have in mind?
   To what extent are YOU that kind of reader?
10 How does the kind of reader he has in mind affect:
   a the content of the text
   b the style of the text

(B) **1** 👥 **Think of another subject you feel strongly about and which you have some personal knowledge of: e.g., traffic problems in your city, bureaucracy, energy conservation, etc. Make notes on your experiences and your views.**

2 🖉 **Write a paragraph in a similar style to the text. Use the first person and answered or unanswered questions.**

A 1 Discuss these questions:
- Which of the things look easier to use? Why is this?
- Can you programme a video recorder to record a TV programme? Have you ever set one wrong? Was it your fault or the designer's?

2 Now one of you should look at Activity 6, one at 19 and one at 28. You'll have some more questions to ask each other about the design of everyday equipment (based on the ideas of Donald A. Norman).

B 1 Spend some time researching and thinking about the ideas you discussed earlier, looking at the way you and other people interact with doors, watches, switches, numbers, etc.

2 Find out about each other's ideas and experiences. Discuss how you will organise and sequence your ideas for an article with this headline:

User-friendly? I don't think so!

(300–350 words)

3 Write your article, giving examples from what you discussed in A2 and discovered in your research. Make notes before you start.

"A virus ate my homework."

13

Just good friends?

13.1 Friends ... and enemies   LISTENING & TOPIC VOCABULARY

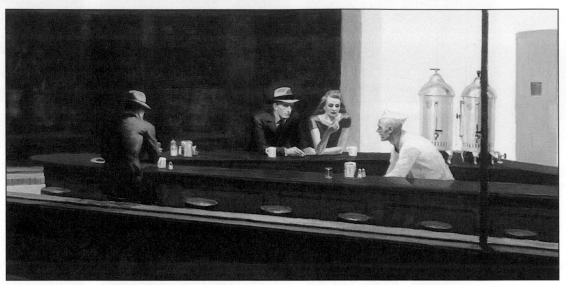

Edward Hopper: Nighthawks, *1942 (detail)*

A 👥 **Discuss these questions about the picture:**

- Where are the people? Who are they? How do they feel?
- What has happened earlier, what's happening now and what's going to happen?
- What have they said to each other earlier? What are they saying now? What are they going to say? What is their relationship?
- How does the picture make YOU feel? Would you like to be one of the people? Why (not)?

B 👥 **One of you should look at Activity 7, the other at 20. You'll each have another picture to look at and describe. Ask each other questions to find out how the picture illustrates the relationships between the people.**

C 🔊 **You'll hear Ruth, William and Sarah talking about friendship. Indicate which of the speakers expresses each of the opinions listed by writing the appropriate letter in each box.**

Write R **for Ruth, or** W **for William, or** S **for Sarah. Write more than one letter in the box if a view is expressed by more than one person.**

1 A good friend can support you when you're feeling sad. ⬜ **1**

2 A good friend can tell you if you're behaving stupidly. ⬜ **2**

3 I don't like the partners my best friend chooses. ⬜ **3**

4 I have known by best friend since we were children. ⬜ **4**

5 I still spend a lot of time with my best friend. ⬜ **5**

6 It's hard for an adult to make new friends. ⬜ **6**

7 It's hard to break into an established circle of friends. ⬜ **7**

8 My best friend likes to do different things from me now. ⬜ **8**

D 👥 **Discuss these questions:**

- Which of the experiences you heard about in **C** struck a chord with you?
- Describe the person who was your own best friend as a child – how has your relationship changed since you first got to know each other?
- What do you appreciate about the friends you have now? Explain why you get on well.
- Is it better to have just one or two close friends, or friends you don't know so well?

E **1** 👥 Discuss the relative importance of the following qualities in a friendship or a relationship. Note down THREE important qualities that are missing from the list.

> cheerfulness   commitment   compassion   compatibility   consideration   enthusiasm
> generosity   good looks   intelligence   kindness   loyalty   optimism   passion   patience
> politeness   punctuality   realism   reliability   responsibility   sincerity   thoughtfulness

2 And how important are the following factors in a friendship or a relationship?

> age   family background   mutual interests   a sense of humour   social class
> shared attitudes to religion, politics, etc.   similar personalities

3 Which FIVE features from the two lists in E1 and 2 are the most important and why? Which are the five LEAST important features?

F **1** 🔊 You'll hear the same words spoken in different ways. Decide which word from the list on the right best describes each speaker's mood or tone.

1	
2	
3	
4	
5	

> annoyed   jaded
> anxious   patient
> businesslike   sarcastic
> despondent   timid
> eager   impatient

2 👥 Discuss how each speaker's TONE OF VOICE conveyed their mood. Consider their speed of delivery, the amount of hesitation, the pitch of their voice, the way they emphasised words, the way they sighed or laughed or made other noises, etc.

Well, good evening. Thank you both for getting here on time and for waiting so patiently. Everyone else seems to be rather late, or maybe they haven't been able to make it. Anyway, we'll make a start I think, and if any of the others do come we can always fill them in on what's happened so far...

3 👥 Take it in turns to read the speech aloud in different ways. Can your partner guess what mood you're trying to convey?

13.2 As the saying goes... GRAMMAR REVIEW

A These sayings and proverbs all have something to do with relationships. Rewrite each one starting with the words on the right, keeping the meaning as similar as possible to the original sentence. (This exercise revises some of the points covered in the Grammar review sections earlier in the book.)

1 A friend in need is a friend indeed.   Someone who _helps you if you're in trouble_ is a true friend.
2 It takes two to make a quarrel.   When there .... , both parties ....
3 Actions speak louder than words.   What really .... do, not .... say.
4 It takes all sorts to make a world.   The world is .... people.
5 Live and let live.   Be .... and .... what they want to do.
6 It's easy to be wise after the event.   You couldn't .... happen.
7 Blood is thicker than water.   Family .... other relationships.
8 Like father like son.   A son tends .... father.
9 Many a true word is spoken in jest.   A remark ....
10 Out of sight, out of mind.   Absent friends ....
11 Absence makes the heart grow fonder.   When people ....
12 One good turn deserves another.   After someone ....
13 Where there's a will there's a way.   If you ....
14 Love is like the measles, we all have to go through it.   Everyone .... , but they . ... eventually.

B 👥 Discuss which of the sayings you agree with, comparing them with your own experiences.

Proverbs should be used sparingly in conversation, and they can sound very odd when used inappropriately. We can soften their effect by adding ...
– *as they say* or ... – *as the saying goes:*
    "Well, it's easy to be wise after the event – *as the saying goes*."

13.3 / Family life

A Read the three extracts and discuss the questions that follow.

CHAPTER ONE

THIS is the story of a five-year sojourn that I and my family made on the Greek island of Corfu. It was originally intended to be a mildly nostalgic account of the natural history of the island, but I made a grave mistake by introducing my family into the book in the first few pages. Having got themselves on paper, they then proceeded to establish themselves and invite various friends to share the chapters. It was only with the greatest difficulty, and by exercising considerable cunning, that I managed to retain a few pages here and there which I could devote exclusively to animals.

I have attempted to draw an accurate and unexaggerated picture of my family in the following pages; they appear as I saw them. To explain some of their more curious ways, however, I feel that I should state that at the time we were in Corfu the family were all quite young: Larry, the eldest, was twenty-three; Leslie was nineteen; Margo eighteen; while I was the youngest, being of the tender and impressionable age of ten. We have never been very certain of my mother's age, for the simple reason that she can never remember her date of birth; all I can say is that she was old enough to have four children. My mother also insists that I explain that she is a widow for, as she so penetratingly observed, you never know what people might think

I did not kill my father, but I sometimes felt I had helped him on his way. And but for the fact that it coincided with a landmark in my own physical growth, his death seemed insignificant compared with what followed. My sisters and I talked about him the week after he died, and Sue certainly cried when the ambulance men tucked him up in a bright-red blanket and carried him away. He was a frail, irascible, obsessive man with yellowish hands and face. I am only including the little story of his death to explain how my sisters and I came to have such a large quantity of cement at our disposal.

In the early summer of my fourteenth year a lorry pulled up outside our house. I was sitting on the front step rereading a comic. The driver and another man came towards me. They were covered in a fine, pale dust which gave their faces a ghostly look. They were both whistling shrilly completely different tunes. I stood up and held the comic out of sight. I wished I had been reading the racing page of my father's paper, or the football results.

'Cement?' one of them said. I hooked my thumbs into my pockets, moved my weight to one foot and narrowed my eyes a little. I wanted to say something terse and appropriate, but I was not sure I had heard them right

I was born poor in rich America, yet my secret instincts were better than money and were for me a source of power. I had advantages that no one could take away from me – a clear memory and brilliant dreams and a knack for knowing when I was happy.

I was at my happiest leading two lives, and it was a satisfaction to me that the second one – of the dreamer or the sneak – I kept hidden. That was how I spent my first fifteen years. Fifteen was young then and I knew this: The poor don't belong. But one summer out of loneliness or impatience my second self did more than wake and watch, and more than remember. He began to see like a historian, and he acted. I have to save my life, I used to think.

Early that summer I was walking down a lovely crumbling little street lined with elms, called Brookview Road. The city of Boston, with its two tall buildings

Discuss these questions and note down your answers:

1 Which extract comes from which of these books:

2 Which of the extracts makes you want to read on? Give your reasons.
3 What do the extracts have in common?
4 What are the main differences between the three extracts?
5 What kind of young person does each narrator seem to be?
6 In the first extract, how did the narrator's family *invite various friends to share the chapters*? And what does he mean by *'their more curious ways'*?
7 In the second extract, why do you think the narrator was *'rereading a comic'*? Why did he *'wish he had been reading the racing page of his father's paper'*?
8 In the third extract, what is meant by *'The poor don't belong'*?
9 What do we learn of the relationship between the narrator and his family in each extract?

B 👥 → 👥 **Compare your answers to the questions. Then discuss which of the qualities in 13.1 E1 are most important in FAMILY relationships between parents and children, and between sisters and brothers.**

C Highlight **any words in the extracts in A which you didn't understand (or had to guess). Use a dictionary to check their meanings.**

13.4 Conditionals – 2   ADVANCED GRAMMAR

A **1** 👥 **Discuss any differences in style or meaning between the sentences in each group:**

1 If it weren't for the children they would have split up by now.
   If it wasn't for the children they would have split up by now.
   Were it not for the children they would have split up by now.
   If they didn't have children they would have split up by now.
2 If you should see Terry could you give him my regards?
   When you see Terry could you give him my regards?
   If you happen to see Terry could you give him my regards?
   If you see Terry could you give him my regards?
   Should you see Terry could you give him my regards?
3 If you wouldn't mind waiting I'll let them know you're here.
   If you don't mind waiting I'll let them know you're here.
   If you wait I'll let them know you're here.
4 Had it not been for your help I couldn't have done it.
   Without your help I couldn't have done it.
   If it hadn't been for your help I couldn't have done it.
   If you hadn't been so helpful I couldn't have done it.
   I'm glad you helped me otherwise I couldn't have done it.

2 There are NO COMMAS in any of the above sentences. Which of them would be easier to understand if they were to have commas?

B **Finish the incomplete sentences in such a way that each one means the same as the complete sentence before it:**

1 Please do take a seat and I'll bring you some coffee.   If you ....
2 Their relationship was doomed because of their incompatibility.   Had ....
3 I might miss my connection, if so I'll try to call you to let you know. Should ....
4 They didn't get married because their parents were against it.   But ....
5 You probably won't have time – but I'd like you to come and see us.   If ....
6 There was such a lot of traffic: that's why we're late.   Had ....
7 She could tell him she's leaving, but it would upset him.   If ....
8 They have a wonderful relationship, and have decided to get married.   Were ....
9 She's very patient and loyal, that's why she hasn't left him.   If it ....
10 If you don't work hard at a relationship it's not likely to last.   Without ....

C **1** 👥 ✎ **Write FIVE sentences about your own friends and relatives, and your relationships with them using the following structures:**

   Had...   If it weren't for...   Were...   Should...   Without...

2 👥 → 👥 **Compare your sentences.**

13.5 ... till death us do part?

A **1** Read this extract through carefully, preferably before the lesson.

Whenever Henry Wilt took the dog for a walk, or, to be more accurate, when the dog took him, or to be exact, when Mrs Wilt told them both to go and take themselves out of the house so that she could do her yoga exercises, he always took the same route. In fact the dog followed the route and Wilt followed the dog. They went down past the Post Office, across the playground, under the railway bridge and out on to the footpath by the river. A mile along the river and then under the railway line again and back through streets where the houses were bigger than Wilt's semi and where there were large trees and gardens and the cars were all Rovers and Mercedes. It was here that Clem, a pedigree Labrador, evidently feeling more at home, did his business while Wilt stood looking around rather uneasily, conscious that this was not his sort of neighbourhood and wishing it was. It was about the only time during their walk that he was at all aware of his surroundings. For the rest of the way Wilt's walk was an interior one and followed an itinerary completely at variance with his own appearance and that of his route. It was in fact a journey of wishful thinking, a pilgrimage along trails of remote possibility involving the irrevocable disappearance of Mrs Wilt, the sudden acquisition of wealth, power, what he would do if he was appointed Minister of Education or, better still, Prime Minister. It was partly concocted of a series of desperate expedients and partly in an unspoken dialogue so that anyone noticing Wilt (and most people didn't) might have seen his lips move occasionally and his mouth curl into what he fondly imagined was a sardonic smile as he dealt with questions or parried arguments with devastating repartee. It was on one of these walks taken in the rain after a particularly trying day at the Tech that Wilt first conceived the notion that he would only be able to fulfil his latent promise and call his life his own if some not entirely fortuitous disaster overtook his wife.

Like everything else in Henry Wilt's life it was not a sudden decision. He was not a decisive man.

from Wilt by Tom Sharpe

2 Note down your answers to these questions:

1 Who decided what time Clem should go for a walk?
2 Who decided on the route for the walk?
3 What do you think a *semi* (line 6) is?
4 Why did Clem feel more at home where the houses were larger?
5 Why did Wilt feel uneasy there?
6 What did Wilt do during the rest of the walk?
7 What were the three directions in which his thoughts took him?
8 How do you think Wilt fared in arguments in real life?
9 What do you think Wilt does at *the Tech*?
10 What might *some not entirely fortuitous disaster* be?
11 Why aren't we told Mrs Wilt's first name?
12 Why is Henry Wilt referred to as *Wilt* (rather than Mr Wilt or Henry)?

B **1** Now read this extract and compare it with the extract above. Find out what the two extracts have in common. How are they different?

Henry Farr did not, precisely, decide to murder his wife. It was simply that he could think of no other way of prolonging her absence from him indefinitely.

He had quite often, in the past, when she was being more than usually irritating, had fantasies about her death. She hurtled over cliffs in flaming cars or was brutally murdered on her way to the dry cleaners. But Henry was never actually responsible for the event. He was at the graveside looking mournful and interesting. Or he was coping with his daughter as she roamed the now deserted house, trying not to look as if he was glad to have the extra space. But he was never actually the instigator.

Once he had got the idea of killing her (and at first this fantasy did not seem very different from the reveries in which he wept by her open grave, comforted by young, fashionably dressed women) it took some time to appreciate that this scenario was of quite a different type from the others. It was a dream that could, if he so wished, become reality.

One Friday afternoon in September, he thought about strangling her. The Wimbledon Strangler. He liked that idea. He could see Edgar Lustgarten narrowing his eyes threateningly at the camera, as he paced out the length of Maple Drive. 'But Henry Farr,' Lustgarten was saying, 'with the folly of the criminal, the supreme arrogance of the murderer, had forgotten one vital thing. The shred of fibre that was to send Henry Farr to the gallows was –'

What was he thinking of? They didn't hang people any more. They wrote long, bestselling paperback books about them.

from The Wimbledon Poisoner by Nigel Williams

2 👥 **Discuss these questions:**

- Which parts of the two passages amused you? Can you explain why? (If neither passage amused you at all, what did you find annoying about them?)
- Both books were written by men – but what kind of readers were they written for? Would they appeal more to men or women, or to both?
- Look at the first sentences: Are they both 'nodders' (see 11.7)?
- What do you think is going to happen in each story? Will either of the Henries actually succeed in murdering his wife, or not?

13.6 Underlying meanings   VOCABULARY DEVELOPMENT

A 👥 Some words have particular associations with other words and ideas. Highlight these examples in the extract from Wilt in 13.5A. Decide what CONCEPT or UNDERLYING MEANING the writer expects the reader to associate each phrase with.

yoga exercises	parried
a semi (= semi-detached house)	a pilgrimage
Rovers and Mercedes	the Tech (= technical college)
an itinerary	fulfil his latent promise

B Read these notes and then decide which of the words in each pair below seem to have more pejorative associations:

Some words have pejorative or uncomplimentary associations:
    That's a stupid mistake!   She's a very fussy person.

Some words have less pejorative or more positive associations:
    That's a silly mistake!   She's a very discerning person.

> Associations very much depend on the context in which words are used.

cautious · prudent	cooperative · obedient	difficult · challenging
dreamer · idealist	frank · sincere	gullible · trusting
humble · modest	laid back · lazy	light-hearted · frivolous
moody · depressed	naive · innocent	optimistic · impractical
oversight · mistake	realistic · pessimistic	solemn · serious
stubborn · resolute	studious · hard-working	tease · mock

C 1 Choose FIVE of the following ideas and write down five nouns or adjectives that you associate with each of them. Pick words that reflect your feelings – as in the examples:

> For example, *clever* and *bright* are generally complimentary, but to call someone *a clever dick* or a *bright spark* is disparaging. It's also possible to use complimentary words in a sarcastic or ironic way: *That was <u>very</u> clever of you!*

Being at home	*security predictable reassurance mother warmth*	
Away from home	*freedom danger excitement interesting cold*	
Being with a friend	Meeting a stranger	Being alone
Parents	Marriage	Children
Taking an exam	Learning English	Music
Earning a living	Holidays	School
Shopping	Reading	Television

2 👥 Compare your ideas. Which of the words you wrote down seem to have negative and which have positive associations?

"Leave those… Kevin will do the washing up."

13.7 **The narrator**

A Read the passage and then discuss the questions below with a partner.

My career has always been marked by a strange mixture of confidence and cowardice: almost, one might say, made by it. Take, for instance, the first time I tried spending a night with a man in a hotel. I was nineteen at the time, an age appropriate for such adventures, and needless to say I was not married. I am still not married, a fact of some significance, but more of that later. The name of the boy, if I remember rightly, was Hamish. I do remember rightly. I really must try not to be deprecating. Confidence, not cowardice, is the part of myself which I admire, after all.

Hamish and I had just come down from Cambridge at the end of the Christmas term: we had conceived our plan well in advance, and had each informed our parents that term ended a day later than it actually did, knowing quite well that they would not be interested enough to check, nor sufficiently au fait to ascertain the value of their information if they did. So we arrived in London together in the late afternoon, and took a taxi from the station to our destined hotel. We had worked everything out, and had even booked our room, which would probably not have been necessary, as the hotel we had selected was one of those large central cheap-smart ones, specially designed for adventures such as ours. I was wearing a gold curtain ring on the relevant finger. We had decided to stick to Hamish's own name, which, being Andrews, was unmemorable enough, and less confusing than having to think up a pseudonym. We were well educated, the two of us, in the pitfalls of such occasions, having both of us read at one time in our lives a good deal of cheap fiction, and indeed we both carried ourselves with considerable aplomb. We arrived, unloaded our suitably-labelled suitcases, and called at the desk for our key. It was here that I made my mistake. For some reason I was requested to sign the register. I now know that it is by no means customary for wives to sign hotel registers

from *The Millstone* by Margaret Drabble

1 What kind of person does Rosamund, the narrator, seem to be?
2 Find an example of the narrator poking fun at herself.
3 How would you describe the tone or style of the passage?
4 What do you think is going to happen in the rest of the novel? What clues are given in the passage? Why is it called *The Millstone* do you think?

B 1 The author wrote the story in the first person. Why do you think she did this? What would be the effects of changing *my* to *her*, *I* to *she*, *we* to *they* and *our* to *their*?

2 Look again at 13.5. If the extracts from *Wilt* and *The Wimbledon Poisoner* were in the first person, what effect would this have on them?

If the extracts in 13.3 were in the third person, what effect would this have?

C 1 Think of an embarrassing, amusing or memorable experience you've had (or can imagine having). Write TWO versions of the opening paragraph of a story about the experience: one in the first person (using *I/me/my*), the other in the third person as if you're writing about a 'character' (about 50 words each).

2 Compare your paragraphs. Discuss which version was easier to write and which is most convincing.

If you're writing an article or a letter in the exam, narrative can help to engage the reader.

A fictional or semi-fictional story can be easier to handle than one which sticks strictly to the truth, because you can make the events fit the time and space available – and it may be easier to restrict the vocabulary to words you know.

A A proposal is like a report, except that the focus is on the future. Proposals include recommendations for discussion or for action. Proposals include section headings. Read this information and then MAKE NOTES on your ideas for the facilities the proposed students' centre should provide.

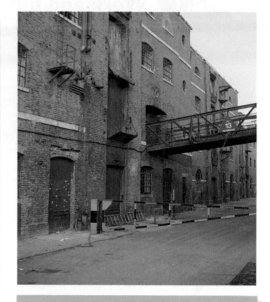

Lion Yard to become International Student Centre?

The owners of Lion Yard, which has been empty for over a year, have offered the building to the city on condition that it is converted into an international student centre.

Lion Yard was built in 1800 as a leather warehouse and is a historic building. Any conversion of the building would have to retain its exterior and remain faithful to the historical nature of the interior.

The Mayor is asking students to submit economically viable proposals on what facilities the new Centre should provide, to make the best use of the building whilst retaining its historic character.

International Student Centre?

Students find it hard to make friends

A recent survey among students revealed that many feel that they have a narrow circle of friends and that their social life would be much better if they could widen this circle. Many students say that their only friends are their class-mates. They find it hard to make contact with students from other faculties and other year groups and institutions.

A new Student Centre, which would enable students from different colleges and institutions to meet socially, could help to bridge that gap.

B Write your proposal (300–350 words). Use section headings.

"Trust me, he'll come running home when he hears the can opener"

14

All in a day's work

Work and business   VOCABULARY AND LISTENING

A **1** 🔊 **You'll hear a doctor, a butler/house-manager, and a photographer describing their jobs. MAKE NOTES on which aspects of their work each one enjoys most and which aspects they don't enjoy.**

2 👥 **Discuss these questions:**

- What are the pros and cons of each person's job?
- Which of the jobs would you prefer to have? Give your reasons.
- What would be the ideal job for you – and why?

B **Choose the best word or phrase to fill each gap in each text. Look at the example first:**

In Part I of the Reading Paper you'll have to do three vocabulary exercises similar to these. Some of the questions in the exam will be harder than these.

A large company is owned by its ___⁰___, who may be individual ___¹___ or major financial ___²___, but it is controlled by a board of ___³___. Many ___⁴___ corporations are divided into different divisions. For example Vivendi, a French-based corporation, has ___⁵___ all over the world, including Universal Studios and Connex, who run trains. But the ___⁶___ of the company is in France.

0	**A** staff	**B** shareholders ✓	**C** managers	**D** customers
1	**A** unions	**B** clients	**C** banks	**D** investors
2	**A** societies	**B** institutes	**C** institutions	**D** guilds
3	**A** bosses	**B** managers	**C** presidents	**D** directors
4	**A** multi-national	**B** nationalised	**C** local	**D** cosmopolitan
5	**A** branches	**B** departments	**C** subsidiaries	**D** offices
6	**A** directors	**B** headquarters	**C** bosses	**D** factories

When designer Jane Rodgers was ___⁷___ up by the boss of an internet start-up company serving the film industry, she thought she knew what she was in for. "I researched the guy and his ___⁸___ businesses, bought a new suit and lied to my boss about having to leave early for a doctor's appointment on Tuesday evening." Rodgers met her ___⁹___ new employer not in his office but in a bar in Hoxton, an up-and-coming area of East London. "Imagine my surprise when, after five minutes of chitchat, first date questions really, he leaned towards me, stared earnestly into my eyes and told me: 'Jane, I think you're the one.' I felt like it was me as a person that was being ___¹⁰___." He had neither seen her CV nor told her what the job ___¹¹___, but he was determined to ___¹²___ her. She declined the offer.

7	**A** e-mailed	**B** called	**C** telephoned	**D** contacted
8	**A** previous	**B** further	**C** past	**D** prior
9	**A** future	**B** probable	**C** prospective	**D** likely
10	**A** seen	**B** scrutinised	**C** addressed	**D** interviewed
11	**A** earned	**B** consisted	**C** included	**D** involved
12	**A** rent	**B** interview	**C** fire	**D** hire

The selection and   ¹³ staff is the responsibility of the human   ¹⁴ department.
They carry out interviews after looking at the suitability of all the applicants, looking at their   ¹⁵ and making a short list of candidates to interview. This department is also responsible for the   ¹⁶ and welfare of staff. If the company is in financial   ¹⁷ and has to cut back on its staff and make people   ¹⁸ , they are also responsible for dealing with this.

13 A finding	**B** recruitment	**C** advertising	**D** choice
14 A personnel	**B** awareness	**C** personal	**D** resources
15 A photographs	**B** portfolios	**C** CVs	**D** referees
16 A instruction	**B** training	**C** education	**D** induction
17 A difficulties	**B** hardships	**C** dilemmas	**D** embarrassments
18 A idle	**B** jobless	**C** redundant	**D** unemployed

14.2 Collocations: verb phrases   VOCABULARY DEVELOPMENT

A **1** **Which of the following things _break_? And which can _change_?**

waves   traffic lights   a boy's voice   a storm   the weather   your mood   day

2 **Which of the following things can you _break_? And which can you _change_? (Some can be used with either verb, with different meanings.)**

a promise   a world record   an appointment   a tablecloth   crockery   direction
gear   money   someone's heart   the bed or the sheets   a habit   the ice   the law
the news to someone   the silence   the subject   trains   your arm   your clothes
your leg   your mind   your shoes

And in what circumstances might you break or change each of them?

B **Which of the following things can you _follow_? And which can you _lose_? (Some can be used with either verb, with different meanings.)**

an argument   a line of argument   a route or directions   a story   trade or profession
advice or instructions   someone's example or their lead   an idea   control over something
face   heart   a football team   a football match   interest in something
the fashion or a trend   the thread of a story   track of something   weight   your job
your nerve   your temper   your voice if you have a cold   your way or bearings

And in what circumstances might you follow or lose each of them?

C **Fill the gaps in these sentences with suitable words from the list below, changing the form of the verb as necessary.**

This section deals with only a small portion of a vast topic. The only way to learn collocations of this kind is by reading and listening carefully – and by referring to a dictionary to check up when necessary.

1 Can I .... you a favour? I'd like you to .... me a hand with .... this heavy package.
2 If you want to .... a bank account, they may ask you to .... references.
3 I'd like to .... the order which I .... last week – I've .... my mind about wanting it.
4 Always .... careful attention to what the interviewer says. You should answer clearly but there's no need to .... your voice above the normal level. Don't reply too quickly: give yourself time to .... your thoughts.
5 When he .... me the chocolates, I couldn't .... the temptation to .... them even though I was trying to .... weight.
6 Although she .... a very busy life, ... her own business, she tries to .... a balance between the demands of her work and her private life.
7 She tried to .... light on the situation by .... our attention to the fact that we would have to .... the costs of the scheme.
8 No one .... any objection when we .... the decision to .... the next meeting on Sunday.

accept   ask   bear   cancel   change   collect   draw   hold   lead   lend   lift   lose
offer   open   pay   place   raise   raise   reach   resist   run   strike   supply   throw

14.3 A good ending

A 👥 Which of these students' endings to a job application letter are most effective? Which encourage the reader to look favourably on the application?

1

```
In order to improve my English skills
I would like to work for about two
years in England and I think the
position as a junior commercial
banker would fit with my imagination.
I am ready for further discussions.
Give me a ring or write to me.
```

3

```
I have a good knowledge of English and
German, and I am learning Spanish.
   I enclose my curriculum vitae and will
be available for interview any day after
September 1. My present position is subject
to one month's notice.
   I look forward to your reply.
```

2

```
Besides my mother tongue, German, I can
also speak English and Japanese fairly well.
   If you feel that my qualifications meet
with your requirements, I shall be pleased
to come for an interview.
   Please find enclosed a curriculum vitae,
educational reports and certificates of
training.
```

4

```
I can type and take shorthand, I
enjoy contact with people and I am
a willing and responsible person.
   I am very interested in the job
you are offering and reckon myself
to be the right person for it.
   I look forward to hearing from
you,
```

B 👥 Look at the final paragraphs of the passages in 9.3, 9.7, 10.7, 12.3, 12.4B, 12.8 and 14.5, taking account of the very last sentence in particular. Discuss these questions:

- Which one has the least effective ending? Which one has the most effective ending? Why?
- Do short sentences seem more effective than long, complex ones? Why (not)?
- Why is a good ending important?

C ✐ Now look at the final paragraphs of your own recent compositions:

- Which of them are you most pleased with? Why?
- Which of them could be improved? Rewrite the last sentences of these.

14.4 Word order: phrasal verbs

A Study the notes and examples and fill the gaps in the sentences below. Highlight any phrasal verbs that you're unfamiliar with and look them up.

1 Some phrasal verbs are **intransitive** (they don't take an object):

When we challenged him to justify his point of view he backed down.
He wasn't being serious, but I didn't catch on until he started smiling.

But not: I didn't catch immediately on. ✗

check up	*climb down*	*cool off*	*close in*	*die out*	*fall apart*
fall behind	*pass away*	*pay up*	*ring off*	*settle down*	*settle up*
shop around	*speak up*	*stand out*	*stay on*	*stop over*	*wear off*

a If you want to save money you should .... before making a purchase.
b After a few moments' silence, one of them .... and asked a question.
c The effects of the wine .... by the next morning.

2 With most **transitive** phrasal verbs (i.e. verbs that take an object), the object can come in various positions, but not if the object is a pronoun:

They've brought the meeting forward.   They've called the meeting off.
They've brought forward the meeting.   They've called off the meeting.
They've brought it forward. They've called it off.
The meeting's been brought forward.   The meeting's been called off.
But not: They've brought forward it. ✗   They've called off it. ✗

> carry out   cut back   dream up   drive out   explain away   follow up
> hand in   leave behind   pay back   rip off   send up   sort out   think up
> tone down   trade in   try out   use up   win over   write out

a Thanks for lending me the money, I promise I'll .... on Friday.
b Everyone was .... by the force of her arguments.
c The little boy was very upset because his mother ....

3 With some transitive phrasal verbs the **object** must come immediately **after** the verb:
They tried to catch me out by asking me a trick question.
They tried to catch the interviewees out by asking them trick questions.
But not: They tried to catch out me. ✗

> call back   count in   cut off   give up   invite out   order about   see out   show around
> start off   tear up

a When they left I went downstairs with them and ....
b Pam is a new student, could one of you .... , please?
c I wanted to .... on Friday night, but she said she was washing her hair.

4 Some phrasal verbs can be followed by a <u>preposition</u>:
I was trying to catch up <u>on</u> the work I'd missed.
  (**but**   I've missed a lot of work and I'm trying to catch up.)
He disliked having to clean up <u>after</u> his guests.
  (but   He disliked having to clean up.   He disliked having to clean everything up.)

> tidy up <u>after</u>   check up <u>on</u>   crack down <u>on</u>   creep up <u>on</u>
> miss out <u>on</u>   play along <u>with</u>   wait up <u>for</u>

a I wasn't invited to the party and I was afraid I might be .... the fun.
b I'm just interested in how you're getting on – I'm not ....

5 Some phrasal verbs **MUST** be used with a <u>preposition</u>:
You shouldn't talk down <u>to</u> children.
He finds it hard to live up <u>to</u> his mother's expectations.

> come up <u>against</u>   face up <u>to</u>   grow out <u>of</u>   lead up <u>to</u>   stick up <u>for</u>

a When they set up their new business they .... a lot of problems.
b She was being unusually polite to me and I wondered what it was all ....

The object of a **verb + preposition** (see 12.4) **MUST** come after the preposition:
We were counting on him to help us.   We were counting on Bill to help us.
  But not: We were counting him on. ✗   We were counting Bill on. ✗
I talked her out of giving up.   I talked Jo out of giving up.   She was talked out of giving up.
  But not: I talked her giving up out of. ✗   She was talked giving up out of. ✗

B Fill each of the blanks with a suitable phrasal verb from 1 to 5 above.

1 If you've got a parking ticket you can't just .... – you'll have to ....
2 It was clearly my fault but I was able to .... an excuse to ....
3 He was threatening to .... his notice, but I managed to .... and persuade him to ....
4 I'm relying on you to .... if there's any trouble.
5 Let's hope you aren't .... by this question!
6 If you already have a car, you can .... when you buy a new one.
7 I'm going to be back very late tonight – don't ....
8 He eventually .... after we'd presented all the arguments.
9 Customs officers have been .... people who are over the duty free limit.
10 She used to be a very sulky little girl, but she .... eventually.

14.5 **Learning to be happy**

A   Read the first paragraph of this article: what are YOUR answers to the questions?

Learning to be happy

WHY DO some people exude humour and good cheer while others seem to treat every day like a funeral? What makes the elderly more contented with their lot than the young? And why isn't winning the National Lottery necessarily a good thing?

As another grey Monday morning dawns, these are some of the questions that make Michael Argyle, Emeritus Professor of Psychology at Oxford Brookes University, go into work with a spring in his step.

While his colleagues work themselves into a frenzy measuring the effects of Prozac on depressed lab rats, Professor Argyle, who is a youthful 71, is turning his mind to a far more rewarding area of study: happiness.

B   Read the rest of the article and then answer the questions that follow:

1. Who has it and who doesn't? And how do those of us with less of it get more? It is a riddle that has exercised philosophers ever since Aristotle first identified happiness as the end of all human activity. Wealth and health are thought to be a means to it, but the thing itself always seems to be just beyond our grasp.

2. After a decade studying happiness or "subjective well-being", to give it its proper psychological term, Argyle concludes that the best guarantee of long-term happiness is something called "serious leisure" – a hobby or activity that involves your whole being.

3. It could be bridge or it could be bungee jumping. Or it could be an activity as innocuous as reading or housework.

4. It could even be Scottish country dancing – a passion the professor admits to indulging twice a week.

5. "It's extremely invigorating and a great source of euphoria," says Argyle. "It's also a highly social activity, which is a very important component of happiness. The music is cheerful. The point is it doesn't really matter what you do as long as you find the activity challenging and absorbing."

6. Other experts, like Mihaly Csikszentmihaly, Professor of Psychology at the University of Chicago, concur. He has a similar theory called "flow". This is what a chess player senses at the most intense point in a game or skiers feel when they hit a particular groove on a black run, a feeling they describe as being "at one with the slope".

7. "Flow is produced by the balance between the demands of what you are doing and the skill which you have to do it," explains Argyle. "It's a state of loss of self-awareness, brought about by facing challenges with necessary skills."

8. Because most people are by nature lazy and undisciplined, the majority find it easier to achieve flow when they are forced to rise to challenges imposed on them from outside, hence the importance of work as a source of happiness.

9. But work can also be a huge source of stress and there seems to be less time than ever for the simple pleasures of life.

10. This is where Professor Argyle's theories come in. Flow, he argues, is all very well for the adrenalin-driven commodities traders of this world, but those of us who don't have a high-powered job in the City – or any job for that matter – may have to look elsewhere for contentment.

11. "There really is a problem here," he writes in his latest book, *The Social Psychology of Leisure*, "in that free time has greatly increased but those who have the greatest increase have not been able to convert it into satisfying forms of leisure."

12. The best example is TV. Recent studies have shown that Britain is in danger of becoming a nation of couch potatoes and Argyle agrees that because of its essential passivity TV is one of the activities least likely to produce flow. "The bad thing about TV is it means you are not doing something else, like talking to your friends."

13. On the other hand, Argyle points out that TV is often the focus for family gatherings and that soap operas can provide a sort of "fantasy social life".

14. So what sort of "serious leisure" activities should we be considering if we want a slice of Nirvana?

15. One answer is to ask the subject to write down what they do at each hour of the day, and how it makes them feel. This technique, known as "pleasant activities therapy", was invented by Peter Lewinsohn. The data is fed into a computer which comes up with the activities that tend to produce the greatest happiness for the greatest number.

16. Professor Argyle's own study of leisure groups put dancing at the top of the contentment charts, which

you may or may not see as a happy coincidence given the professor's own passion for hopping about in a kilt ("it's a bit of an in-joke in the department, actually," says Argyle, grinning).

Next comes church, not so much for its religious aspects, although these are important (belief in the afterlife and all that), as mingling with other worshippers.

"Church is a great source of comfort and companionship, particularly for the elderly and isolated," says Argyle, who happens to be a devout Anglican and an active member of the university congregation.

Next is any other activity that involves contact with people – such as volunteer work, or simply sitting around and relaxing with family and friends – followed by reading, making or fixing things and team sports. Cooking, housework and shopping are all ranked above watching TV.

But isn't all this ranking of different leisure activities beside the point? After all, there are plenty of compulsive-depressive types (bond dealers come to mind) who work all hours, go skiing every weekend and still end up committing suicide at 35.

For a moment Argyle looks as if he might frown.

"Just as there are happy people, there are unhappy people," he says, answering one of the questions posed at the outset of this article. The difference is that unhappy people look at themselves when things go wrong, but happy people only look at themselves when things go right. "The Americans call it the Pollyanna effect – always looking on the bright side."

Argyle can even demonstrate this phenomenon using something he calls the Oxford Happiness Inventory. This was compiled by inverting items from something called the Beck Depression Inventory. There are 29 multiple-choice questions like: "Do you laugh never/sometimes/a lot/all the time?" and: "Are you optimistic about the state of the world?"

Whatever personality type you are, however, he argues that a happy marriage can more than make up for it. Indeed, Argyle, who has been married 46 years and has four children and eight grandchildren, argues that a loving relationship is by far the greatest single source of contentment (conversely, an unhappy marriage is one of the greatest sources of distress).

So what about the answers to some of those questions posed at the outset: why are the old more content than the young and why isn't winning the National Lottery necessarily a good thing?

The answer to the first is the flipside of flow: what Professor Argyle calls "a cognitive appraisal of the goal-achievement gap".

"When you're young the gap between your goals and your ability to achieve them tends to be wider hence anxiety. But when you're older you've achieved more and don't aspire to as much."

Okay, but surely winning the Lottery can't make you any more anxious?

"Actually, lots of people's lives seem to be wrecked by it," says Argyle, deadly serious "They give up their work, so they lose their job aspirations. Then they move house and their new neighbours ignore them. Finally, they row with their family."

Argyle is getting gloomier by the minute.

"Look," he says. "If wealth were the source of happiness you would expect that as societies got richer the sum of happiness would increase. In fact that's not the case at all. Unfortunately, the only thing that seems to matter to some people is being better off than the next person."

Mark Honigsbaum

Choose the best alternative to fill each gap.

1 According to Prof Argyle 'serious leisure' is something you ....
are passionate about   spend all your spare time doing   take up when you're older

2 In principle, Prof Csikszentmihaly and Prof Argyle ....
see eye to eye   see things differently   have nothing in common

3 Prof Csikszentmihaly believes that work brings happiness to ....
few people   most people   some people

4 Prof Argyle says many people can't find happiness at work because they don't have ....
enough free time   demanding jobs   enough time to enjoy their work

5 People can be helped to find happiness by ....
being told jokes   reflecting on how they spend their time   observing others having fun

6 Prof Argyle believes that ....
everyone can be happy   happiness can be learnt   not everyone can be happy

7 Older people tend to be happier than younger people because they ....
are less worried about being successful   have learnt that it's no use worrying about failure

8 Lottery winners often ....
spend all their money very quickly   become very unhappy   give their money away

C Find each of the phrases below in the article and highlight them. Then decide which of the meanings on the right is correct in the context:

¶1	exercised	*kept fit · kept busy*
¶1	end	*finish · goal*
¶2	concludes	*judges · finishes*
¶3	innocuous	*dull · innocent*
¶5	euphoria	*exhilaration · excitement*
¶10	adrenalin-driven	*motivated by excitement · motivated by fear*
¶12	couch potatoes	*people who watch too much TV · people who eat too much*
¶17	mingling	*combining · socialising*
¶18	devout	*believing · benevolent*
¶23	inverting	*reversing · devising*
¶26	flipside	*opposite · less good side*

D Discuss your reactions to the article. Which of Prof Argyle's views do you agree with most strongly – and which points do you disagree with?

14.6 **Beat the clock**

READING

A Five paragraphs have been removed from this article. Choose the most suitable paragraph from the list A–E for each gap (1–5) in the article.

Beat the clock

When designer Jane Rodgers was called up by the boss of an internet start-up company serving the film industry, she thought she knew what she was in for. "I researched the guy and his previous businesses, bought a new suit and lied to my boss about having to leave early for a doctor's appointment on Tuesday evening." Rodgers met her prospective new employer not in his office but in a bar in Hoxton, an up-and-coming area of East London. "Imagine my surprise when, after five minutes of chitchat, first date questions really, he leaned towards me, stared earnestly into my eyes and told me: 'Jane, I think you're the one.' I felt like it was me as a person that was being scrutinised." He had neither seen her CV nor told her what the job involved, but he was determined to hire her. She declined the offer.

1

"Personality is becoming increasingly important" observes Andrew Swift of recruitment consultants Price Jamieson. "There's a chronic staff skills shortage in areas such as new media, so companies are looking at who will fit in with their culture, rather than who has experience. Technology is changing so fast anyway that there's no point recruiting people who have today's skills. What we need are people with creative, dynamic personalities who are not afraid to push forward into the unknown. "Traditional interview rules are all well and good, but when people need staff in a hurry, they learn the benefits of intuition."

2

London-based psychologist Ros Taylor has just interviewed the chief executives of 80 blue-chip companies about the human side of running a successful business. "Really, to make a good impression, you don't even get time to open your mouth," she says, pointing out that often employers will be observing a candidate from the moment they park their car outside the office. "An interviewer's response to you will generally be pre-verbal – how you walk through the door, what your posture is like, whether you smile, whether you have a captivating aura, whether you have a firm, confident handshake. You've got about half a minute to make an impact and after that all you are doing is building on a good or bad first impression." Thirty seconds is hardly enough time to think consciously, Taylor adds: "It's a very emotional response."

3

Ben Williams, an occupational psychologist involved in interview training, doesn't agree that a candidate has the luxury of 30 seconds. "I'd argue that it's more like a third of a second, which is basic human reaction time. In that time, like animals, we make a judgement based on whether there is a perceived threat, in which case our instinct is to run, or a favourable response, when we feel it's safe to approach. Everything that happens after only backs that up."

4

Psychologists call this tendency to fixate on character traits and overlook context the Fundamental Attribution Error – that the way a person will behave in an interview situation reflects the way that person will always behave. In other words, we don't need to know someone in order to believe that we do know them.

5

Perhaps the job interview itself has become an outmoded concept. There's a joke doing the rounds of personnel departments at the moment. A human resources officer gets a call from Satan: would she like to work in Hell? She pops down for a meeting and likes what she sees – wild partying and champagne flowing. "OK, when do I start?" On Monday morning when she reports for work, Hell is a very different place. There's no party, everyone is depressed. "What's happened to this place?" she asks. Satan laughs. "Oh that – that was just the job interview. You're an employee now."

Anita Chaudhury

A

Experts like Williams are often called in by employers to bring a more objective approach to recruitment; intuition is not a skill he seeks to encourage in his clients. "Things like psychometric testing are designed to limit the effect of first impressions. We also train interviewers to be a case of the 'halo effect' – when you instantly like someone and everything they subsequently reveal becomes a self-fulfilling prophecy because you only want to believe the good stuff."

B

The New Yorker recently looked into this issue. Malcolm Gladwell observed that job interviews are increasingly becoming encounters in which charisma and gut reaction are vital. "Hiring someone is essentially a romantic process. We are looking for someone with whom we have a certain chemistry, we want the unlimited promise of a love affair." The structured interview, by contrast, seems to offer only the dry logic and practicality of an arranged marriage.

C

In fact, Rodgers' experience is not as unusual as it sounds. As the skills shortage in the new economy spirals out of control, your CV is likely to be the last thing on a prospective employer's mind. Last weekend, a study presented to the American Psychological Society in Miami revealed that most interviewers decide within a minute whether someone is suitable for the job. But this is by no means an American trend. Stressed-out British executives, faced with the longest working hours in Europe, are waking up to the wisdom of employing people who may not be qualified for the job but at least will be fun to work with when the team has to pull off an all-nighter.

D

Addie Churchill, who runs a PR company with clients including Carlton TV and Disney, admits she always goes on gut feeling. "It sounds like a dangerous thing to rely on but I have learned the hard way that if you get a strong vibe about someone, 99% of the time it's accurate. I recently hired an account executive within moments of him walking through the door. I knew he was the right person because we just clicked, but I also knew he didn't have the right experience, that it would take three months to knock him into shape. It was the right decision. It happens the other way round, of course – you instantly know someone is wrong for the job but have to go through the interview process anyway. Using gut feeling isn't risky, but you need to know how to use it."

E

So is the job interview dead? Not quite. But research from the University of Toledo in America reveals that only the first 15 seconds really matter. Researchers interviewed 98 volunteers of various ages and backgrounds for 20 minutes; each interviewer then filled out a six-page evaluation of the candidate. Originally the study was to establish whether applicants who had been coached in body language would get better ratings than those who hadn't (they didn't) – but then another student decided to use the interview videos to test out the idea that "the handshake is everything". She took 15 seconds of footage, showing applicants as they knocked on the door, came in, shook the hand of the interviewer and sat down. Then she got a series of strangers to rate the applicants based on that clip, using the same criteria as were used in the longer interviews. Even with such a short tape, their ratings were very similar.

B **1** **Highlight** the most important point made in each paragraph of the article.

2 Then join a partner and compare what you've both highlighted. What kind of training would you give to people who are going to attend interviews?

14.7 Looking for a job?

LISTENING AND COMPOSITION

A You'll hear part of a seminar for job-seekers. Listen to the recording and tick only the advice and information that the speakers actually give.

This is similar to Part 4 of the Listening Paper – except that in the exam there are only 6 opinions to choose between.

In each box write:

	Anne	for a view expressed only by Anne
or	**Kerry**	for a view expressed only by Kerry
or	**Both**	for a view expressed both by Anne and Kerry
or	**Neither**	for a view expressed by neither of them

■ THE APPLICATION FORM ....

1	Photocopy it and practise filling in the copy first.		1
2	Write your final version neatly and clearly.		2
3	Use a separate sheet for any extra information you want to give.		3
4	Personnel officers read application forms very carefully.		4
5	Use words that show you want to be successful.		5
6	Mention any unusual hobbies or jobs.		6

■ THE INTERVIEW ....

7	Be confident.		7
8	Avoid answering questions about your leisure interests.		8
9	Do some research into the company's competitors.		9
10	Ask the interviewer to explain what his or her company does.		10
11	Expect to be surprised.		11
12	You may have to have lunch with the interviewer.		12
13	The interviewer may insult you.		13
14	Remain calm whatever happens.		14
15	Arrange to participate in some mock interviews beforehand.		15
16	Tell the interviewer that you are sensitive and clever.		16

■ 'CREATIVE JOB SEARCHING' ....

17	This technique is better than applying in the conventional way.		17
18	Get in touch with employees in companies in your chosen field.		18
19	You will get a job if you are persistent enough.		19
20	If you're personally known to a company you stand a better chance.		20

B 🏃🏃🏃🏃 Discuss these questions:

- Which of the advice do you disagree with? What other advice would you give to job-seekers?
- If you were looking for an employee, what qualities would you be looking for?
- What do you find most difficult about EXAM interviews? What aspects of your performance would you most like to improve?

C ✍ **Write a letter of application.** Find an advertisement for a job you find attractive, or which is suitable for someone with your talents, experience and qualifications.

Describe yourself and explain why you are the ideal person for the job (300–350 words).

"Thanks, and I assure you you've picked the right man for the job, Dad."

A

Read this text and think of the word that fits best in each space. Use only one word.

This exercise is similar to Part 1 of the Use of English Paper. In the exam, you should write your answers in CAPITAL LETTERS on the Answer Sheet.

Grounds for optimism

Brazil's coffee growers had a problem in the 1930s – record harvests had caused the coffee price to plummet. Growers were ⎽⎽⎽⎽ [1] to burn or dump millions of tons of coffee beans into the sea.

The Brazilian Coffee Institute ⎽⎽⎽⎽ [2] Nestlé, the Swiss food company, to see if it could come up with new ⎽⎽⎽⎽ [3] based on coffee. Nestlé had already made a ⎽⎽⎽⎽ [4] for itself by producing powdered milk and chocolate, and preserving other perishable foodstuffs.

Nestlé's scientists, after several years of ⎽⎽⎽⎽ [5], found that they were able to retain the aroma and taste of coffee in a soluble form by adding hydrocarbons. The result went on ⎽⎽⎽⎽ [6] in 1938 as Nescafé.

UK production began the following year at Nestlé's factory in west London. But the war intervened, slowing ⎽⎽⎽⎽ [7] of Nescafé and other Nestlé products. The group's ⎽⎽⎽⎽ [8] crashed from $20m in 1938 to $6m in 1939, and it moved part of its operations from isolated Switzerland to the USA.

But help was at ⎽⎽⎽⎽ [9]. US troops pouring across Europe and Asia found Nescafé in their ration packs. Liberated populations, many of whom had been drinking ersatz coffee made from acorns and had little ⎽⎽⎽⎽ [10] of real coffee imports for some time to come, quickly ⎽⎽⎽⎽ [11] a taste for the instant coffee carried by their liberators.

In one year the whole ⎽⎽⎽⎽ [12] of the Nescafé's US plant went to the armed forces.

Continued research at Nestlé led to a new ⎽⎽⎽⎽ [13] producing a soluble residue which was 100% coffee. This was ⎽⎽⎽⎽ [14] under the Nescafé name in 1952, just in time to ⎽⎽⎽⎽ [15] from the boom in coffee drinking as young people flocked to coffee bars to listen to the new rock and roll music.

B

Read the second part of the article. Use the word given in CAPITALS at the end of some of the lines to form a word that fits in the space in the same line.

This exercise is similar to Part 2 of the Use of English Paper, but in the exam there are only 10 spaces to fill. In the exam, you should write your answers in CAPITAL LETTERS on the Answer Sheet.

Further research by Nestlé's ⎽⎽⎽⎽ [16] to capture more fully the taste of home-made coffee resulted in the ⎽⎽⎽⎽ [17] of the freeze-drying process in 1966 and the launch of Nescafé Gold Blend.   **SCIENCE** **INVENT**

In simple terms, Nescafé is made by selecting the right mix of beans, extracting liquid coffee in much the same way as the conventional coffee machine, and then freeze-drying the results. The ⎽⎽⎽⎽ [18] skills lie in the roasting, extracting and dehydrating processes employed.   **TECHNOLOGY**

There are two basic coffee plants: arabica, a highly ⎽⎽⎽⎽ [19] variety grown in central and south America and the east coast of Africa at altitudes between 600 and 2,000 metres, and robusta, a more pungent, stronger-tasting coffee grown below 600 metres in parts of Africa and Asia. Arabica accounts for two-thirds of world coffee ⎽⎽⎽⎽ [20], robusta for the rest.   **AROMA** **PRODUCE**

Nestlé estimates that on average 3,000 cups of Nescafé are drunk every second, with an overall ⎽⎽⎽⎽ [21] of no fewer than 100bn cups per year. More than 40m cups of Nescafé are drunk every day in Britain.   **CONSUME**

In 1974 the Nestlé board, concerned about the company's ⎽⎽⎽⎽ [22] upon ⎽⎽⎽⎽ [23] commodity prices and sources of supply in politically and economically unstable regions, decided to ⎽⎽⎽⎽ [24] outside its core food business. The company bought a large stake in the French cosmetics group L'Oréal.   **DEPEND** **CERTAIN** **DIVERSE**

In the next three years the price of coffee quadrupled and the price of cocoa tripled. Nevertheless, Nescafé continued to be a big ⎽⎽⎽⎽ [25], and a greater variety of coffee drinks was brought out under its brand name. These included Blend 37, with a more ⎽⎽⎽⎽ [26] coffee taste, an after-dinner coffee using just arabica beans, ⎽⎽⎽⎽ [27] Nescafé and an instant cappuccino.   **SELL** **CONTINENT** **CAFFEINE**

In the 1960s Nescafé started to replace its tins with glass jars. More ⎽⎽⎽⎽ [28] was its 1980s–90s Gold Blend TV campaign, a mini soap opera about the developing ⎽⎽⎽⎽ [29] between a young couple. It grabbed the nation's attention, perhaps more for its story line than the ⎽⎽⎽⎽ [30].   **STRIKE** **RELATION** **PRODUCE**

15 Is it art or entertainment?

15.1 The tingle factor

READING

A Read this article and then answer the questions that follow:

The tingle factor

Music makes us emotional – but how?
Psychiatrist Raj Persaud finds out

We've all felt something like it – a lump in the throat at a romantic song, a tingle up the spine from a Beethoven quartet or a rush of energy at a club. Music, perhaps more than any other art form, has a direct line to the emotions. The question is, how? Serge Dorny, artistic director of the London Philharmonic Orchestra, has taken a psychological approach in programming the orchestra's forthcoming festival, Regeneration, using music to interpret the anticipated emotional upheaval of the new century. He has juxtaposed Bernd-Alois Zimmerman's dark piece Photoptosis, for instance, which explores anxiety and desperation (the composer eventually killed himself) with Scriabin's heady, excitable Poem of Ecstasy and Beethoven's life-affirming, optimistic violin concerto.   1

There can be little doubt that music has a profound impact on mood. A recent startling study from America found a strong association between suicide rates and the amount of air time devoted to country and western music on local radio. Were the mournful themes of country music causing listeners to feel low, or did they choose the music because it reflected their negative mood?   2

One popular theory is that music provokes our emotions because of the context in which we normally hear it – so a funeral march, for instance, produces sadness because we hear it at depressing times. But researchers into the psychology of music can predict what sequences of notes reliably provoke the same emotional reactions in different people. For example, it has been found that sadness and even tears tend to be produced by repetitive phrases which lead to predictable sequences, but which then vary leading to anticipated resolutions. Shivers and goose pimples tend to be a result of unexpected harmonies. It seems that expectancy and violation of expectancy play a major part in emotional reactions to music, and rhythm seems key.   3

Conventionally, fast tunes have energetic connotations, and slow tunes more leisurely ones. Since when events occur rapidly more energy is consumed than when they take place slowly, it seems that there is something intrinsically energetic and positive about fast music. Slow music therefore could be associated with low energy, and perhaps sadness. This could explain the consensus about the emotional content of pieces of music, even when these pieces are unknown to different listeners. As musicologist and psychiatrist Dr Anthony Storr puts it: "No one calls Rossini's overture to The Barber of Seville tragic; no one thinks of Beethoven's Fifth Symphony as merely pretty."   4

Music also intensifies emotions already present – think of a chanting football crowd, or the rabble-rousing sounds of a military band. Storr points out that because music brings about similar emotional responses in different people at the same time, it is relied on to create a sense of unity – which also highlights the political use of music to unite and so perhaps control a crowd.   5

Storr argues that this power derives from the way music structures time, imposing order and ensuring that the emotions aroused by a particular event peak at the same moment. In fact the rhythmical nature of music may hold the secret to its emotional impact, since rhythm is so rooted in our bodies in the form of breathing, heart beat, walking, even sex.   6

It is possible, too, that our choice of music could reveal the emotional states we prefer, and so provide clues to personality. Dr William McCown and colleagues at the department of psychology at Northeast Louisiana University, noting the spread of bass-enhancing technology in personal audio equipment, found that the preference for exaggerated bass in music was associated with impulsiveness and a preference for unusual experiences.   7

They argue that since, in what they term "primitive" cultures, the bass is associated with warfare and uninhibited actions, exaggerated bass may actually encourage wild behaviour – which could explain why such music is frequently heard in clubs. Something to think about, perhaps, next time you strut your stuff at Home or Fabric.   8

1 Music is more likely to evoke .... than other art forms.
   A uncomfortable feelings   C an emotional response
   B strong memories   D a violent reaction
2 People who listen to country and western music on the radio ....
   A enjoy feeling sad   C choose it because they feel sad
   B are driven to feel suicidal D are more likely to kill themselves than others
3 An emotional response to music is triggered when ....
   A you are feeling tired   C you are feeling vulnerable
   B what you expect doesn't happen D you are shocked by it
4 It is .... certain pieces of music evoke the same response in everyone.
   A untrue that   C agreed that
   B doubtful whether   D quite certain that
5 Some music can lead groups of people to ....
   A disagree with each other intensely C start marching
   B feel the same way as each other   D join together and start singing
6 People who like deep notes tend to be more ....
   A active   C likely to make quick decisions
   B emotional   D indecisive

B 🚶🚶🚶🚶 **Discuss these questions:**

- What kinds of music send a tingle up your spine? Can you think of specific examples of favourite songs or pieces of music?
- What kinds of music leave you cold? What kinds of music do you dislike – and why?
- Do you choose music to suit your mood? Do you like a heavy bass rhythm?

15.2 'You're being paid to be a child!'

LISTENING

In Part 3 of the Listening Paper you'll have to answer multiple-choice questions like these. In the exam, there are only five questions to answer.

Simon Russell Beale has performed at the Royal National Theatre and with the Royal Shakespeare Company, most recently in the part of Iago in Shakespeare's *Othello*. Listen to the interview and choose the alternative which fits best according to what he says.

1 On the world tour, the audiences' response to *Othello* was ...
   A friendly   B unpredictable   C slow   D enthusiastic   ☐ 1
2 Shakespeare's plays are different from modern plays because the actor and audience are subconsciously aware of a continuous ...
   A relevance to today   B stream of imagery   C beat   D series of emotions   ☐ 2
3 Performing Shakespeare in modern dress can be effective as long as ...
   A guns aren't used instead of swords   B it doesn't distract from the language
   C there are no anachronisms   D the actors really make the play believable   ☐ 3
4 The actors Simon has worked with are very ...
   A creative   B cheerful   C funny   D intelligent   ☐ 4
5 Simon finds acting in front of a camera difficult because he ...
   A doesn't have the right kind of energy   B is mainly a stage actor
   C finds it hard to suddenly begin performing   D doesn't enjoy filming   ☐ 5
6 The pace of a screen performance is controlled by the director and the ...
   A scriptwriter   B actors   C editor   D camera operator   ☐ 6
7 For Simon, one of the pleasures of his job is that he enjoys ...
   A playing   B showing off   C standing on stage   D being famous ☐ 7
8 What advice would Simon give a would-be actor?
   A Be careful!   B Don't do it!   C Have a go!   D Wait until you're older! ☐ 8

15.3 Prepositions – 2

A Fill the gaps in these sentences with a suitable preposition from the list. Some are used more than once.

after at before below beside besides by during for from in into
in front of next to on on top of opposite over to under with

1 There's a free seat .... me here – sit .... me and keep me company.
2 The temperature .... the South Pole .... winter is usually .... 50 degrees .... zero.
3 The *Mona Lisa,* which is .... the Louvre .... Paris, was painted well .... 400 years ago.
4 Would you prefer to go .... car, ... the bus or .... foot?
5 The Odeon is directly .... the bus station, a few metres .... the square. If you're approaching it .... the west, turn .... the left when you see the university .... your right.
6 'Try to arrive .... time .... future,' he said to me .... a whisper.
7 I couldn't see very well because someone .... a big hat was sitting .... me .... the cinema. And I couldn't hear the soundtrack because some people were talking .... loud voices .... the film.
8 .... painting lovely pictures she's very good .... sculpture.
9 G comes .... F .... the alphabet, and .... H.
10 She was working .... the painting .... five weeks .... the spring.
11 Instead of keeping his money .... the bank he hides it .... the carpet. He keeps his small change .... a biscuit tin .... the wardrobe.
12 When they walked .... the room hand .... hand, they saw her sitting .... an armchair .... the window .... a big smile .... her face.

B Fill each of the gaps in this text with a suitable preposition or prepositional phrase:

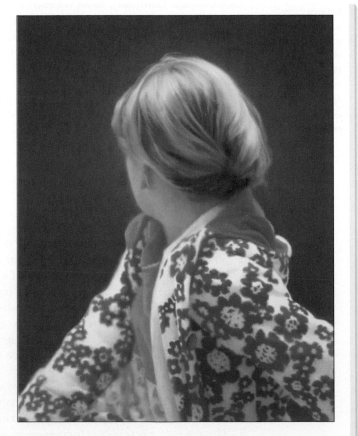

The artist's daughter Betty is painted ¹ photographic detail. She sits very near ² the surface ³ the picture, as ⁴ a close-up camera shot. The painting could not really be called a portrait ⁵ Betty, however, as it teaches us very little ⁶ her. Richter has chosen to paint his daughter as she turns away; her face is invisible. Instead he has concentrated ⁷ the red, white and pink patterns ⁸ her jacket and dress, and her hair gathered ⁹ the back ¹⁰ her head. Richter has undermined accepted notions ¹¹ painting and representation, giving us a painting that literally turns its back ¹² convention. Continually discovering new ways ¹³ expression, Richter's work is extremely diverse. The wall ¹⁴ the background ¹⁵ this painting resembles some of the very abstract works that Richter creates. These monochrome, thickly painted canvases evoke sadness and despair and were executed ¹⁶ response ¹⁷ the Vietnam war.

Gerhard Richter: Betty, 1988 (oil on canvas – 102 × 72 cm)

from *The Art Book* (Phaidon Press)

C Discuss your reactions to the painting reproduced above and the description you've read.

A **Replace the conjunctions in these sentences with the words given in red:**

1 I don't know much about art but I know what I like.   Despite ....
2 Not only does he paint in oils, but he also paints watercolours.   Besides ....
3 You won't get seats for the show unless you go to the box office today.   Without ....
4 The performance was cancelled because the tenor and soprano were both ill.   Due to ....
5 I like all kinds of music but I don't like jazz.   Except for ....
6 He was missing his wife and he was missing his children too.   As well as ....
7 You didn't enjoy the film, and neither did I.   Like ....
8 The pianist gave a wonderful performance, so I enjoyed the concert.   But for ....

B **Read these notes. Then fill the gaps in the sentences below – and then write a CONTINUATION for each sentence using some of the phrases in red.**

These phrases are used when making generalisations:

as a rule   *broadly speaking*   *everyone would agree that*   *generally speaking*   *in many cases*
in most cases   *in some cases*   *it is often said that*   *it is recognised that*
it is sometimes said that   *many people believe*   *on the whole*

These phrases are used when explaining exceptions:

apart from   *but all the same*   *but every so often*   *but now and then*
but in other cases   *but in this one case*   *but there are exceptions to every rule*
except for   *however*   *on the other hand*   *to some extent*   *to a certain extent*

1 <u>Some people say that</u> modern art is overrated, but ....
2 .... artists lead a good life: their hobby is their profession, but ....
3 .... Hollywood movies are ephemeral, ... you see one you can't forget.
4 .... watching television is rather a waste of time, ...
5 .... politicians are honourable, dedicated people, ...
6 .... reading is a wonderful source of pleasure; ....
7 .... people work because they have to, not because they want to, ...
8 .... I enjoy all kinds of music, ...

C **1** 👥 **Look at this picture: why is it called *The Fall of Icarus*? Talk about the various things that are going on in the picture and make notes on the main points.**

Pieter Brueghel (1527–1569) *The Fall of Icarus* (oil on canvas – 73.5 × 112 cm)

2 👥 **Look at the poem in Activity 1 and then discuss these questions:**

- What did you find out about the picture that you hadn't noticed already?
- Did the poem make you think differently about the picture? In what ways?
- What are the main points made in the poem?

3 ✏️ **Write a description of the painting, explaining what it shows and what you think about it (about 150 words). Try to use some of the conjunctions and connectors in red on page 159.**

Try to use some of the conjunctions and connectors in red on page 159.

| 15.5 | **Use of English Part 5: *Guernica*** | EXAM PRACTICE |

Pablo Picasso's *Guernica* was painted after the bombing of a Basque town in 1937 during the Spanish Civil War. The painting itself is nearly eight metres across, but the reproduction below gives an idea of what it looks like.

Pablo Picasso (1891–1973) – *Guernica* (oil on canvas – 350 × 777 cm)

Ⓐ 1 👥 **Before you read this text, discuss your reactions to the picture.**

2 👥 **Read the text and answer each of the questions that follow in a word or short phrase:**

In Part 5 of the Use of English Paper you'll have to read two texts, answer questions and write a 50–70 word summary. In this section there is only one text to read.

Guernica was the last great history-painting. It was also the last modern painting of major importance that took its subject from politics with the intention of changing the way large numbers of people thought and felt about power. Since 1937, there have been a few admirable works of art that contained political references – some of Joseph Beuys's work or Robert Motherwell's *Elegies to the Spanish Republic*. But the idea that an artist, by making a painting or sculpture, could insert images into the stream of public speech and thus change political discourse has gone, probably for good, along with the nineteenth-century ideal of the artist as public man. Mass media took away the political speech of art. When Picasso painted *Guernica*, regular TV broadcasting had been in existence for only a year in England and nobody in France, except a few electronics experts, had seen a television set. There were perhaps fifteen thousand such sets in New York City. Television was too crude, too novel, to be altogether credible. The day when most people in the capitalist world would base their understanding of politics on what the TV screen gave them was still almost a generation away. But by the end of World War II, the role of the 'war artist' had been rendered negligible by

looked like bad, late German Expressionism, or the incontrovertible photographs from
Belsen, Majdanek, and Auschwitz? It seems obvious, looking back, that the artists of Weimar
Germany and Leninist Russia lived in a much more attenuated landscape of media than ours,
and their reward was that they could still believe, in good faith and without bombast, that art
could morally influence the world. Today, the idea has largely been dismissed, as it must be
in a mass media society where art's principal social role is to be investment capital, or, in the
simplest way, bullion. We still have political art, but we have no *effective* political art. An artist
must be famous to be heard, but as he acquires fame, so his work accumulates 'value' and
becomes, ipso facto, harmless. As far as today's politics is concerned, most art aspires to the
condition of Muzak. It provides the background hum for power. If the Third Reich had
lasted until now, the young bloods of the Inner Party would not be interested in old fogeys
like Albert Speer or Arno Breker, Hitler's monumental sculptor; they would be queuing up
to have their portraits silkscreened by Andy Warhol. It is hard to think of any work of art of
which one can say, *This* saved the life of one Jew, one Vietnamese, one Cambodian. Specific
books perhaps; but as far as one can tell, no paintings or sculptures. The difference between
us and the artists of the 1920s is that they thought such a work of art could be made. Perhaps
it was a certain naïveté that made them think so. But it is certainly our loss that we cannot.

15

20

25

30

from *The Shock of the New* by Robert Hughes

<table>
<tr><td>In Part 5 of the Use of English Paper there aren't as many questions as this. These are to give you extra practice!</td><td>
1 What does the writer mean by *insert images into the stream of public speech* in line 6?
2 How do people in the West nowadays form their political opinions, according to the writer?
3 Why does the writer say so much about television in lines 9 to 14?
4 Why is the word *effective* in italics in line 21?
5 Why is the word *value* in inverted commas in line 22?
6 According to the writer, what is the function of art today?
7 How does the writer feel about the ineffectiveness of political art today?</td></tr>
</table>

B **Discuss these questions:**

- To what extent do you agree with the writer's views?
- What do you think is the purpose of a work of art?
- What influence can a painting, or any other work of art, have on your own feelings and attitudes?
- Does a critic like Robert Hughes perform a useful function in explaining and interpreting works of art as well as evaluating them?
- Does the same hold good for a music critic, a film critic, a TV critic, a restaurant critic or a sports writer?

C **Discuss these exam tips with a partner. Which of them might work for you? Are there any other tips you can add?**

---

1 Part 5 of the Use of English Paper is worth 22 marks (30% of the marks for the whole paper). Aim to spend about 20–25 minutes on it – but don't spend too long on it at the expense of the other questions.

2 The 4 questions on language awareness (style, emphasis or vocabulary) are worth 2 marks each. These can be answered briefly – in a word or short phrase. Don't bother to write full sentences for these answers. Use a highlighter or a pencil to help you to focus on the quoted phrases in context in the text.

3 The summary task is worth 14 marks (4 for content and 10 for summary writing skills). You have to extract information from both texts for this – and you must write fewer than 70 words. Check for any irrelevancies in your notes before you start writing.

4 Make notes before you put pen to paper – space is limited and there may not be enough room for extensive corrections later.

5 In the summary, try to rephrase some of the information in your own words, but don't waste too much time trying to think of a synonym for every word – just avoid direct quotation as far as possible!

Read these reviews and then answer the questions below:

Jakob the Liar by CLARK COLLIS

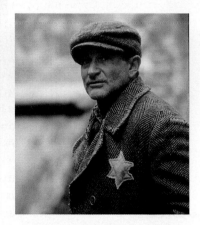

There was once a time when a comedy about the holocaust would have been considered an audaciously brave and/or audaciously stupid move. Unfortunately for *Jakob the Liar*, the conclusion of that particular period in cinema history occurred last year, with the release of Roberto Benigni's *Life is Beautiful*.

As a result, what would otherwise have been, if nothing else, at least controversial, simply comes across as a vehicle for Robin Williams at his most unpleasantly sentimental.

The artist formerly known as Mork plays the economically truthful Jakob, a mild-mannered Jewish baker-cum-boxing manager who we discover failing to make ends meet in a Polish ghetto towards the end of World War II.

After accidentally learning that Germany is losing the battle for the Eastern front, Williams spreads the good news – and before you can say, 'Gooooooooooood morning, Warsaw!' the entire community is under the misapprehension that he has somehow saved a radio from Nazi confiscation.

Which presents something of a dilemma for our supposedly unheroic hero. Should he tell the truth and destroy his increasingly suicidal friends' last hopes?

Or should he risk execution by pretending that he does have a radio, enabling him to do a lot of funny voices behind a screen for the entertainment of the cute little concentration camp-escaping child that he stumbled across way back in Act One?

Anyone who bets on the first option has clearly never seen a Robin Williams movie – although they would certainly be well advised not to make this their first.

Since it was based on a book by camp survivor Jurek Becker, no one could argue that director Kassovitz's intentions are less than noble. But as entertainment, the end product is as turgid a film about mass genocide as we are ever likely to see.

Moreover, while the support from fellow players Alan Arkin, Liev Schreiber and Nina Siemaszko, as Williams' fellow persecutees, is competent enough, the entire enterprise has been smothered with such a sickly layer of glutinous Hollywood sentimentality – replete with a predictably semi-happy ending – that diabetics should probably consult their doctor before even seeing the trailer.

● ●

1 *Jakob the Liar* is ....
  a a controversial film   c not controversial
  b a moving film   d better than *Life is Beautiful*

2 The writer finds Williams' performance ....
  a distasteful   c better than in his previous films
  b charming   d dull

3 What does Jakob do when his fellow-inmates think he has a radio?
  a He has a lot of fun   c He tells them that Germany is losing the war
  b He keeps up the pretence   d He tells the truth

4 Which of these phrases is NOT used humorously or sarcastically?
  a the cute little concentration camp-escaping child that he stumbled across
  b they would certainly be well advised not to make this their first
  c no one could argue that director Kassovitz's intentions are less than noble
  d diabetics should probably consult their doctor before even seeing the trailer

What Dreams May Come by KIM NEWMAN

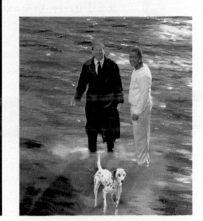

One advantage of recent advances in special effects technology is that films can take you to places you've never seen before, and couldn't even imagine. *What Dreams May Come* takes you somewhere you may not want to experience quite yet. Chris Nielsen (Robin Williams), a doctor whose happy marriage has already been blighted by the deaths of his kids, is killed in an accident and wakes up in a private universe which takes the shape of his wife's semi-Impressionist paintings. Death isn't so bad, especially with guide Albert (Cuba Gooding Jr.) around to give tips and reunite him with his put-down dog and lost little girl. However, Chris' wife Annie (Annabella Sciorra) can't take another bereavement and commits suicide. Since this condemns her to the Hell section of this afterworld, Chris strives – guided by Max Von Sydow – to haul her out of the slough of despair and bring her to the happy lands, even though everyone says this is futile.

Adapted from a cranky mystic novel by Richard Matheson and directed with visual genius by Vincent Ward, this is one of those failures that has so many near-great things that it almost gets by on guts. Few films have the nerve or the imagination to create a world beyond, and the settings are consistently incredible, whether in the idyllic heaven or the paved-with-agonised-faces hell.

The problem is that, despite mostly strong performances, there's something not right about the central perfect relationship so you get distracted arguing with all the religious guff. It feels like what you'd get if you took the legend of Orpheus and previewed it in Pasadena, then rewrote the classical tragedy as a feelgood Hollywood hug-fest. After the underrated excellence of *Map Of The Human Heart*, Vincent Ward is entitled to a misstep and we probably ought to be grateful that this one is as interesting as it is.

5 When Dr Nielsen dies and wakes up in the afterworld .... ,
   a he is all alone   **c** he meets his dog again
   b he is very unhappy   **d** his wife is by his side
6 What does the writer mean by *incredible* in the second paragraph?
   a absurd   **c** not believable
   b very strange   **d** wonderful
7 Why does Annie kill herself?
   a She wants to join Chris in heaven   **c** Too many of her nearest and dearest have died
   b She is all alone in the world   **d** She doesn't realise she'll go to Hell
8 The writer thinks that *What Dreams May Come* is .... ,
   a a brave attempt   **c** well worth seeing
   b not worth seeing   **d** nearly as good as the director's previous film

B **1** 👥 **Discuss these questions:**

* Which of the films would you LEAST like to see? Why?
* What was the WORST film you've ever seen? Tell your partners about it.
* How seriously do you take reviews? How much do they influence your decision whether to see a movie, buy a CD, eat at a restaurant or go to a show?

2 👥 **Before one of you looks at Activity 5, and the other at 18, read this introduction:**

Movie clichés

Apparently there are only half a dozen basic movie plots. However, the list of movie clichés is endless. Many of them are necessary short cuts (movie people never ask for change in a shop or from a taxi driver, for instance), but the rest are gratuitous. Still, they can alleviate the tedium of watching a bad film.

15.7 Writing Part 2 EXAM PRACTICE

A Discuss this exam advice for Paper 2 with a partner. Which pieces of advice are the most useful? Which might not work for you? Can you add any more advice to the list?

1 Follow the instructions exactly. If the instructions say 'Write a letter to a friend', for example, your work must look like a personal letter and NOT like a business letter! This may sound obvious but it's easy to overlook important instructions when you're in a hurry.

2 Make sure you understand the instructions for each question. If you don't fully understand a particular question, it's best not to answer it. Answers that 'wantonly misinterpret the question' are penalised.

3 If you choose a question which asks you to tell a story, such as an article about a memorable journey, you don't have to tell the truth. In fact, it may be more interesting and easier to use your imagination and make up a story.

4 Decide which of the questions are the easiest for you to answer – maybe cross out the ones you don't want to do and then choose between the ones that remain.

5 Make notes for both questions. If at this stage you find you haven't got enough ideas on one of them, there may be time to choose another one.

6 Check if any particular grammatical structures seem to be needed for the subject: conditionals, modal verbs, past/present perfect, etc.

7 Examiners prefer compositions that are easy to read (and neatly written). If in doubt, use a straightforward neutral style – generally this is preferable to a very informal or very formal style.

8 Allow enough time at the end for editing your work and proof-reading it, i.e. checking it through for spelling mistakes, grammatical errors and slips of the pen.

B 1 Re-read the two movie reviews in 15.6. Choose the ONE which you prefer and make notes on these aspects of the movie that are mentioned by the writer:

	information	favourable view	critical view
the plot			
the script			
the actors			
the look			
the director			
the music			
comparisons			
conclusion			

- Which aspects were NOT mentioned in the review? Why weren't they mentioned?
- What is the main impression the review gives? Does it make you want to see the film or not?

2 Pick a film you've both seen and discuss all the aspects noted above. Which of the points you discuss would be worth mentioning in a 300–350 word review – and which would be best omitted?

C Write a review of a film you have seen recently (300–350 words).

"Are you sure this is a film noir"

Part 1 of the Reading Comprehension Paper consists of 18 multiple-choice questions on missing words from three texts. The questions focus on different aspects of vocabulary and grammar. Look at the annotated questions (1–6) and then answer questions 7–12 unaided.

The Beach by ANGIE ERRIGO

Getting away from it all on an ___¹ tropical beach is not the idyll of your lottery winning dreams in this unnerving drama of a hidden Eden where obsessive travellers disassociate from the world.

Leonardo DiCaprio is backpacker Richard, who thinks he's worldly-wise, but is so "the young American abroad" when he seeks adventure and danger in Thailand. A strange ___² with crazed Daffy (Robert Carlyle), who rants of a perfect, secret beach, seems the travel tip for him. And he recruits a French girl he fancies rotten (Virginie Ledoyen) and her amiable boyfriend (Guillaume Canet) to ___³ him on a mysterious, funny, scary journey to the spectacularly beautiful (take a bow, cinematographer Darius Khondji) haven. There Sal (Tilda Swinton) holds sway over a community of drop-outs who are kind of a ___⁴ between the *Swiss Family Robinson* and an apocalyptic water sport cult. Like Garland's novel, the film will be compared with *Lord Of The Flies* as the absence of societal constraints and concerns creates a moral vacuum for wild things to rumpus mightily. *The Beach* is more a ___⁵ of the modern world, though, with a more experienced gang and their alternative attempts to connect with ___⁶ riven by their secrets, desires, jealousies and competitiveness. They import their own serpents into this paradise.

Choose the best word or phrase to fill each gap in the text:

In the exam it's a good idea to put a pencil mark beside the questions you can't answer and come back to them later. It's usually best to eliminate the answers you know to be wrong first,

1 **A** abandoned
    not appropriate
  B unspoilt
    ✓
  C tropical
    not grammatical
  D Asian
    OK but not the best

2 **A** meeting
    OK but not the best
  B rendezvous
    not quite right
  C date
    not appropriate
  D encounter
    ✓

3 **A** encounter
    doesn't make sense
  B join
    ✓
  C travel
    not grammatical
  D escort
    not appropriate

4 **A** mixture
    OK but not the best
  B blend
    not appropriate
  C cross
    ✓
  D association
    different meaning

5 **A** microcosm
    ✓
  B symbolic
    not grammatical
  C comparison
    doesn't make sense
  D reflection
    OK but not the best

6 **A** themselves
    doesn't make sense
  B a team
    silly
  C each
    not grammatical
  D one another
    ✓

Richard is more than a little disturbed, as we learn from a voiceover that ___⁷ on intrusive but underlines his alienation. His fixation with Vietnam movies could be spelled out more clearly to ___⁸ his solitary stint in the jungle turning into a pathological commando game, Heart Of Darkness for the Sega generation.

DiCaprio's ___⁹ as the smartarsed thrill-seeker and the more wry narrator with ___¹⁰, but he works very hard for his reputed $20 million fee when required to turn into a bug-eating nutter. ___¹¹ the dodginess of this interlude, however, Boyle's direction holds a true line between allure and horror, and John Hodge's ___¹² is intriguing and forceful. It's much better than rumoured: entertaining, engrossing, and ripe for discussion – somewhere civilised – afterwards.

then if you're still unsure you may have to guess. It's better to make a wild guess than not to answer at all.

7 **A** frontiers **B** borders **C** approaches **D** comes close
8 **A** explain **B** justify **C** interpret **D** describe
9 **A** role **B** part **C** voice **D** perfect
10 **A** foresight **B** hindsight **C** retrospect **D** knowledge
11 **A** Although **B** In spite **C** Despite **D** Because of
12 **A** script **B** book **C** story **D** plot

Use of English Part 4

Part 4 in the Use of English Paper also tests both vocabulary and grammar. Look at the annotated answers to the first questions and then do the rest unaided. Complete the second sentence so that it has a similar meaning to the first sentence, using the word given. Do not change the word given. You must use between three and eight words, including the word given.

1 Because of the rain the only thing we could do was go to the art gallery.
alternative
As it .... go to the art gallery.

was raining there was no alternative but	✗ 'to' omitted
was wet we decided to	? 'alternative' omitted
was raining there were no alternatives so we had to	✗ word changed + too many words
was raining we had no alternative but to	✓ correct
was raining our only alternative was to	✓ correct

2 I remember very few things about the film.
scarcely
I .... the film.

(can) scarcely remember a thing about	✗ brackets not advisable
can scarcely remember	✗ meaning changed
can scarcely remember anything about	✓
scarcely remember anything about	✓
can scarcely remember a thing about	✓

3 A silent movie can't be compared to a modern film.
comparison
There .... a modern film.

can be no comparison between a silent movie and	✗ too many words
isn't a comparison to be made between a silent movie and	✗ meaning changed + too many words
is difficulty in comparing a silent movie with	✗ word altered
is no comparison between a silent movie and	✓
's no comparison between a silent movie and	✓ contractions are OK

When doing a transformation exercise like this, make absolutely sure that you've included all the information given in the original sentence, and that you haven't inadvertently changed the meaning or emphasis of the sentence. And make sure the grammar in your rewritten sentence and the spelling are OK.

4 Not many people are expected to attend the show.
poorly
The show .... attended.

5 You can't possibly expect me to pay for the tickets.
question
There .... the tickets.

6 After making *Titanic*, Leonardo DiCaprio appeared in *The Beach*.
previous
Leonardo DiCaprio .... *Titanic*.

7 It was stupid of her to turn down the offer of free tickets for the opera.
fool
She .... of free opera tickets.

8 I never thought of taking up painting as a hobby.
occurred
It .... painting as a hobby.

A Find synonyms for the phrases in red, or explain their meanings. Refer to a dictionary if necessary.

1 I know it's a very old car but I think it's still good for a few more years.
2 'What do you enjoy most about your work?' 'That's a good question!'
3 I asked him to apologise and he did so, but with bad grace.
4 I made ten photocopies and then one more for good measure.
5 Don't do someone a good turn in the hope of getting something in return.
6 Have you finished in the shower, or are you planning to stay in there for good?
7 I'm not myself today – I had rather a bad night.
8 Is it bad manners to read while you're eating a meal?
9 After that things went from bad to worse.
10 I didn't get the job, but it's all to the good because it wasn't really right for me.
11 He can't be trusted: he's good for nothing and a thoroughly bad lot.
12 'Work hard and play hard' is an old saying that still holds good today.

B Fill the gaps in these sentences with suitable phrases from the list on the right. The verbs may need to be changed to fit the context.

1 You can .... as an entertainer, if you're successful.
2 Make sure you arrive .... for the interview – that usually ....
3 She promised to phone me first thing today and she was ....
4 I've had the machine overhauled and serviced – now it's ....
5 I can't run because I've got ....
6 The company is .... : more staff are being made redundant.
7 The service here is terrible – I .... to complain to the manager.
8 I know the managing director personally, so I'll .... for you.
9 I took the machine to pieces but couldn't fix it – in the end I ....
10 Things may go wrong if we continue, I think we should stop now ....
11 We made the offer .... and didn't expect these problems would arise.
12 Lunchtime already! It's .... I brought some sandwiches.

a bad leg/ankle/ knee
give up as a bad job
in a bad way
a good job
as good as new
as good as her word
make good money
have a good mind
in good faith
in good time
make a good impression
put in a good word
while the going's good

"OK, 'Leo', break's over."

16 Look after yourself!

16.1 A healthy life?

READING AND VOCABULARY

A Read this article and then answer the questions that follow:

Programme
for Natural Healing

Everyone worries about their health. For some it's about losing a bit of weight, others that they'll inherit diseases which afflicted their parents. But what if someone told you in just two short months you could be feeling on top of the world? That's exactly what Andrew Weil has to say in his latest book, *8 Weeks to Optimum Health*. Weil – a doctor and bestselling author of *Spontaneous Healing* – believes we can all optimise the functioning of the body's natural healing system, not just on a day-to-day basis but also in responding to everyday illnesses and more serious medical conditions. He has drawn up a programme which makes simple changes to our lifestyle in terms of diet, exercise, supplements and mental and spiritual development, in turn prompting "long-lasting and dramatically beneficial effects for our health". Of course, everyone is different so Weil also provides specific guidance for men and women, pregnant women, people under 20, over 50 and over 70, those who are overweight, people at risk from cardiovascular disease and cancer and those who have young children. There are even sections devoted to the health of those who live in big cities and who travel frequently.

So how does it work? Weil says it has much to do with the body's own healing system. "Health is wholeness and balance, an inner resilience that allows you to meet the demands of living without being overwhelmed. If you have that kind of resilience, you can experience the inevitable interactions with germs and not get infections, you can be in contact with allergens and not suffer allergies and you can sustain exposure to carcinogens and not get cancer."

Week one begins with a general cupboard clearance – out must go all unhealthy foods like oils and artificial sweeteners – and an introduction to vitamin C, walking and eating more broccoli – a nutrient and fibre-rich vegetable. Breath observation – pay attention to your breathing patterns – also starts now.

As the weeks progress, so Weil steps up the demands. Week two calls for an increase in your consumption of whole grains and an end to drinking chlorinated water. He also suggests attempting a one-day "news-fast". With each week comes the adoption of new supplements and fresh dietary habits. Exercise is increased and more mental and spiritual tasks are set. Alongside each chapter he includes true stories of those 'healed' by the plan, plus various healthy recipes. But he warns: "Perfect health is not possible – beware of persons and products that promise it. Health is not static: it is normal to lose it periodically in order to come back to it in a better way."

Weil says the eight-week programme gives users the information needed to keep their healing system in working order. "It shows you how to build a lifestyle that will protect you from premature disability and death and it teaches practices and skills that will enable you to prepare body, mind and spirit for any eventual health crisis you may face. Start it now and reap the benefits for the rest of your life."

1 People are concerned about...
   A receiving conflicting advice from medical experts
   B suffering from the same illnesses as their parents
   C their parents falling ill
   D gaining too much weight
2 Dr Weil believes that everyone should...
   A be sceptical about his methods
   B use different methods
   C follow the same programme
   D eat less and exercise more

3 Dr Weil believes that everyone...
   A can develop immunity to germs   **C** should avoid contact with germs
   B can cope with potential sources of illness   **D** is at risk from infection
4 Following Dr Weil's methods over the weeks...
   A you have to put more and more effort into it   **C** you shouldn't watch the news on TV
   B you must expect to be ill occasionally   **D** you will never suffer from illness
5 Dr Weil's programme will be effective if you...
   A don't expect results for at least two months   **C** begin at once
   B have faith in it   **D** follow every step rigorously

In the exam read each text in Paper 1 twice: once quickly to get the gist and again more carefully to find the answers. In Parts 2–4, each correct answer gains **TWO** marks. Some alternatives in multiple-choice questions are designed to be tricky and distract you from the right answer – so don't jump to conclusions.

Use a highlighter or pencil to mark any questions that you're still unsure about. It may be best to come back to them later on, rather than read the text again straight away.

B   **Discuss these questions:**

• What do you think about Dr Weil's programme? Would it work for you?
• How do YOU stay healthy and fit? What kind of exercise do you take?
• How careful are you about your diet?
• Do you worry about your health? What special precautions do you take against falling ill?

C   Choose the THREE best answers to fill the gap in each sentence.

1 He will have to go on a diet because he is getting ....
   dense   flabby   buxom   robust   plump   stout

2 If he still feels ill after taking this treatment, he should see ....
   a consultant   a midwife   a specialist   his GP   a quack

3 She needs to put on some weight after her illness because she is too ....
   fragile   lean   light   skinny   slim   thin   slender

4 Many illnesses today are related to ....
   grief   stress   tension   worry   sadness   suffering

5 What treatment should be given to someone who has .... ?
   fainted   lost consciousness   passed away   passed out   passed through

6 I'm a bit worried about the .... I've been having in my back.
   agony   twinges   ache   pain   suffering   wound

7 Illness can be stopped before it happens by means of ....
   after care   vaccines   preventive medicine   therapy   healthy living

8 The nurse made her take .... to help her sleep better.
   a lotion   a sedative   a pain-killer   an ointment   a tranquilliser

9 Take two of these .... three times a day after meals.
   drugs   capsules   sweets   tablets   pills   placebos

10 Everyone hoped that he would .... after the operation.
   pull out   pull through   get better   pull over   get well   get up

11 You really must see a doctor about that ....
   pimple   rash   blister   scratch   swelling   inflammation

12 Keep away from other people if you have a disease that is ....
   catching   contagious   antiseptic   catchy   infectious

13 Once a year it's a good idea to go to the doctor for ....
   an examination   a check-up   an operation   a post-mortem   a medical

14 She had to go to hospital when she ....
   had a break   broke up   pulled a muscle   sprained her ankle   fractured her wrist

15 Medical experts take the claims of .... medicine more seriously nowadays.
   alternative   complementary   conventional   fringe   mainstream   orthodox

D **In these sentences only ONE of the four alternatives given is correct. Choose the correct alternative.**

1 An illness that is caused by the mind is known as a .... illness.
pschyosamatic   pschyosomatic   psychosamatic   psychosomatic

2 Before the operation the patient was given a general ....
anaesthetic   anesthaetic   anasthetic   anisthetic

3 The doctors examined the patient and came to the conclusion that he was ....
a loony   off his rocker   silly   unbalanced

4 Malaria is .... by the female anopheles mosquito.
broadcast   sent   transmitted   transported

5 Realising that she was probably pregnant she consulted a ....
chiropodist   gynaecologist   osteopath   pediatrician

6 We realised he must be ill when he ....
threw down   threw out   threw in   threw up

7 Hayfever is a very common type of ....
allergy   antagonism   symptom   therapy

8 Smallpox, once responsible for millions of deaths, has been completely ....
abolished   erased   eradicated   exterminated

9 The consultant operated on the patient when he complained of pains in his ....
insides   paunch   tummy   stomach

10 He has a morbid fear of going outside his home, known to doctors as ....
agoraphobia   arachnophobia   claustrophobia   xenophobia

E 🔊 **You'll hear ten 'Doctor, doctor' jokes – which do you think is the funniest?**

16.2 Speaking   EXAM PRACTICE

In the Speaking Paper candidates are assessed on their:

grammatical resource (accuracy and range of grammar) · lexical resource (vocabulary) · discourse management · pronunciation of sentences · interactive communication · vocabulary resource

Part 1: The interlocutor talks with each candidate about general topics (3 minutes).

Part 2: The candidates look at visual prompts and the interlocutor leads them into a discussion (4 minutes).

Part 3: Each candidate is given a written question. They have to talk uninterrupted for 2 minutes each, then a discussion follows (12 minutes).

A 👥 **Conversation with interlocutor**   One of you should look at Activity 11, the other at 21. You'll have some general questions to answer.

B 👥 **Conversation about pictures**   One of you should look at Activity 12, the other at 22. You'll each have a picture to describe and discuss.

C 👥 **Long turns and discussion**   One of you should look at Activity 13, the other at 23. You'll each have a topic to talk about for two minutes and then discuss together.

In the exam, don't be the passive partner – take the initiative just as you would in a normal conversation. If you're reticent, it may be quite difficult for the assessor to assess how well you speak English. Remember that it's how well you communicate that's being assessed, not whether your answers are correct, intelligent or sensible – or even wholly true!

A cheerful, confident manner is also very helpful. The assessor will try to put you at your ease, but the best way to feel confident is to have plenty of practice before the exam. Team up with another student and try the Speaking tests in *Cambridge Proficiency Practice* 1. You can practise giving a two-minute talk on your own, preferably recording your voice onto cassette or minidisc.

16.3 Relative clauses

  Discuss any differences in meaning or style between these sentences:

1 The doctor I spoke to yesterday told me not to worry.
  The doctor, whom I spoke to yesterday, told me not to worry.
  The doctor, who I spoke to yesterday, told me not to worry.
  The doctor to whom I spoke yesterday told me not to worry.
2 He told us about the treatment, which made him feel better.
  He told us about the treatment that made him feel better.
3 They operated on the first patient who was seriously ill.
  They operated on the first patient, who was seriously ill.

B Fill the gaps with *who, whose, which* or *that*. Add COMMAS where necessary.

The Californians have come up with a device for people ¹have their own small swimming pool ² should transform their lives as much as those indoor exercise bikes ³ were so popular in the 1970s did. Swimming ⁴ is recognised to be one of the best ways of keeping fit is impractical in pools ⁵ are too small for serious swimming. But the *Hydroflex* is a new device ⁶can keep swimmers in the same spot and still allow them to do all the strokes. It consists of a plastic bar ⁷ is attached to the side of the pool by two lines and to the swimmer by a waist belt. The swimmer ⁸ legs are protected from the lines by the bar remains stationary while swimming It sounds like an activity ⁹ is only suitable for people ¹⁰ desire to keep in shape helps them to ignore the taunts of neighbours ¹¹happen to spot them in the pool.

C Complete each sentence with suitable words. Add COMMAS wherever they are needed.

1 He's the only person I know .... ten kilometres a day before breakfast.
2 I swam twenty lengths .... me a long time.
3 He has two sisters both .... doctors. The younger of the two .... Jane qualified last year. He also has two brothers neither .... know anything about medicine.
4 One of the children must have swallowed the pills .... left in the bathroom.
5 All .... people say about hospitals is true.
6 She loves talking about her operation .... us all feel ill.
7 The matron is the .... is in overall charge of the nursing staff.
8 Taking a degree in medicine .... longer than most other university courses is the only method .... one can become a doctor.

16.4 Listening Part I

EXAM PRACTICE

In Part I of the Listening Paper you hear four extracts, each with two multiple-choice questions. Make sure you read the questions before you listen to the recording. (You'll hear each clip twice.)

Extract One

You hear a doctor talking to her patient.

1 When was the patient injured?
  A Tuesday   **B** Wednesday   **C** Thursday   [1]

2 The doctor is
  A helpful   **B** sympathetic   **C** unsympathetic   [2]

Extract Two

You hear part of a radio programme about homeopathy.

3 Samuel Hahnemann's purpose of 'proving' substances was to ...
  A cure his patients   **B** discover the effects of different substances
  C test his technique of dosage   [3]

4 The efficacy of homeopathy depends on ...
   A the similarities between symptoms and the effects of various substances
   B patients getting worse before they get better
   C giving patients very small doses of poison

4

Extract Three

You hear a doctor talking about his relationship with patients.

5 A patient is more likely to believe that practitioners can cure them if they have ...
   A a good bedside manner   B smart consulting rooms
   C letters from cured patients

5

6 The doctor's own patients recovered, he suggests, because ...
   A their own bodies cured them   B they trusted him
   C they were not really ill

6

Extract Four

You hear two friends talking about dreams.

7 According to the man, dreaming is like
   A being another person   B visiting other countries
   C running from place to place

7

8 Compared to our waking lives, dream experiences are more
   A interesting   B vivid   C intense

8

16.5 Use of English Part 2

EXAM PRACTICE

In Part 2 of the Use of English Paper you have to form a word that fits in the space. Make absolutely sure the word is grammatically correct in the context. Each question of the ten questions is worth one mark. Here, to give you extra practice, there are 15 questions.

Use the word given in capitals at the end of some lines to form a word that fits in the space in the same line. Write your answers in CAPITAL LETTERS.

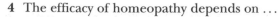

More than half the world's population consider ___¹ shy, delegates   **THEM**
to the first international ___² on shyness, being held in   **CONFER**
Cardiff, will be told today. One in 10 cases is severe. Effects include
mutism, speech problems, ___³, blushing, shaking and   **LONELY**
trembling, lack of eye contact, ___⁴ in forming relationships and   **DIFFICULT**
social phobia – the most extreme form of shyness, defined by the
American Psychiatric Association as a pronounced and ___⁵ fear   **PERSIST**
of social or performance situations in which ___⁶ may occur. Shy   **EMBARRASS**
people tend to blame themselves for social ___⁷ and attribute   **FAIL**
success to ___⁸ factors. They expect their behaviour to be   **OUT**
___⁹, remember only negative information about themselves   **ADEQUATE**
and accept without challenge adverse comments from others.

The causes are complex and not fully understood. The latest theory is
that it can be traced to genes as well as to social ___¹⁰.   **CONDITION**
One estimate, based on research with twins, is that around 15 per cent
of the population are born with a ___¹¹ to shyness. Some   **DISPOSE**
___¹² believe there are two types: an early developing, fearful   **PSYCHOLOGY**
shyness and a later developing, ___¹³ shyness. The fearful   **CONSCIOUS**
version emerges often in the first year of life and is ___¹⁴ to be   **THINK**
___¹⁵ inherited.   **PART**

In Part 2 of the Listening Paper you have to complete nine sentences with specific information or an opinion. You'll hear just one person speaking, or one person being interviewed.

A 🔊 **In the recording Professor Carl Abrahams is talking about Sigmund Freud. Complete the sentences with a word or short phrase:**

Sigmund Freud (1856–1939)

1 According to Professor Abrahams, some patients [_____1_____] after psychoanalysis.

2 Freud's own account of the wolf man case was [_____2_____] .

3 Although Freud was not a good doctor, he was a good [_____3_____] .

4 An innocent [_____4_____] is commonly believed to betray conccalcd sccret desircs.

5 When they first came out, Freud's books got [_____5_____] .

6 Freud asserted that sexuality and [_____6_____] were directly related.

7 Freud's technique of 'free association' was [_____7_____] .

8 The popularity of Freud has [_____8_____] research into mental disorders.

9 People who consult psychoanalysts are being [_____9_____] by them.

In the exam you'll hear each recording twice. You'll have about 45 seconds to read the questions through beforehand and about 15 seconds between each playing to check your answers. Answer the easier questions during the first listening and make a pencil mark beside the ones you can't get and listen carefully for them during the second listening. Don't leave any blanks – make a guess if you really don't know an answer.

Beware of distractingly plausible answers and don't rely on what you already know. Concentrate on what the speakers actually say, not what you'd say if you were talking about the same topic.

B 👥 **Discuss these questions:**
- How would you describe Professor Abrahams' attitude during the interview? Write down three descriptive adjectives to characterise your impression of him.
- To what extent were you convinced by what he said?
- How can a psychiatrist (or psychoanalyst or psychotherapist) help someone with their problems?
- What is the difference between a psychologist and a psychiatrist?

16.7 **Synonyms and homonyms** VOCABULARY DEVELOPMENT

Synonyms are useful in Part 5 of the Use of English Paper, where you are expected to use your own words as far as possible and to avoid quoting directly from the text. In your compositions you can avoid repetition or an over-simple style by choosing suitable synonyms.

When you're writing, and you can't think of a suitable synonym on the spur of the moment, leave a gap (like this:), or p il in the word you want to replace, and come back later to fill it in.

A 🔊 **You'll hear the same words spoken in eight different ways – pay attention to the underlying meaning conveyed by each speaker's tone of voice:**

> *Ah, there you are. I was wondering where you'd got to. Luckily I had some work to get on with so I wasn't bored. Anyway, even if the film has started by the time we get there, I don't think it'll matter, do you?*

1 Decide which word from the list on the right best describes each speaker's tone:

1	
2	
3	
4	

5	
6	
7	
8	

amused   bored
cross   friendly
furious   kind
sad   unemotional

2 🔊 Listen to the recording again and note down at least one other adjective (or phrase) to describe the tone of each speaker. Compare ideas with your partners.

B **Look at these words and match them with their synonyms below.**

amazed   annoyed   clever   confused   cured   depressed   determined   different
disappointed   dull   encouraged   exciting   frightened   glad   respected   revolting
shocked   upset   worried   worrying

*admired   anxious   astonished   better   bewildered   delighted   despondent   disgusting
disillusioned   distressed   disturbing   diverse   dreary   heartened   horrified   indignant
persistent   scared   talented   thrilling*

C **Replace each word in red with a synonym which might impress the examiners – or which can help you to avoid repetition. (You may have to rewrite the whole sentence.)**

1 Surfing can be dangerous, but hang-gliding is much more dangerous.
2 There are many good ways of keeping fit – jogging is very good.
3 I was happy to meet my old friends again. It was good to talk about old times.
4 I'm sorry that you were unwell yesterday. You look all right today.
5 It was kind of you to offer to help, but the work wasn't difficult.
6 We went for a nice walk at the weekend, ending up at a nice restaurant.
7 The original novel was interesting, but the film they made of it was boring.
8 The meal we had last night was good, but the wine wasn't good.

D **Replace the verbs in red with suitable phrasal verbs. (This exercise revises some of the phrasal verbs you have come across in previous units.)**

1 Freud had the theory that pleasure and sexuality were directly linked.
2 I couldn't make them understand that I was tired and this really depressed me.
3 I withdraw that remark I made about you.
4 If you have a pain in your back you'll just have to endure it.
5 I find that stress at work often causes a headache.
6 I hope you aren't delayed in the rush-hour traffic.
7 She invented the whole story and she deceived us all!
8 His suitcase disintegrated on the luggage carousel.
9 Having heard all the arguments I've decided to support your idea.
10 Would it inconvenience you if I stayed for dinner?

A 👥 **Discuss the notes below and add your own views to them. Decide which of the points you'll include and which you'll leave out in an essay on this topic:**

We are constantly bombarded with advice from experts on ways of staying healthy and surviving to a ripe old age. Which aspects of their advice do you think it is practicable to follow? Read this leaflet and then write an essay giving your views on this topic. (300–350 words)

Look after yourself! Dos and Don'ts

DO...

| eat a well-balanced diet and control your weight.
| eat less salt and lower your blood pressure.
| eat less fat and make your heart healthier.
| eat less sugar and lose weight.
| eat a high fibre diet to improve your digestion.
| get plenty of regular exercise – improve your feeling of well-being and fitness.
| find ways to relax – avoid getting stressed.

DON'T...

| smoke cigarettes – they give you cancer and lung disease.
| drink alcohol – it can be addictive and give you liver disease.
| eat too much.
| drive somewhere when you can walk or cycle.
| get stressed – stress can lead to migraines, mental illness and depression.

B **1** ✏️ Make your own notes and then write the essay. Try to do everything in ONE HOUR: making notes, writing the composition and checking your work.

2 👥 Show your completed essay to your partner and ask for comments.

What are the examiners looking for in the Writing Paper?

1 How well you have fulfilled the task set. (The five questions in Part 2 provide five different tasks: each demands different responses and techniques.)

2 The relevance and organisation of your composition as a whole, as well as the quality of the individual paragraphs.

3 The quality of the language you use: the range and appropriateness of vocabulary and sentence structure; the correctness of grammar, punctuation and spelling.

4 Your ability to display a breadth of experience or background knowledge, and your use of illustration and allusion.

5 A 'balance between accuracy and imagination' in each composition: the examiners try to give equitable treatment to compositions which are 'pedestrian but accurate' and those which are less accurate but 'lively and imaginative'.

16.9 Reading Part 3: Taking the waters

EXAM PRACTICE

In Part 3 of the Reading Paper you have to decide which paragraph fits in the spaces in the text. To add to the difficulty, there's one extra paragraph which doesn't fit anywhere. In the exam there are seven paragraphs missing, but here only six are missing.

Six paragraphs/sentences have been removed from this article. Choose the most suitable paragraph/sentence from the list A–G for each gap (1–6) in the article. There is one extra paragraph you don't need to use.

Jane Clarke

Taking the waters

While we can survive for some time without food, we can only live for a few days without water. A persistently dehydrated body can lead to lethargy, poor skin, high cholesterol levels, urinary-tract infections such as cystitis and bowel problems such as constipation.

1 [   ]

Even high blood fat (cholesterol and triglycerides) levels can be aggravated by lack of water; without it, fibre (found in whole grains, pulses, oats, fruits and vegetables) cannot swell and stimulate the body to produce High Density Lipoprotein, aka 'good cholesterol'. HDL picks up Low Density Lipoprotein – 'bad cholesterol' – and takes it to the gut, where it is excreted.

2 [   ]

Most adults should drink two or three litres (about four or five pints) of water every day. Those who exercise, and pregnant women, need even more. Exercise causes the body to lose fluid, which can lead to over-heating, dizziness and tiredness. During pregnancy, the fluid requirement increases to nourish the foetus, while breast-feeding mums need extra fluid to produce milk. Children can lose a lot of water through their skin, because they're generally more active. Urine is one of the best guides to the adequacy of fluid intake.

3 [   ]

When you boost your water intake, you will find yourself using the loo more frequently, but your body will soon adapt. If you have other symptoms – a need to pass urine excessively, blood in urine, pain or extreme itchiness or discomfort – it may mean that you have a urine infection, which will need medical attention.

4 [   ]

With digestive disorders such as a hiatus hernia or oesophagitis (inflammation of the oesophagus), having too much liquid can cause the stomach contents to leak up into the oesophagus, irritate the oesophagus walls and bring on heartburn. To avoid this, take only small sips with your meal to refresh your palate, but make up your fluid requirement between meals.

5 [   ]

Some people find bottled water unnecessary and uneconomical. A litre of tap water costs 0.06 pence, approximately – that's up to a thousand times cheaper than bottled water. There is also the cost to the environment (plastics for packaging and energy for transport). If the taste puts you off tap water, your water supplier will be able to test for contamination (which can occur in old pipes, for example) or bacterial overgrowth. Water companies now have a legal duty to meet safety standards and are 'committed to improvements in the palatability of water, particularly taste and clarity', according to Water UK.

6 [   ]

Also, it doesn't have to be served cold – there are many fruit and herbal teas and tisanes on the market; you could even make your own using fresh mint, or root ginger with lemon and honey. Remember that water that contains caffeine – from coffee, tea, colas or hot chocolate – does not count towards your daily two- to three-litre intake because caffeine is dehydrating. Enjoy two or three cups (the daily recommendation), but then take care to keep up necessary levels of pure water – your best liquid asset.

A A water filter can remove some of the undesirable tastes, but make sure it is regularly serviced, otherwise you will be contaminating your water by passing it through an unclean filter. Bottled water is handy to carry around with you, to give to your child to take to school or to have sitting on your desk – all good ways of reminding you to drink a glass an hour. You can make water more interesting by adding shavings of fresh ginger, slices or squeezes of fresh lemon or lime, a few drops of orange-blossom water or a dash of elderflower or lime cordial.

B An adult's body is made up of about 65 per cent water, and this has to be topped up to keep it healthy, flexible and young-looking. We need water to keep the body flushing waste products, maintain healthy skin, hair and organs, produce digestive enzymes, regulate our temperature (cooling by evaporation through the skin) and aid uptake of essential nutrients such as vitamins, minerals and natural sugars.

C For people who have a poor appetite, or who need to put on weight or maximise their calorie intake, it is important not to drink large amounts of water at meal times. Water itself does not disturb digestion, but if you fill yourself up with fluid, you'll have less room for food.

D I recently discovered when advising a high-altitude level climber (Mount Everest, K2, etc.) that checking the colour of urine can be a life-saving exercise. Urine should be pale in colour, and you should go to the loo regularly throughout the day. If urine is dark, you are not drinking enough water – which can quickly lead to death if you're 24,000ft above sea level. If you think two litres of water is a lot, imagine having to drink eight to 10 – the average daily fluid requirement for high-altitude climbers!

E We lose water mainly through our kidneys and skin (the skin's inner layer, dermis, is made up of 70 per cent water and acts as a natural reservoir). We also lose a lot of water when we suffer sickness, diarrhoea or any infection that causes fever. Now that the majority of us live in centrally heated houses and work in offices with heating and air conditioning, we lose more water through our skin than people did in the past. Our diets now also contain higher levels of salt, additives and sugars, all of which place extra strain on the body's water reserves.

F Many people wonder why doctors and medical people make so much fuss about water, but the reason is clear: water is good for you. And the more you drink the better it is for your health. Most people drink far less than they should and they are not aware of this.

G Whether you get your water from a tap or a bottle is up to you. Mineral and spring water are ground waters, which means they landed as rain, seeped through rocks and collected in underground pools. When this water reaches the surface, it can be bottled and labelled as spring water. 'Natural mineral water' is more rigidly defined and is better regulated; it has to come from a source which is naturally protected, of a constant composition and free from pollution. A small amount of water can be found to be naturally sparkling, but most sparkling water has had carbon dioxide pumped into it. This poses no threat to health.

16.10 Use of English Part 3 EXAM PRACTICE

In Part 3 of the Use of English Paper there are six sets of three sentences, each with a missing word. You have to think of a word that fits in all three sentences. If you can only think of a word that fits in two of them, it might be worth guessing that this is the missing one in the third.

Make sure the word you choose is grammatically correct – does it need an 's' or 'ed' on the end?

Think of ONE WORD which can be used appropriately in all three sentences.

1 I suppose you think my opinions don't .... – well, they do!
  He was found guilty on one .... of murder and two of assault.
  I hope it won't .... against me if I don't come to your party.

2 When his health deteriorated the surgeon decided to ....
  You can find instructions on how to .... the machine in the manual.
  Parking restrictions only .... from 8 am to 6 pm.

3 The .... of the organisation was born two hundred years ago.
  The crew abandoned ship when it began to .... on the rocks.
  Their plans are going to .... if they don't keep to their budget.

4 Her constant criticism .... my enthusiasm.
  Pollution is exacerbated by the fumes from car and lorry ....
  Going up a mountain .... even experienced climbers.

	1
	2
	3
	4

5 She hates working for other people, and prefers to run her own ....
Young people .... less and less respect for their elders these days.
Recent reports .... a sharp rise in the numbers of overweight people.

| 5 |

6 The headings are usually printed in bold ....
She doesn't want to see him again because he isn't her ....
I wish I had learned to .... when I was younger, it's so difficult now.

| 6 |

16.11 Use of English Part 5: Floating   EXAM PRACTICE

In Part 5 of the Use of English Paper you have to read two texts and answer four language awareness questions (each worth two marks). You then have to write a 50–70 word summary of some information contained in the two texts (worth 14 marks).

There are more than four questions here, to give you extra practice.

A   Read the text and answer the questions below:

Fee floating

STRESSED executives used to unwind with a few cigarettes and a pint of lager. No longer. Fear of the two big Cs – cancer and corpulence – has encouraged them to take to more exotic therapies. The big hit of
5 the moment is floating about in tanks of salt water. Today only slobs smoke and slurp; sensible people float and free-associate.

The idea behind floating is simple: deprive the body of physical sensations and you free the mind
10 for meditation. The fad started 20 years ago in California. While he was investigating the side-effects of sensory-deprivation, a neuro-physiologist called John Lilley had the bright idea of immersing his assistants in tanks of salt water. They emerged
15 euphoric, jabbering about inner peace and mystical visions.

The first British tank was set up six years ago in a seedy bit of south London. There are now more than 40 of them open to the public and almost as many
20 private ones – a tank can be yours for just £2,000 ($3,400). They have even found their way into night clubs. Seasoned floaters report a recent surge in interest. "Neighbours", a television soap-opera, has featured it; Jason Donovan, a pop star, has
25 discovered it; even the medical profession has put in a good word for it.

Floating is certainly a weird sensation. The tank is a light-proof and sound-proof closed shell about the size of a small sauna. You lie (alone) in the
30 darkness, with your head resting on a floating pillow and your body suspended in ten inches of warm water, salted about as heavily as the Dead Sea. For the first few minutes you listen to a tape of warbling flutes and twittering birds. Then everything falls
35 silent.

At first, you concentrate on the physical sensation of floating. Next you start to worry about unpaid bills and unfinished jobs. Finally, you drift off into a meditative limbo – the middle-zone, the cognoscenti
40 call it. Snatches of music and exotic images – some of them startlingly vivid – drift in and out of your mind. Floaters usually lose track of time, unaware of whether they have been in the tank for five minutes or five hours. Not so the proprietors: after your
45 allotted hour, a tape of bellowing whales and crashing waves summons you out of your reverie. Even in the new age, time is money.

Floating leaves you feeling spaced-out without the physical side-effects of chemicals or the mental
50 tedium of meditation. But beware the lure of salt water. The contrast between the womb-like security of the tank and the bustle of the street sends the pulse racing and the senses reeling – and undoes the benefits of an hour in less than ten minutes. Frequent
55 floaters go to ever greater lengths to attain nirvana: some float for up to eight hours a day. And none of this comes cheap: an hour in the tank will set you back £20.

from *The Economist*

For questions 1–7 write a word or short phrase. You do not need to write complete sentences.

1 Why did the writer use the word *jabbering* in line 15?
2 What impresssion does the writer give by using the word *seedy* in line 18?
3 Why did the writer use the expression *warbling flutes* in lines 33–4?
4 Why is the word *alone* in brackets in line 29?
5 What are said to be the disadvantages of taking drugs and meditation?
6 Why might floaters feel worse after a session in the tank?
7 Explain in your own words how floaters are informed that their time is up.

8 In 50–70 words, summarise the history of floating.

B 👥 **Compare your answers.**

The summary writing task tests information selection, linking and sentence construction. Four of the 14 marks are awarded for including the relevant points, the rest are for summary writing skills.

16.12 *mind, brain and word* IDIOMS

A **Find synonymous words or phrases to replace the phrases in red, using a dictionary if necessary.**

1 Don't expect him to spare your feelings: he always speaks his mind.
2 Being insured costs a lot of money but it gives you peace of mind.
3 I was so annoyed that I couldn't resist giving him a piece of my mind.
4 She gave me her word that she would pay me back the next day.
5 She's so indecisive: she can never make up her mind what to do.
6 We were in two minds whether to phone you or not.
7 He's so garrulous that you can't get a word in edgeways.
8 It'll all end in tears, mark my words!
9 I can still see the whole scene in my mind's eye.
10 I'm sorry I didn't post the letter, it slipped my mind, I'm afraid.
11 Their new car is the last word in luxury.
12 'No, you can't stay out all night,' 'Is that your last word?' 'Yes.'

B **Fill the gaps in these sentences with suitable phrases from the list below. You may need to change the form of the verbs.**

1 Actors have to be .... before they go on the stage.
2 You're an expert on this subject, would you mind if I .... ?
3 He's usually so trustworthy, he's the last person I'd expect to ....
4 I couldn't think what to do, then suddenly I had a ....
5 Sit down, listen to some music and try to .... your problems.
6 I'm so angry about the way I was treated that I .... write a letter of complaint.
7 Idioms like these can't be translated .... into another language.
8 Who are you going to believe? We both denied responsibility so ....
9 You look preoccupied, as if you ....
10 Many English jokes depend on a ....
11 If you .... about coming with us, just give me a call.
12 I was .... but I couldn't solve the problem.

> brainwave   change your mind   go back on her/his word   have a good mind to
> have something on your mind   take your mind off   word for word   word perfect
> it's his/her word against mine   pick your brains   play on words   rack my brains

"He pretends to throw the stick, I pretend to chase it.
Is this normal?"

© Mike Baldwin / Cornered

17

The past is always with us

Use of English Part I and Reading Part 2

EXAM PRACTICE

A **Look at the pictures and discuss these questions:**

- What is each person famous for? What were his achievements?
- Why do we hear about so few women in history? Who are the most famous women in your country's history? What are they famous for?
- How interested are you in history? Give your reasons.

B **Fill each gap with ONE suitable word.**

In Part I of the Use of English Paper you should read the whole text through before filling any of the blanks. If you can't think what to put in some of the gaps, leave them blank and allow yourself enough time to come back to them later. If you're unsure of an answer, write it in pencil and come back to it later. Remember to write your answers in CAPITAL LETTERS on the Answer Sheet.

Make sure the words you choose not only make sense in the context but are grammatically correct – and that you spell them correctly. If you aren't sure, try to decide what kind of word is missing: noun, adjective, adverb, verb, etc.

JEANS

'G ÈNES' is the French name for Genoa, and by extension for a traditional
¹ of trousers worn by Genoese sailors. Serge de Nîmes was the
² of a tough blue sailcloth, now corrupted to 'denim', traditionally ³
in the French town. Levi Strauss (1829–1902) was a ⁴ of Bavaria who
⁵ to New York at the age of fourteen and who ⁶ his brothers in
their ⁷ of supplying the prospectors and frontiersmen of the Californian
Gold Rush. Some time in the 1860s Levi's company had the ⁸ of matching
the denim cloth with the Genoese trousers, and of ⁹ the pockets and
seams with brass horse-harness rivets.
Thus was produced the most durable and universal item in the ¹⁰ of fashion
design – a German immigrant using French materials and Italian style to invent an
archetypal American ¹¹.
'Blue jeans' remained workaday clothing in North America for almost a ¹²
, before taking Europe (and the ¹³ of the world) by ¹⁴ in the 1960s,
a prime ¹⁵ of 'Americanization'.

from Europe A History by Norman Davies

C **Read this text and then answer the multiple choice questions that follow:**

You'll have to answer multiple choice questions like these in the Reading Paper Parts 2 and 4 (and also in the Listening Paper Parts I and 3). If you don't know which answer is right, first eliminate the ones you think are wrong. Then choose between the ones that might be right. If in doubt, guess! Don't leave a blank.

MURANO

1   MURANO is an island in the Venetian lagoon. It is the site of a Romanesque church, Santa Maria e Donate, dating from 999, and the glassworks of the former Venetian Republic.

2   Glass-making has been practised in Europe since ancient times, but Greek and Roman glass was coarse in texture and opaque in colour. It was only at Murano, near the turn of the thirteenth century, that the glass-masters created a product that was both tough and transparent. For several decades the formula remained secret, but then it leaked to Nuremberg, whence it spread to all corners of the continent.

3   Transparent glass made possible the science of optics, and was crucial in the development of precision instruments. The principles of the lens and the refraction of light were known by the time, c.1260, that Roger Bacon was credited with designing the first pair of spectacles. (There is a portrait of the Emperor Henry VII (d. 1313) wearing spectacles in one of the stained glass windows of Strasburg cathedral.) Glass windows gradually came into fashion between the fourteenth and sixteenth centuries, first in churches and palaces and later in more humble dwellings. Glass flasks, retorts, and tubes facilitated the experiments of alchemy, later of chemistry. Glass cloches and greenhouses transformed market-gardening. The microscope (1590), telescope (1608), barometer (1644), and thermometer (1593), all glass-based, revolutionized our views of the world. The silvered mirror, first manufactured at Murano, revolutionized the way we see ourselves.

4   The social consequences of glass were far-reaching. The use of spectacles extended the reading span of monks and scholars, and accelerated the spread of learning. Windows increased the hours and efficiency of indoor work, especially in northern Europe. Workplaces could be better lit and better heated. Greenhouses vastly improved the cultivation of flowers, fruit, and vegetables, bringing a healthier and more abundant diet, previously known only in the Mediterranean. Storm-proof lanterns, enclosed coaches, and watch-glasses all appeared, whilst precision instruments encouraged a wide range of scientific disciplines, from astronomy to medicine.

5   The mirror had important psychological consequences. People who could see a sharp image of their own faces developed a new consciousness. They became more aware of their appearances, and hence of clothes, hairstyles, and cosmetics. They were also led to ponder the link between external features and the inner life, in short, to study personality and individuality. They developed interests in portraiture, biography, and fashion. The very unmedieval habits of introspection were strongly reflected in Rembrandt's paintings, for example, and ultimately in the novel.
The *Galerie des Glaces* (Hall of Mirrors) at the palace of Versailles was opened on 15 November 1684. It was a wonder of the age. Spanning the full façade of the central pavilion and overlooking the park, its colossal mirrors reflected the light of seventeen huge windows and seventeen colossal chandeliers. It was the secular counterpart to the medieval stained glass of Chartres.

6   The ancients had seen through glass darkly. The moderns saw through it clearly, in a shocking, shining cascade of light that reached into their innermost lives.

from *Europe A History* by Norman Davies

1 The method of making glass one could see through ...
A was already practised in Ancient Greece
B developed slowly between 999 and 1200
C was perfected in Nuremberg
D was, for many years, only known to Murano glassmakers

2 The new type of glass was first used in ...
A windows for religious buildings
B bottles and containers
C windows in normal houses
D reading glasses

3 Glass improved everyday life in the north of Europe because ...
A spectacles helped people to read
B flowers could be grown in cold weather
C it was easier to see indoors
D the study of medicine developed

4 Before people used mirrors they ...
A didn't care how they looked
B didn't examine their own behaviour
C had no idea how they looked
D behaved inconsiderately

5 Without the new type of glass there would have been no ...
A cathedrals   B paintings   C bottles   D scientific instruments

D   **Discuss these questions:**
- Name three significant events in your country's history. When did they happen and why are they memorable?
- What was the most significant world event of the last ten years?

A Read and listen to these poems before you look at the questions in B below.

THE SOLDIER

If I should die, think only this of me;
   That there is some corner of a foreign field
That is for ever England. There shall be
   In that rich earth a richer dust concealed;
A dust whom England bore, shaped, made aware,
   Gave, once, her flowers to love, her ways to roam,
A body of England's breathing English air,
   Washed by the rivers, blest by suns of home.

And think, this heart, all evil shed away,
   A pulse in the eternal mind, no less
      Gives somewhere back the thoughts by England given;
      Her sights and sounds; dreams happy as her day;
   And laughter, learnt of friends; and gentleness,
     In hearts at peace, under an English heaven.

Rupert Brooke

THE GENERAL

'Good-morning; good-morning!' the General said
When we met him last week on our way to the Line.
Now the soldiers he smiled at are most of 'em dead,
And we're cursing his staff for incompetent swine.
'He's a cheery old card,' grunted Harry to Jack
As they slogged up to Arras with rifle and pack.

But he did for them both with his plan of attack.

Siegfried Sassoon

FUTILITY

Move him into the sun –
Gently its touch awoke him once,
At home, whispering of fields unsown.
Always it woke him, even in France,
Until this morning and this snow.
If anything might rouse him now
The kind old sun will know.

Think how it wakes the seeds, –
Woke, once, the clays of a cold star.
Are limbs, so dear-achieved, are sides,
Full-nerved – still warm – too hard to stir?
Was it for this the clay grew tall?
– O what made fatuous sunbeams toil
To break earth's sleep at all?

Wilfred Owen

B 👥 **Discuss which of the alternatives best reflects the meaning and mood of each poem.**

1 In Rupert Brooke's *The Soldier*, the poet is praising...
  A England's brave soldiers   **C** England's scenery and people
  B England's free and democratic society   **D** England's heritage and history

2 The England described in the poem is England...
  A during peacetime   **C** in spring or summer
  B during the poet's youth   **D** during the previous century

3 If he dies the poet is sure that...
  A he will be remembered   **C** his Englishness is immortal
  B England will remain unchanged   **D** his friends and relations will remember him

4 If the idea of 'England' were replaced by 'Germany' or another country, the poem would...
  A no longer make sense   **C** still mean the same
  B have a different significance   **D** be more moving

5 The tone of *The Soldier* is...
  A sentimental   **B** optimistic   **C** pessimistic   **D** detached

6 In Wilfred Owen's *Futility*, the soldier described...
  A has only just died   **C** has been dead for a long time
  B is sure to die soon   **D** is likely to survive

7 According to the poem it is pointless that...
  A any man should die in war   **C** a dead man should be moved into the sun
  B a man should grow up to die in this way **D** a dead body should be buried

8 The tone of *Futility* is...
  A resigned   **B** sardonic   **C** lyrical   **D** emotional

9 In Siegfried Sassoon's *The General*, the smiling general is...

   A insincere   **B** incompetent   **C** happy   **D** brave

10 'Harry and Jack' are...

   A two typical private soldiers   **C** two now-dead friends of the poet

   B two young officers   **D** two living friends of the poet

11 The soldiers who marched past the general last week...

   A disliked him   **B** respected him   **C** liked him   **D** didn't notice him

12 The tone of *The General* is...

   A serious   **B** humorous   **C** sarcastic   **D** emotional

C One of you should look at Activity 9, one at 25 and the other(s) at 30. You'll each have some information about each poet's life to share with your partners. Then discuss these questions:

- How does knowing more about each poet's life influence your response to the poems?
- Which of the poems made the greatest impact on you? Why?
- Which poems or works of literature came out of wars that your country has been involved in?
- Why is it that some people find films and books about war fascinating?

17.3 Modifying adjectives and participles

VOCABULARY DEVELOPMENT

A 1 Which of these sentences look right – and which are wrong?

They were extremely pleased with my work.
It was very delightful to have met you.
It is extremely important to read the question carefully.
It is very essential to make notes before you start writing.
It is extremely vital to check your answers for slips of the pen.

2 Tick the words that are 'GRADABLE' (i.e. they can be intensified by words like *very* or *extremely*) and put a cross by the ones that are 'non-gradable' or 'ABSOLUTE' (not usually intensified by *very*).

livid [✗] indignant [✓] good [✓] perfect [✗]   identical ☐ similar ☐
absurd ☐ preposterous ☐ improbable ☐   interesting ☐ fascinating ☐
intelligent ☐ sensible ☐ brilliant ☐   priceless ☐ valuable ☐
amazed ☐ surprised ☐ astounded ☐   worthless ☐ futile ☐ inexpensive ☐
terrifying ☐ frightening ☐   delightful ☐ pleasant ☐
fatal ☐ hazardous ☐ deadly ☐ harmful ☐   essential ☐ important ☐
happy ☐ euphoric ☐
genuine ☐ believable ☐

B Fill each gap with a suitable modifier from the list, but don't repeat the same one in the same sentence.

absolutely badly considerably deeply exceptionally extraordinarily fully highly
perfectly quite really remarkably thoroughly totally unexpectedly utterly

1 He was .... determined to succeed, and he was .... disappointed when he didn't. We were .... amused, but pretended to be .... sympathetic.

2 The amount of work that is required is .... greater than we expected, and we'll have to make a(n) .... great effort to finish it on time.

3 We were .... delighted to hear he was marrying such a(n) .... nice woman.

4 He was feeling .... depressed after his illness, but he made a .... quick recovery, and was .... cheerful after that.

5 We felt we had been .... let down when they told us our application had been rejected. We were .... embarrassed because we'd told all our friends.

6 I'm sure her business will be .... successful, as she is a .... capable person, even though it's .... true that most new businesses don't succeed.

7 It was a(n) .... wonderful film and I thought the performances were .... moving. It was .... different from any other film I've ever seen.

8 The role of women in history is not .... recognised by many historians, who tend to be .... traditional in their attitudes.

C For each sentence, write a new sentence as similar in meaning as possible to the original sentence, using the word given but without altering the word in any way. Use three to eight words.

impossible

1 Some people simply can't remember historical dates at all.
Some people find that .... remember historical dates.

delighted

2 We should be very happy indeed to accept your invitation.
We should .... accept your invitation.

forgotten

3 It happened so long ago that no one remembers it at all now.
It happened so long ago that ....

futile

4 There's no point at all in asking him to be tactful.
It is .... to be tactful.

livid

5 She was very angry indeed when she found out about our plans.
She .... find out about our plans.

improbable

6 There is no likelihood at all of his succeeding.
It is .... succeed.

essential

7 You must *not* forget to check your work through for mistakes.
It is .... to check your work through for mistakes.

fascinating

8 We really were extremely interested in the lecture.
We ....

17.4 The end of the war   READING

A Read this extract, which describes the last months of the First World War, as seen from one young man's point of view. Then answer the questions on the next page.

Nancy's brother, Tony, had also gone to France now, and her mother made herself ill by worrying about him. Early in July he should be due for leave. I was on leave myself at the end of one of the four-months' cadet courses, staying with the rest of Nancy's family at Maesyneuardd, a big Tudor house near Harlech. This was the most haunted house that I have ever been in, though the ghosts, with one exception, were not visible, except occasionally in the mirrors. They would open and shut doors, rap on the oak panels, knock the shades off lamps, and drink the wine from the glasses at our elbows when we were not looking. The house belonged to an officer in the Second Battalion, whose ancestors had most of them died of drink. The visible ghost was a little yellow dog that would appear on the lawn in the early morning to announce deaths. Nancy saw it through the window that time.

The first Spanish influenza epidemic began, and Nancy's mother caught it, but did not want to miss Tony's leave and going to the London theatres with him. So when the doctor came, she took quantities of aspirin, reduced her temperature, and pretended to be all right. But she knew that the ghosts in the mirrors knew the truth. She died in London on July 13th, a few days later. Her chief solace, as she lay dying, was that Tony had got his leave prolonged on her account. I was alarmed at the effect that the shock of her death might have on Nancy's baby. Then I heard that Siegfried [Sassoon] had been shot through the head that same day while making a daylight patrol through long grass in No Man's Land; but not killed. And he wrote me a verse-letter from a London hospital beginning: *I'd timed my death in action to the minute . . .*

It is the most terrible of his war-poems.

Tony was killed in September. I went on mechanically at my cadet-battalion work. The new candidates for commissions were mostly Manchester cotton clerks and Liverpool shipping clerks – men with a good fighting record, quiet and well behaved. To forget about the war, I was writing *Country Sentiment,* a book of romantic poems and ballads.

In November came the Armistice. I heard at the same time of the deaths of Frank Jones-Bateman, who had gone back again just before the end, and Wilfred Owen, who often used to send me poems from France. Armistice-night hysteria did not touch our camp much, though some of the Canadians stationed there went down to Rhyl to celebrate in true overseas style. The news sent me out walking alone along the dyke above the marshes of Rhuddlan (an ancient battlefield), cursing and sobbing and thinking of the dead.

Siegfried's famous poem celebrating the Armistice began:

Everyone suddenly burst out singing,
And I was filled with such delight
As prisoned birds must find in freedom . . .

But 'everyone' did not include me.

from Goodbye to All That by Robert Graves

1 According to the writer, the invisible ghosts...
   A really did not exist
   B were visible only to Nancy
   C really did exist
   D were the ghosts of soldiers who had died at the Front
2 The doctor who came to see Nancy's mother...
   A knew she was dying
   B did not examine her thoroughly
   C did not realise she was very ill
   D gave her tablets to bring down her temperature
3 The writer mentions the deaths of...
   A five people he knew well
   B three people he knew well
   C four people he knew well
   D two people he knew well
4 The writer, at the time, was...
   A fighting at the Front
   B training new recruits
   C training soldiers who wanted to be officers
   D training would-be officers, fresh from school
5 When the Armistice was announced the writer...
   A was overjoyed
   B became hysterical
   C had mixed feelings
   D was overwhelmed with grief
6 The tone of the writing in the extract seems...
   A emotional   B cynical   C detached   D careless

B **Discuss your reactions to the text with a partner.**

When tackling a reading text in the exam, you may prefer to read it quickly through to get the gist before looking at the questions – or look at the questions first and then read the text through.

Some of the alternatives given in the questions may be tricky or deceptively plausible, which may distract you from the best alternative – so don't jump to conclusions. Be ready to eliminate the wrong answers and find the right one by a process of elimination.

Read carefully through the text to find the answers, highlight any relevant parts so that you can find them again quickly later. In the exam each correct answer gains two marks.

17.5 Adjectives + prepositions   GRAMMAR REVIEW

A Discuss the differences in meaning between the adjectives in these sentences. **Who or what might *it* or *them* refer to at the end of each sentence?**

1 Drink up: it's good for you.
  He was very good about it.

  She is very good at it.
  She was very good to them.

2 She was angry with them.

  He was angry about it.

3 I knew I was right about them.

  The choice was right for them.

4 We were pleased with them.
  He sounded pleased about it.

  We were pleased for them.

5 She was sorry for them.

  He was sorry about it.

B Decide whether *of* or *to* is used after each of these adjectives:

accustomed   ahead   allergic   ashamed   aware   capable   comparable   conscious
courteous   critical   cruel   devoid   devoted   envious   equivalent   guilty   hurtful
identical   impolite   indifferent   inferior   intolerant   irrelevant   kind   loyal
preferable   proud   scared   sensitive   short   similar   superior   susceptible
unfaithful   unworthy   wary   weary

C Which of the prepositions is used after each of these adjectives?

absent	annoyed	apprehensive	bewildered	comparable	compatible	consistent
conversant	curious	***about***	***for***	***from***	***on***	***with***	dependent	dubious
familiar	famous	far	free	fussy	guilty	indignant	intent	keen	level
	patient	responsible	sceptical	vague	

D Fill each gap with one word only, chosen from the previous two exercises:

1 We felt .... about the reception we might get, even though we knew that we'd be forgiven when we explained how .... we were for being late.

2 He is .... to his children and feels .... of them, but he does get .... with them if they are ever .... to people. Usually he feels .... about this afterwards, even though he knows it is .... for them.

3 I know I'm being .... of your staff but I'm not .... to being treated in this way. Who is the person who is .... for this?

4 She pretended to be .... to our sarcastic remarks, but in fact she's quite .... to being made fun of. Personally I'm .... about the effectiveness of sarcasm and I'm .... of the fact that it can be very .... to people.

5 Although he's usually .... on getting his own way, he didn't seem to be .... of convincing anyone at the meeting – on this occasion I felt quite .... for him, but I was .... of telling him so.

17.6 Listening Part 3: Emigration   EXAM PRACTICE

Part 3 of the Listening Paper is an interview or discussion. There are five multiple-choice questions which focus on only some of the information or opinions given. Read the questions carefully before you hear the recording, so that you know what to listen out for. (In the exam there are only five questions to answer.)

A You'll hear part of a lecture about emigration. Choose the alternative which fits best according to what you hear.

1 The total number of emigrants from Great Britain in the 19th century was ...
   A about 2 million   C around 11 million
   B under 6 million   D over 13 million   ⬚ 1

2 Soon after their arrival in the United States, most immigrants were ...
   A homesick   C pleasantly surprised
   B hungry   D disillusioned   ⬚ 2

3 Most Irish emigrants left their country because they didn't have enough ...
   A money   C food
   B religious freedom   D independence   ⬚ 3

4 Most Indians did not go to other countries intending to ...
   A work   C make their fortunes
   B become labourers   D settle   ⬚ 4

5 The total number of US immigrants between 1830 and 1930 was ...
   A 30 million   C 53 million
   B 35 million   D 105 million   ⬚ 5

6 One can deduce the origins of American citizens of European origin by ...
   A noticing their foreign accents   C looking at the colour of their skin
   B looking through a telephone directory D asking what kind of food they like   ⬚ 6

7 According to the speaker, more recent immigrants in the 20th century ...
   A were less likely to integrate   C don't mix with former immigrants
   B send money home to their families   D are less successful   ⬚ 7

8 The speaker implies that immigration has contributed to ...
   A prejudice against immigrants   C a rich mixture of different cultures
   B the loss of immigrants' cultural heritage D the language of the host country   ⬚ 8

B Discuss these questions:

• Which countries have people from your country emigrated to in the past?
• Do you have any relatives who have emigrated? Do you keep in touch?
• Would you consider emigrating to another country? Give your reasons.
• Which countries have immigrants to your country come from? Why did they come?

Part 4 of the Listening Paper is a discussion. The three-way matching questions require you to decide which of the speakers expressed a particular opinion – or whether they both did. Read the questions carefully before you hear the recording, so that you know what to listen out for.

This is the last Listening exercise. Before the exam, practise doing some Listening tests from Cambridge Certificate of Proficiency in English 1 – under exam conditions if possible.

You will hear part of a radio discussion. Indicate which of the speakers expresses each of the opinions listed by writing the appropriate letter in each box.

In each box write:
- **A** for a view expressed only by Alan
- or **J** for a view expressed only by Jane
- or **B** for a view expressed both by Alan and Jane

1 The First World War was inevitable. ☐ **1**

2 Britain was neutral until Belgium was invaded. ☐ **2**

3 In 1914 the German plan to encircle the French forces misfired. ☐ **3**

4 The Western Front hardly shifted from 1915 to 1918. ☐ **4**

5 Things that happened in the First World War made the Second World War inevitable. ☐ **5**

6 The Russian Revolution began with the support of Germany. ☐ **6**

In Part 1 of the Writing Paper you have to answer a compulsory question based on a short text and, perhaps, a diagram or picture. Make sure your answer sticks to the instructions closely and that you have a clear idea of who your supposed reader is. You may have to write an article, an essay, a letter or a proposal.

A

 Prepare and write this composition task, allowing yourself sixty minutes only. This hour includes: time to think, time to make notes, time to write the letter – and, afterwards, to check your work through for mistakes. Do this without using any reference books (300–350 words).

This extract is part of a newspaper article about teaching history. Readers were asked to send in their own opinions. You decide to write a letter responding to the points raised and expressing your own views.

Looking to the future?

Moves are afoot to reform the syllabus in secondary schools. The Education Minister has said that history has no place in a forward-looking society. Its place in the curriculum will be taken by extra lessons in information technology, maths and science.

"History had a place when this country could look back proudly on its past. Now we are looking to the future and history has had its day."

There is as yet no word from the Minister on the fate of the country's history teachers, most of whom are not qualified to teach more "forward-looking" subjects.

In Part 2 of the Writing Paper you have a choice of questions, including questions on each of the set texts (not included here). You may have to write an article, a proposal, a report, a review or a letter.

B **Write 300–350 words on one of these topics:**

1 Write a report of a historical event in the style of a modern newspaper article.
2 Describe the life and achievements of a famous historical figure from your country.
3 Write a first-person narrative about a historical event, as if you were one of the people present at the time, ending with the words: ". . . only then did I realise that I had been involved in a significant moment in history."

Checking your work: Look carefully for any mistakes or slips of the pen you may have made, like the ones illustrated here:

Its important to emphasise that . . .   *Rarely it is possible to . . .*
Perhaps it should pointed out that . . .   *I decided to do a long journey . . .*
Historie can be a facsinating subject.   *We enjoied the peformance.*

By now you're probably familiar with the kind of 'silly mistakes' that you make yourself when you're under pressure. As long as these are spotted and corrected before your work is handed in, there's nothing to worry about – but make sure you do allow yourself enough time for this!

Look back at two or three of your most recent compositions and highlight any 'silly mistakes' you made. Make sure you check your work for mistakes like these in the exam.

17.9 Speaking   EXAM PRACTICE

In Part 1 of the Speaking Paper you give information about yourself and are asked to give some opinions. In Part 2 (two-way conversation) you are given visual and spoken prompts, which generate a discussion. In Part 3 (long turns and discussion) you have to talk for two minutes, working from a prompt card. Then a discussion ensues, exploring the topics of the long turns further.

A Conversation about pictures. **Look at the pictures and discuss these questions together:**

- What's happening in the pictures? What kind of people do you think they are?
- What would it have been like to be a member of each family, do you think?
- What other aspects of family life in the first half of the 20th century would you like to see photos of? Why?

B **1** Long turns and discussion.

Student A	Student B
Talk for two minutes about this topic:	**Talk for two minutes about this topic:**
What changes have happened in the home since the first photo was taken?	What changes have happened in travel and transport since the second photo was taken?
➢ food and cooking	➢ cycling
➢ family life	➢ motoring
➢ hobbies and leisure activities	➢ travel abroad

2 Now discuss these questions:

- How has life improved since those days?
- Is it worth studying history and finding out how people used to live?
- What is your favourite period of history? Why?

To help you feel more confident about the procedure for the exam, spend some time doing practice Speaking tests from one of the Cambridge Proficiency Examination Practice Books with a partner.

Try to give a good impression of your spoken English. Don't just wait to be asked questions – behave and speak as you would in a real conversation. Each part of the Speaking test is all based on the same general topic, but you won't lose marks if you go off at a tangent.

---

18 Modern life

18.1 Reading Part 2

In Part 2 of the Reading Paper you read four texts on the same theme: these may be articles from newspapers or magazines, advertisements, fiction or non-fiction. You should expect all kinds of questions, focusing on content, detail, attitude, opinion – as well as questions about the style of the text. There are eight questions, each worth two marks.

A Read these four texts and choose the answer which you think fits best according to the text.

GIRL PAYS THE PRICE FOR LETTER TO PUTIN

A grammar school student in a tiny village deep in the Russian countryside who made the mistake of sending a letter to the president, Vladimir Putin, found herself stripped of the graduation honours she deserved and enrolled in a dairy academy instead of heading for medical school.

The letter was not political, and its author, Anya Provorova, certainly meant no disrespect. She and five graduating classmates of the little school in Vorobyovo, about 250 miles north of Moscow, had only fallen back upon centuries of Russian tradition and sent the Kremlin a request for help.

It wasn't that crucial – all they wanted was a video camera so they could record their graduation – but it seemed worth a try. It couldn't hurt to ask, could it?

It could, and it did.

The problem was this: in her salutation to "The Esteemed Vladimir Vladimirovich Putin", Ms Provorova neglected to finish the phrase with an exclamation point. Moreover, she used the Russian word for "you" in referring to the president, without giving it a capital letter.

As a result, her grades were lowered and she is heading to the local dairy institute.

"I don't think it's fair, especially because the medal commission had already confirmed my marks," she said. "I don't think these mistakes should be enough of a reason to lower my score."

She learned of her reprimand on June 15, at her graduation, after the school commission had condemned the letter to Mr Putin, and chastised the students for their immaturity.

There the story might have ended had not the regional correspondent for the national newspaper, Izvestia, learned of what had happened.

After the story appeared on Tuesday, school officials in the northern district denied that the withdrawal of the medals had anything to do with the letter.

Will Englund

1 Why did Anya fail to graduate?
  A She didn't sign the letter correctly.   **C** Writing to the president was against the rules.
  B Because of her poor spelling.   **D** She made two small punctuation errors.

2 What did Anya hope to do after leaving school?
  A Meet the president in person.   **C** Become a graduate.
  B Win a medal for being a good student.   **D** Study to be a doctor.

Boy falls victim to town with no scents

WHEN Gary Falkenham ran a few smears of Dippity-Do gel through his hair it was simply with the intention of enhancing his appearance. Not unnaturally, the 17-year-old also applied a dab of deodorant under each armpit.

Almost anywhere else these events might have passed without attracting undue attention, but Mr Falkenham lives in Halifax, Nova Scotia. Halifax has what its city council calls a "no-scent encouragement programme".

The schoolboy was expelled for two days after a teacher complained about the aroma he brought with him to the classroom. She said that it made her feel ill.

The elected representatives of the city – noted for the pungent fragrance of newly landed fish – believe that commercially produced scents contain untested carcinogenic chemicals and have banned them in public places.

The perfumes industry says their policy stinks.

Betty Bridges, a nurse from Virginia who travelled to the Canadian city to bolster the war on cologne, said: "The end result is that you have products that are being used by virtually the entire population but nobody knows what they'll do."

Ms Bridges, who often wears a breathing mask, has suffered for the past five years from multiple chemical sensitivity. She says that substances from perfumes have been found in breast milk and are linked to neurological disorders.

Conversely, Charles Low, the president of the Canadian Cosmetic, Toiletry and Fragrance Association, said: "The question we're here to answer fundamentally is: 'are fragrances and scented products safe for human use?' Our answer is yes."

As for Mr Falkenham, he was arrested by the Royal Canadian Mounted Police – who always get their man, whether or not he is wearing Dippity-Do – and released without charge.

Michael Ellison

3 Which of the following supports the 'no-scent encouragement programme' most strongly?
- **A** Gary Falkenham
- **B** Charles Low
- **C** Gary's teacher
- **D** Betty Bridges

4 What smell predominates in Halifax?
- **A** deodorant
- **B** chemicals
- **C** fish
- **D** fragrances

Year in jail for airliner mobile phone man

A man who repeatedly refused to turn off his mobile phone during an international flight was jailed for 12 months yesterday.

Airlines, police and the pilots' association welcomed the prison term imposed on Neil Whitehouse, 28, an oil worker, by a judge at Manchester crown court.

He was convicted of "recklessly and negligently" acting in a manner likely to endanger the British Airways Boeing 737 flight from Madrid to Manchester in September last year.

Judge Anthony Ensor told him: "Clearly you have no regard to the alarm and concern of passengers by your stubborn and arrogant behaviour. Any sentence must not only punish you but act as a warning to others."

He called on the Civil Aviation Authority to conclude investigations into legislation specifically banning mobile phones on planes.

"Proliferation of ownership of mobile phones and an increasing number of reports from pilots of electro-magnetic interference makes this a priority," he said.

At his trial last month the jury heard how Whitehouse, of Mansfield, Nottinghamshire, refused to switch off the phone despite requests from the captain and cabin crew.

Jamie Wilson

5 Who is looking into the possibility of introducing a law prohibiting mobile phones on planes?
- **A** The police
- **B** The Civil Aviation Authority
- **C** The pilots' association
- **D** The airlines

6 Why did the judge impose such a heavy sentence?
- **A** Because Whitehouse was arrogant.
- **B** Because the plane nearly crashed.
- **C** Because the plane made an emergency landing.
- **D** To discourage others from copying Whitehouse.

When high life was just a carousel

IT SOUNDED like the kind of glamorous job most people dream of. It required Geoffrey Senior to dress in smart suits, stay in expensive hotels and travel like a model executive back and forth to Heathrow airport.

In 12 months Mr Senior, aged 21, saw £300,000 pass through his hands, but the high life ended yesterday in a three-year prison sentence. The young, penniless, homeless man's luck ran out when a policeman stopped him pushing a trolley loaded with luggage away from a domestic flight terminal's carousel.

Mr Senior's version of the Generation Game – selecting his favourite items from a moving belt but without having to memorise them first – was the sort of profitable low-risk enterprise which has earned Heathrow the nickname Thiefrow and left senior police officers agog at criminal takings estimated at between £4 million and £10 million a week.

At the peak of summer nearly 200,000 people pass through the airport every day, making the remotest parts of the Piccadilly Line an El Dorado for the criminals working the terminals.

"Those like you who haunt Heathrow stealing people's baggage are an absolute menace to society," said Judge George Bathurst Norman in sentencing Mr Senior, who pleaded guilty to eight charges of theft.

Michael Orsulik, prosecuting, told the court that Mr Senior used to go smartly dressed to Terminal One and watch the domestic flight baggage carousel from an upstairs balcony. "If there was baggage going round on it and not many people about he would go down and help himself to items of luggage which took his fancy. He would then take them somewhere quiet, search through and help himself to things worth selling."

In one suitcase Mr Senior found £7,000 in cash. The money was spent on food, clothes and living it up.

David Sharrock

7 Who did Geoffrey Senior steal luggage from?
  A His fellow-passengers.
  B Passengers arriving from abroad.
  C Passengers who were delayed at passport control.
  D Passengers from British cities.
8 What did he do with most of the things in the luggage?
  A He took them home and kept them.
  B He stored them in a locker.
  C He sold them.
  D He left them behind.

B **Discuss these questions:**

- What do you find most difficult about answering questions like these?
- Is there any advice you can offer each other?
- What tips from previous units do you try to follow when doing this kind of test?
- Do you prefer to read all the texts quickly through first, before looking at the questions?

18.2 Use of English Part 3   EXAM PRACTICE

In Part 3 of the Use of English Paper you have to find a word that fits in all three sentences. The words are likely to be different parts of speech and may well have quite different meanings.

A   Think of ONE WORD which can be used appropriately in all three sentences. Write your answers in CAPITAL LETTERS.

1 The bodywork is a bit rusty but the engine is ....
  E-commerce shares are not considered to be a .... investment.
  There was a strange .... followed by complete silence.   [1]

2 There will be a .... drop in temperature when night falls.
  It will be very cold tomorrow in .... contrast to today.
  He has a .... eye for a bargain.   [2]

3 The authorities put up .... all over town about the meeting.
  The barmaid never .... him when he tries to catch her eye.
  The film got very good .... but I found it disappointing.   [3]

4 Everyone had lots of fun at the village ....
We had a .... amount of sunshine last month.
I usually make notes for an essay before I write a .... copy.

	4

5 She hopes to .... a good job when she finishes her studies.
In the 19th century, most people lived off the ....
Why don't we send him ahead to see how the .... lies.

	5

6 I don't know how you can .... it with your conscience, spending so much money on new shoes.
I've just put up this picture, can you tell me if it's .... ?
I'm so hungry, I haven't had a .... meal for ages.

	6

B 👥👥 **Discuss these questions:**
• What do you find most difficult about this kind of task?
• Is there any advice you can offer each other?

18.3 Use of English Part 4 EXAM PRACTICE

In Part 4 of the Use of English Paper, each correct sentence is worth two marks. A partially correct sentence gets one mark.

A Complete the second sentence so that it has a similar meaning to the first sentence using the word given. DO NOT CHANGE THE WORD GIVEN. You must use between two and eight words, including the word given.

1 Without the cooperation of the public, the police cannot prevent crime.
depends The work .... the cooperation of the public.

2 She was afraid to scream because she didn't want to awaken the neighbours.
fear She .... up the neighbours.

3 The number of murders has been going up little by little each year.
gradual There has been .... number of murders every year.

4 Their flat has been broken into twice this year.
had They .... twice this year.

5 She has a one-hour journey to work every day.
takes Her .... every day.

6 If the traffic is bad, we can't predict exactly when we'll get there.
doubt If the traffic is bad, there .... time we'll arrive.

7 He may not be a very dependable person.
rely You may .... him.

8 I hate the stresses and pressures of modern life.
what The stresses and pressures .... hate.

B 👥👥 **Discuss these questions:**
• What do you find most difficult about this kind of task?
• Is there any advice you can offer each other?

The text in Part 3 of the Reading Paper may be an article from a newspaper or magazine, or from a fiction or non-fiction book. There are seven paragraphs or sentences to fit into the spaces, giving a total of 14 marks.

Look for little clues: linking words, names and pronouns, times and places, words like *this*, *that*, *these*. Also consider the overall meaning of the text and the way that the main ideas follow on from each other.

A   Seven paragraphs have been removed from this article. Choose the most suitable paragraph from the list A–H for each gap (1–7) in the article. There is one extra paragraph which you don't need to use.

WHY NO ONE WALKS

I'll tell you this, but you have to promise that it will get no further. Not long after we moved here we had the people next door round for dinner and – I swear this is true – they drove.

1

A researcher at the University of California at Berkeley recently made a study of the nation's walking habits and concluded that 85 per cent of people in the United States are 'essentially' sedentary and 35 per cent are 'totally' sedentary. The average American walks less than 75 miles a year – about 1.4 miles a week, barely 350 yards a day. I'm no stranger to sloth myself, but that's appallingly little. I rack up more mileage than that just looking for the channel changer.

2

I walk to town nearly every day when I am at home. I go to the post office or library or the local bookshop, and sometimes, if I am feeling particularly debonair, I stop at Rosey Jekes Cafe for a cappuccino. Every few weeks or so I call in at the barbershop and let one of the guys there do something rash and lively with my hair. All this is a big part of my life and I wouldn't dream of doing it other than on foot. People have got used to this curious and eccentric behaviour now, but several times in the early days passing neighbours would slow by the kerb and ask if I wanted a lift.

3

'Honestly, I enjoy walking.'

4

People have become so habituated to using the car for everything that it would never occur to them to unfurl their legs and see what they can do. Sometimes it's almost ludicrous. The other day I was in a little nearby town called Etna waiting to bring home one of my children from a piano lesson when a car stopped outside the local post office and a man about my age popped out and dashed inside (and left the motor running – something else that exercises me inordinately). He was inside for about three or four minutes, then came out, got in the car and drove exactly 16 feet (I had nothing better to do so I paced it off) to the general store next door, and popped in again, engine still running.

5

She looked at me as if I were tragically simple-minded and said, 'But I have a programme for the treadmill. It records my distance and speed, and I can adjust it for degree of difficulty.' It had not occurred to me how thoughtlessly deficient nature is in this regard.

According to a concerned and faintly horrified recent editorial in the Boston Globe, the United States spends less than 1 per cent of its $25 billion-a-year roads budget on facilities for pedestrians. Actually, I'm surprised it's that much. Go to almost any suburb developed in the last thirty years – and there are thousands to choose from – and you will not find a pavement anywhere. Often you won't find a single pedestrian-crossing. I am not exaggerating.

6

Although the bookshop was no more than 50 or 60 feet away, I discovered that there was no way to get there on foot. There was a traffic crossing for cars, but no provision for pedestrians and no way to cross without dodging through three lanes of swiftly turning traffic. I had to get in the car and drive across.

At the time it seemed ridiculous and exasperating, but afterwards I realized that I was probably the only person ever even to have entertained the notion of negotiating that intersection on foot.

7

In 1994 Laconia dug up its pretty brick paving, took away the benches and tubs of geraniums and decorative trees, and put the street back to the way it had been in the first place. Now people can park right in front of the shops again and downtown Laconia thrives anew. And if that isn't sad, I don't know what is.

BILL BRYSON

A 'Well, if you're absolutely sure,' they would say and depart reluctantly, even guiltily, as if they felt they were leaving the scene of an accident.

B And the thing is this man looked really fit. I'm sure he jogs extravagant distances and plays squash and does all kinds of exuberantly healthful things, but I am just as sure that he drives to each of these undertakings. It's crazy. An acquaintance of ours was complaining the other day about the difficulty of finding a place to park outside the local gymnasium. She goes there several times a week to walk on a treadmill. The gymnasium is, at most, a six-minute walk from her front door. I asked her why she didn't walk to the gym and do six minutes less on the treadmill.

C The fact is, Americans not only don't walk anywhere, they won't walk anywhere, and woe to anyone who tries to make them, as a town here in New Hampshire called Laconia discovered to its cost. A few years ago Laconia spent $5 million pedestrianizing its town centre, to make it a pleasant shopping environment. Aesthetically it was a triumph – urban planners came from all over to coo and take photos – but commercially it was a disaster. Forced to walk one whole block from a car park, shoppers abandoned downtown Laconia for suburban malls.

D But they always looked so upset when I said this, that I gave in and accepted the lift. I didn't have the heart to make them feel they were leaving me to my fate.

E I had this brought home to me last summer when we were driving across Maine and stopped for coffee in one of those endless zones of shopping malls, motels, petrol stations and fast-food places that sprout everywhere in America these days. I noticed there was a bookshop across the street, so I decided to skip coffee and pop over. I needed a particular book and anyway I figured this would give my wife a chance to spend some important private quality time with four restive, overheated children.

F I was astounded (I recall asking them jokingly if they used a light aircraft to get to the supermarket, which simply drew blank looks and the mental scratching of my name from all future invitation lists), but I have since come to realize that there was nothing especially odd in their driving less than a couple of hundred feet to visit us. Nobody walks anywhere in America nowadays.

G 'But I'm going your way,' they would insist when I politely declined. 'Really, it's no bother.'

H One of the things we wanted when we moved to America was to live in a town within walking distance of shops. Hanover, where we settled, is a small, typical New England college town, pleasant, sedate and compact. It has a broad green, an old-fashioned Main Street, nice college buildings with big lawns, and leafy residential streets. It is, in short, an agreeable, easy place to stroll. Nearly everyone in town is within a level five-minute walk of the shops, and yet as far as I can tell virtually no one does.

 B 👥👥 **Discuss these questions:**
- What do you find most difficult about this kind of task?
- Is there any advice you can offer each other?

"My dog takes his walks pretty seriously"

A Read the two extracts from *Cities Fit To Live In* by Barrie Sherman, and answer the questions. For questions 1–4, answer with a word or short phrase. For question 5, write a summary according to the instructions given.

LONELINESS

Greta Garbo was always crying that she 'wanted to be alone'. In An Enemy of the People Ibsen says that 'the strongest man in the world is the man who stands alone'. Ibsen may be correct, since most people want and need company. Loneliness is a terrible thing, and all the worse in a city with so many people around.

Working men sitting each to his own table, each staring down at his pint of beer. Silence, no eye contact, no movement, no communication, except to order another drink. This is one kind of urban loneliness. An elderly woman, living alone, with her children in another city, barely mobile and visited only by meals on wheels and a once-a-week home help who is too busy to gossip. Her friend is her TV set. This too is modern urban loneliness.

But there is so much more. Young mothers trapped in high-rise flats which could have been designed to promote loneliness. Drug addicts locked into worlds of their own. Unemployed people, children unable to make friends, self-conscious adolescents, visitors, desperately shy people, disabled people, people with speech impediments, people who cannot understand the language, people with psychiatric disorders, and separated and divorced people – they may all need companionship at one time or another, perhaps all the time. 'All the lonely people, where do they all come from?' sang the Beatles. From the cities, where else?

Loneliness is corrosive. A lonely person becomes a withdrawn person and finds it hard to make contact with others. Loneliness feeds upon itself. It is a complex problem. The lonely are not joiners, mixers or clubbable people. So while it is easy to develop clubs, groups, teams, games, parties, card schools and socials, or to promote acquaintanceships, friendships, even love affairs, the truly lonely are never involved.

In some cities the culture mitigates loneliness. Barcelona and Bombay have an extended family system. Liverpool and Dublin have well developed community systems. In Amsterdam, there are public places where people are encouraged to meet and spend time. Other cities make resources available to help old people and disabled people meet other people.

Loneliness is, by and large, preventable and curable. Healthy cities ensure that this is not only recognised but that something positive is done about it.

1 What is implied by the phrase 'Her friend is her TV set' in line 8?

....

2 What is meant by the word 'corrosive' in line 16?

....

EXCITEMENT

Cities are exciting places, or at least they should be. People need excitement. They need to have their adrenalin flowing, and their imaginations stimulated. Excitement provides life's high points which become the memories and conversation pieces of later life. However, excitement can come in many guises, and some are not as good for health as others. For example, danger and 'sin' both breed excitement, but danger is associated with physical assault, and the excitement associated with it is not to be recommended. But taken overall, excitement stimulates, making the body and the psyche tingle with pleasure or anticipation.

Elderly people may find a trip to the shops exciting; for a disabled person any trip from their house may be equally exciting. People from the countryside or small towns tend to find the city exciting. Not only would a city-dwelling young person disagree, but he or she might well describe a night club or an adventure playground as exciting, things which an older person might look upon as a form of torture. Healthy cities provide exciting things to do for all their citizens irrespective of age or physical abilities.

Excitement is also about expectations. Some cities have reputations for excitement. Amsterdam, New York, Paris, Barcelona are all known as exciting cities. Excitement is also about people, especially people in large numbers. If people expect things to happen, more often than not they will, even if the excitement is hardly in evidence to other people. In terms of stimulating the senses or health, it does not matter; it is as valuable as the real thing. This is especially true of the suburbs attached to exciting cities. While these may be as placid and dull as most suburbs, the excitement of the city rubs off on them, sometimes undeservedly.

3 What point is the writer making in the second paragraph?

....

4 What is the meaning of 'rubs off' in the last line?

....

5 In 50–70 words, summarise the advantages and disadvantages of living in a city mentioned by the writer. Use your own words as far as possible.

B 👥👥 **Discuss these questions:**

- What do you find most difficult about this kind of task?
- Is there any advice you can offer each other?

18.6 Writing Parts 1 and 2   EXAM PRACTICE

You have two hours for two compositions in the Writing Paper. Allow yourself enough time to make notes before you start writing – and enough time to check your work through before you hand it in. Don't forget to put the number of the question in the box at the top of the answer paper.

Marking Each piece of work is assigned to a "band" ranging from Band 0 ('Negligible or no attempt at the task set') via Band 3 ('Satisfactory realisation of the task set') up to Band 5 ('Outstanding realisation of the task set'). The examiners' first priority is to assess your efforts at communication and give you credit for that, including the clarity and organisation of your composition. Good spelling, punctuation, paragraphing and easily legible handwriting are important. If you fail to answer the question, there are penalties for reproducing "blatantly irrelevant material learned by heart" or for "grossly or wantonly misinterpreting the question".

Length You must write 300–350 words. You don't get credit for extra length, which anyway will probably increase the total number of inaccuracies in your work.

Question 1 In this directed writing task, structured information is provided. You have to respond to a clearly-defined task and the appropriateness of your response and style and register are particularly important.

Question 5 In Question 5 you have to show that you have read and (hopefully) enjoyed a set text and can demonstrate this in an appropriately illustrated description and discussion. Credit is given for breadth, development and relevance of argument, and for the abundance and appropriateness of illustration and quotation.

In the exam there is a specific question on each set book – not generic questions as here.

A **Part 1**
You must answer this question. Write your answer in 300–350 words in an appropriate style.

1 You have been sent the following newspaper cutting. Prepare a suitable handout for visitors and tourists, to be given when they arrive at airports and frontiers in your country.

> ## 66 Reports in the foreign press
>
> THERE have been a growing number of reports in newspapers abroad that there is a "crime wave" in this country and that tourists are being targeted by muggers, pickpockets and other criminals. The Minister of Tourism fears that foreign visitors may assume they are likely to be robbed once they set foot in the country, and consequently choose different holiday destinations.
>
> The Minister of Tourism stated yesterday, "We want to give all arriving visitors a handout, warning them of the dangers. But we mustn't alarm them unduly. The handout should offer advice on how to minimise the risks by taking the right precautions."
>
> She announced a competition, open to everyone, for a suitable handout which will reassure tourists. The originator of the best handout is to receive a generous cash prize. 99

Part 2

Write an answer to ONE of these questions. Write your answer in 300–350 words in an appropriate style.

2 A travel guide has asked you to write a review of your city, suburb, town or village which will give visitors a good idea of what to do and where to go.

Write your REVIEW.

3 'The punishment should fit the crime.' This has been the theme of a series of articles in your local newspaper. Write a letter to the newspaper, giving your views.

Write your LETTER.

4 A monthly magazine has invited readers to contribute to a special issue on Freedom. Write a story for the magazine beginning or ending with the words: 'Free at last!'

Write your ARTICLE.

5 Basing your answer on your reading of the prescribed book you have studied, answer ONE of the following.

a Describe and give examples of the way in which the writer builds up a sense of excitement and tension as the plot unfolds. Write a letter recommending your book to next year's Proficiency class in your college.

Write your LETTER.

b What makes the book you have read stand out as a 'work of literature' above the common run of popular fiction? Write an article about the book you have read.

Write your ARTICLE.

c 'Any good work of fiction has just the same ingredients as a detective story.' Write an essay explaining to what extent this view is applicable to the text you have read.

Write your ESSAY.

B **Discuss these questions:**

- What do you find most difficult about the Writing Paper?
- Is there any advice you can offer each other?

18.7 One last word . . .

I do hope you've enjoyed using 'New Progress to Proficiency' and I'd like to wish you the best of luck in your exam!
Best wishes,

Leo Jones

Communication Activities

1 **Read this poem and then discuss the questions on page 160.**

MUSÉE DES BEAUX ARTS

About suffering they were never wrong,
The Old Masters: how well they understood
Its human position; how it takes place
While someone else is eating or opening a window or just walking dully along;
How, when the aged are reverently, passionately waiting
For the miraculous birth, there always must be
Children who did not specially want it to happen, skating
On a pond at the edge of the wood:
They never forgot
That even the dreadful martyrdom must run its course
Anyhow in a corner, some untidy spot
Where the dogs go on with their doggy life and the torturer's horse
Scratches its innocent behind on a tree.

In Brueghel's Icarus, for instance: how everything turns away
Quite leisurely from the disaster; the ploughman may
Have heard the splash, the forsaken cry,
But for him it was not an important failure; the sun shone
As it had to on the white legs disappearing into the green
Water; and the expensive delicate ship that must have seen
Something amazing, a boy falling out of the sky,
Had somewhere to get to and sailed calmly on.

W.H. Auden

2
How red wine is made

Ingredients: grape juice, grape skins and stems

- After the grapes have been picked they are taken to the winery where they are put into a machine which crushes them and removes the stems, but not the skins and pips*. This end product is called *must*. It takes 3kg of grapes to make one bottle of wine.
- The must is emptied into tanks or vats. The grape skins have their own natural yeasts which ferment with the sugar in the grape juice to produce alcohol and carbon dioxide. During fermentation, the skins and pips form a thick layer on the surface.
- Fermentation stops after a week or so. The new wine is drained off and the residue of skins and pips is pressed to extract another 20%.
- Wine for everyday drinking is stored in glass-lined cement or stainless steel tanks: the secondary fermentation takes place, making the wine softer and rounder before it is ready to be bottled. Some quality wines may be aged in oak casks, which imparts a special flavour to the wine.
- Before bottling, the wine is *racked* – egg white or another substance is added to carry the sediment to the bottom of the cask.
- The wine is bottled, capped and labelled by machine. Quality wines can be further aged in their bottles, but everyday wine is ready for drinking right away.

* To make white wine, the juice is immediately separated from the skins and pips. To make rosé wine, it is separated after a day or less.

3 In your own words, tell your partners about the ideas in this paragraph:

Handling customers well

The benefits of handling customers well are two-fold. Firstly, your job becomes more rewarding, as you are developing your techniques while using them and thus feel your job is really worthwhile. Secondly, your customers go away happy, which underlines your pride in becoming more competent. Satisfied customers don't just come back to your firm again, they tend to look for you personally and they also tell their friends to seek you out.

from So you think you can cope with customers? – A Video Arts Guide

4 This is the next paragraph of the story in 6.2. In your own words, tell your partner what happened. Then find out from your partner what happened in the end.

The hotel people began to be more pleased with me too, so I thought Mr Yorum must be quite an important man. Several more times on other days I told them I didn't understand Turkish, and each time they rang Mr Yorum and he came, and sometimes I paid for the drinks and sometimes he did. He and the hotel staff must have thought I had taken a great fancy to him or else that I was working up to some deal I wanted to do with him. The fourth time he came I had a bright idea that I would give him one of the missionary manuals that aunt Dot had left behind in her rucksack, because I thought each manual which I got rid of would lighten the rucksack.

5 Don't read the complete sentences aloud – rely on your memory and try to use your own words.

Movie clichés

1 At least one of every pair of identical twins is born evil.
2 It does not matter if your gang is heavily outnumbered in a fight involving martial arts, your enemies will still wait patiently to attack you one by one.
3 When you turn out the light to go to bed, everything in your bedroom will still be clearly visible, and become a slightly bluish colour.
4 If you are a young, pretty woman, it is possible to become a world expert on nuclear fission at the age of 22.
5 During all police investigations, it will be necessary to visit a strip club at least once.
6 You're very likely to survive any battle in any war unless you make the mistake of showing someone a picture of your sweetheart back home.
7 The Eiffel Tower can be seen from the window of any building in Paris.

6 Study these ideas and then ask your partners the questions:

Doors Most doors have to be pushed or pulled:
• Is there an easily visible handle on the side you have to pull and NO handle on the side you have to push? Is it necessary to have PUSH or PULL written on every door?
• Some doors open both ways, but how can you tell?
• Have you ever pushed instead of pulled? Was it your fault or the designer's?
• If revolving doors aren't already moving, how do you know which way to push?
  Do they always go round clockwise or do they go anti-clockwise?
• How do people know whether a door is automatic and doesn't need pushing? If it's 'obvious', why is this so? Have you ever pushed an automatic door?

Clocks and watches Think of the digital watches or clock radios you have used:
• How many different functions do they have?
• Can you make them do everything they're supposed to do? Or do you have to read the instructions?
• Have you ever set the alarm wrong? Was it your fault or the designer's?

7 **Describe this picture to your partner. Find out about your partner's picture by asking the same questions as you discussed in 13.1 B.**

Edward Hopper: *Room in New York*, 1932 (detail)

8 **Retell this news story in your own words, beginning: *There was ...***

Whatever you might say about women drivers, at least they are more responsible than men. Responsibility takes on a whole new meaning, however, when it comes to Ms Chrysanthemum Choo, arguably the world's safest ever motorist. Ms Choo, 30, of Miami had returned to her car after a shopping expedition, started the engine and patiently waited for an opportunity to pull out on to the main road. Eight hours later she was still patiently waiting. 'I like to be careful,' she explained. 'There were many cars around and I didn't want to do anything rash.' Things quietened down considerably during the night, but unfortunately by that point Ms Choo had fallen asleep, waking up just in time for the morning rush hour. It was another four hours before the desperate driver eventually saw her chance. Overcome with relief she slammed her foot on the accelerator and sped on to the road – straight into the side of a passing police car. 'I obviously wasn't careful enough,' she admitted.

9 **Rupert Brooke (1887–1915)** became an army officer at the outbreak of the war in 1914. He died of blood poisoning from a mosquito bite on his way to the Turkish front by ship, and never saw active service. He was buried on the Greek island of Skyros. His best-known poems are patriotic and romantic, contrasting with the bitterness of Owen and Sassoon.

10 **In your own words, tell your partners about the ideas in this paragraph:**

Your behaviour creates an impression

People gain a general impression of you from a combination of your facial expression and head movements, your gestures with your hands and arms, and the rest of your body including your legs. They will tend to see you as defensive if you avoid looking at them, clench your hands or cross your arms, keep rubbing an eye, ear or your nose, lean away from them, cross your legs or swivel your feet towards the door. They will tend to see you as anxious if you blink frequently, lick your lips, keep clearing your throat, put your hand over your mouth while you are speaking, tug at your ear, fidget in your chair or move your feet up and down.

from *So you think you can cope with customers?* – A Video Arts Guide

11

Ask your partner these general questions:

- Where are you from?
- Do you live locally?
- Are you studying or do you work?
- How close to your school/work do you live?
- What do you like about the area you live in?
- Could you tell us something about your work/study?
- What about your early school days? What were they like?
- Could you tell us something about your plans for the future?
- Which countries in the world would you most like to visit?
- What are employment opportunities like in this area?
- How easy do you think it will be to maintain the level of English you have achieved?

12

Look at this picture and then discuss these questions:

- What's happening in this picture?
- How do you think the people are feeling?
- Why are they taking part in this class?
- Would you like to be taking part? Why/Why not?
- How important is keeping fit to you?
- What do you do to keep yourself fit?
- How do you try to stay healthy?

13

Speak for two minutes on this topic:

> **What are your views on living a healthy life?**
>
> ➤ exercise and keeping fit
> ➤ eating the right foods
> ➤ avoiding unhealthy things like alcohol and tobacco

14

cli·ché /'kliːʃeɪ; *US* kliːʃeɪ/ *n* (**a**) [C] phrase or idea which is used so often that it has become stale or meaningless: *a cliché-ridden style.* (**b**) [U] use of such phrases: *Cliché is a feature of bad journalism.*

irony /'aɪərənɪ/ *n* **1** [U] expression of one's meaning by saying the direct opposite of one's thoughts in order to be emphatic, amusing, sarcastic, etc: *'That's really lovely, that is!' he said with heavy irony.* **2** [U, C] situation, event, etc that is desirable in itself but so unexpected or ill-timed that it appears to be deliberately perverse: *the irony of fate ○ He inherited a fortune but died a month later; one of life's little ironies.*

accent /'æksent, -sənt/ *n* **1** [C] an emphasis given to a syllable or word by means of stress or pitch[1](2): *In the word 'today' the accent is on the second syllable.* **2** [C] a mark or symbol, usu above a letter, used in writing and printing to indicate emphasis or the quality of a vowel sound: *'Café' has an accent on the 'e'.* **3** [C, U] a national, local or individual way of pronouncing words: *speak English with a foreign accent ○ a voice without (a trace of) accent.* Compare DIALECT. **4** [C usu *sing*, U] a special emphasis given to sth: *In all our products the accent is on quality.*

sar·casm /'sɑːkæzəm/ *n* [U] (use of) bitter, esp ironic, remarks intended to wound sb's feelings: *her constant sarcasm about his poor work.*

▷ sar·cas·tic /sɑːkæstɪk/ (also *infml* **sarky**) *adj* of or using sarcasm: *a sarcastic person, tone, remark.* **sar·cast·ic·ally** /-klɪ/ *adv.*

slo·gan /'sləʊgən/ *n* word or phrase that is easy to remember, used as a motto eg by a political party, or in advertising: *political slogans ○ 'Power to the people' is their slogan.*

pro·verb /'prɒvɜːb/ *n* short well-known saying that states a general truth or gives advice, eg 'It takes two to make a quarrel' or 'Don't put all your eggs in one basket': *the Book of Proverbs,* ie one of the books of the Old Testament containing the proverbs of Solomon.

dialect /'daɪəlekt/ *n* [C, U] the form of a language used in part of a country or by a class of people with grammar, words and pronunciation that may be different from other forms of the same language: *the Yorkshire dialect ○ a play written in dialect ○ dialect words/pronunciations.* Compare ACCENT **3**.

▶ **dialectal** /ˌdaɪə'lektl/ *adj: dialectal differences between two areas.*

from *Oxford Advanced Learners Dictionary of English*

15

How beer is brewed

Ingredients: water, malted barley, hops and yeast

1 Barley is germinated under controlled conditions, which brings out its sweetness, and then baked: the longer it is baked the darker and more caramelised it becomes.
   This *malt* is then milled and sent to the brewery.
2 At the brewery the malt is mixed with water and boiled.
3 The liquid, called the *wort*, is strained off and piped into a *kettle* where hops are added and it is boiled again. (Hops add flavour and bitterness to the product.)
4 The liquid is strained and cooled and then piped to a fermenting vessel, where a special yeast is added. Fermentation takes place, turning the natural sugar in the malt into alcohol and carbon dioxide. This takes about five days.
5 The beer is filtered and piped into cold sealed tanks where secondary fermentation takes place, improving the flavour of the beer and giving it 'character'.
6 The beer is strained off and then bottled, or piped into metal casks ready to be delivered.

16 **Your partner has the previous paragraph to this one – find out what happened. Then, in your own words, tell your partner what happened in the end.**

> So I went and got this manual, which was called "Why I belong to the Church of England", and was slightly translated into Turkish, and I gave it to Mr Yorum, who thanked me and looked at it with surprise, and it must have dawned on him that I was a missionary and was trying to convert him and that this was why I kept sending for him.
>
> After that he must have told the hotel staff not to ring him for me again, for when I said please to telephone him at once they shrugged and threw out their hands and looked at me despisingly. Soon after this I looked at my phrasebook and saw what I had been saying all the time.

17 **Retell this news story in your own words, beginning: *There was ...***

Nothing is more annoying than parking your car in a car park and then returning to discover you can't remember where you've left it. Imagine how elderly French couple René and Lucille Schubelle felt, therefore, when they returned from a shopping expedition to discover that not just their car but the entire car park had disappeared. Mr and Mrs Schubelle, both 84, of Calais had left their Renault Clio in 'one of those new-fangled municipal parking garages' on the seafront. When they came back two hours later, however, laden down with shopping, they were surprised to discover that the entire car park had vanished into thin air. Thinking perhaps it was 'something to do with terrorists', they contacted the police, who, after a brief investigation, discovered that what the Schubelles had taken to be a multistorey car park was in fact the car deck of a cross-Channel ferry. 'When we told them their car had gone to England they got very confused,' said one official. 'They seemed to think it was a punishment for having a dirty windscreen.'

18 **Don't read the complete sentences aloud – rely on your memory and try to use your own words.**

Movie clichés

8 A man will show no pain while taking the most ferocious beating but will wince when a woman tries to clean his wounds.
9 Even when driving down a perfectly straight road, it is necessary to turn the steering wheel vigorously from left to right every few moments.
10 A detective can only solve a case once he has been suspended from duty.
11 If you decide to start dancing in the street, everyone you meet will know all the steps.
12 When they are alone, all foreign military officers prefer to speak to each other in English.
13 Whenever it rains, the sun is shining in the background.
14 When someone is upset, as soon as they get home, they lean against the front door.

19   Study these ideas and then ask your partners the questions:

Showers   Think of the showers you have used:
- How do you know how to turn it on? How do you know how to make it hotter? How do you know how to increase the flow?
- Do they all follow these conventions?

increase/more   reduce/less

 or   or

- Have you ever been scalded in a shower? Was it your fault or the designer's?

Numbers   Make a list of all the numbers you have to remember, or need to look up quite often: e.g. postcodes, other people's birthdays, passport number, credit card, PINs, phone numbers, etc.
- How many numbers are there? How many can you remember without looking them up?
- Have you ever got any of these numbers wrong? What happened?
- Do you have any special techniques for remembering hard-to-recall numbers?

20   Find out about your partner's picture by asking the same questions as you discussed in 13.1 B. Describe this picture to your partner:

Edward Hopper: *Conference at Night.*

21

Ask your partner these general questions:

* Where are you from?
* Are you studying or do you work?
* Do you live with friends or family?
* Could you tell us something about your work/study?
* Could you tell us something about the house or apartment you live in?
* What about your early school days? What were they like?
* Let's think about not working or studying. What do you do to relax?
* Could you tell us something about why you are learning English?
* Apart from languages, what other skills will it be important to learn in the future?
* If you could change one thing about your education, what would it be?
* How ambitious are you?

22

Look at this picture and then discuss these questions:

* What's happening in this picture?
* How do the people feel, do you think?
* What might the doctor and the woman be saying?
* Why do you think the little girl is having an injection?

* Do you usually consult a doctor if you're unwell, or do you let your body cure itself?
* How important is good health to you?
* How do you feel about injections?

23

Speak for two minutes on this topic:

> **What are your views on doctors and the medical profession?**
>
> ➢ keeping your teeth healthy and dentists
> ➢ the quality of health care in your community
> ➢ alternative medicine (acupuncture, homeopathy, etc.)

24

col·lo·ca·tion /ˌkɒləˈkeɪʃən‖ˌkaː-/ *n tech* **1** [U] the way in which some words regularly collocate with others **2** [C] a habitual combination of words which sounds natural: *"Strong coffee"* is a typical collocation in English but *"powerful coffee"* is not. – see next page.

di·a·lect /ˈdaɪəlekt/ *n* [C,U] a variety of a language spoken only in one area, in which words or grammar are slightly different from other forms of the same language – compare ACCENT[1] (1), IDIOLECT

i·ron·y /ˈaɪərəni/ *n* **1** [U] use of words which are clearly opposite to one's meaning, usu. either in order to be amusing or to show annoyance (e.g. by saying "What charming behaviour" when someone has been rude) – compare SARCASM **2** [C;U] a course of events or a condition which has the opposite result from what is expected, usu. a bad result: *We went on holiday to Greece because we thought the weather was certain to be good, and it rained almost every day; the irony of it is, that at the same time there was a heat-wave back at home!* compare PARADOX; see also DRAMATIC IRONY

jar·gon /ˈdʒaːgən‖-aːr- gaːn/ *n* [C;U] *often derog* difficult or strange language which uses words known only to the members of a certain group; *computer jargon | the jargon of the advertising business*

plat·i·tude /ˈplætəˈtjuːd‖-tuːd/ *n derog* a statement that is true but not new, interesting, or clever; *a very uninspiring speech full of platitudes* – compare CLICHÉ, COMMONPLACE[2] – **-tudinous** /ˌplætəˈtjuːdənəs‖-ˈtuːdənəs‖-ˈtuː-/ *adj*

prov·erb /ˈprɒvɜːb‖ˈpraːvɜːrb/ *n* a short well-known, supposedly wise, saying usu. in simple language: *"Don't put all your eggs in one basket"* is a proverb.

from *Longman Dictionary of Contemporary English*

25

Wilfred Owen (1893–1918) served for three years in Flanders as an officer.

He was killed by machine-gun fire on November 8th 1918, just a few days before the Armistice. Owen's poems exposing the futility and horror of war were not published until after the war had ended.

26

In your own words, tell your partners about the ideas in this paragraph:

Don't use aggressive behaviour

People will tend to see you as aggressive and overbearing if you stare at them, raise your eyebrows in disbelief, look at them over the top of your spectacles, or smile in a 'heard it all before' way; or if you point at them, thump your fist on the table, stride around or stand while they are seated; or, if you are seated, lean right back in your chair with your hands behind your head and your legs splayed.

from *So you think you can cope with customers?* – A Video Arts Guide

27

Retell this news story in your own words, beginning: *There was ...*

One of the most determined and ultimately unsuccessful of all bank robbers was deaf German Klaus Schmidt, currently behind bars after being arrested because he couldn't hear the burglar alarm going off. Courageously refusing to allow his disability to get in the way of his criminal activities, Mr Schmidt, 41, had burst into a Berlin bank armed with a World War Two pistol and screamed, 'Hand over the money or I'll shoot.' Terrified staff had asked if he needed a bag, to which Mr Schmidt confidently replied, 'You're damn right it's a real gun!' 'We knew then that he was deaf as a doorpost,' explained the bank manager, 'so we set off the alarm. It was unbelievably loud, but he didn't seem to notice even when some people put their hands over their ears.' The hard-of-hearing robber waited patiently for five minutes, occasionally waving his gun in the air and crying, 'I'm a trained killer!' until eventually police burst in and arrested him. He is now suing the bank for 'exploiting my disability'.

28

Study these ideas and then ask your partners the questions:

Switches and knobs Think of the electrical equipment and gadgets you use:
- How easy was it for you (and other members of your family) to learn to use each piece of equipment?
- Can you remember how to make the gadgets do everything they're supposed to do? Or do you have to consult the instruction booklet?
- Do you have to look at the labels, or can you intuitively see which switch does what? Do they all follow these conventions:

increase/more ↑ or ⬊   reduce/less ↓ or ⬋

- And what about the ON switch: which way do you push it: IN or UP or DOWN? Does it make a helpful click or not?
- Have you ever used the wrong switch? Was it your fault or the designer's?

Sounds Sounds can provide feedback:
- What noise does a zip make? If a zip was silent, what difference would it make?
- How can you tell if a car door isn't closed properly – can you hear it rattle?
- What other sounds can you think of that provide feedback when you're using a piece of equipment?

29 In your own words, tell your partners about the ideas in this paragraph:

Using body language

If you want to seem friendly and cooperative, look at the other person's face, smile and nod when they are talking, have open hands and uncrossed arms and legs, lean forward slightly or move closer to them. If you want to appear confident, look into their eyes, don't blink, keep your hands away from your face, stay still and don't make sudden movements. If you want to appear thoughtful, tilt your head to one side, stroke your chin or pinch the bridge of your nose, lean forward to speak and back to listen and keep your legs still.

from *So you think you can cope with customers? – A Video Arts Guide*

30

Siegfried Sassoon (1886–1967) served as an army officer on the Western Front in Flanders throughout the war. He survived the war and his collected poems include many written during the Second World War too. He collected and published his friend Wilfred Owen's poems in 1920.

31

ac·cent PRONUNCIATION /ˈæk·sᵊnt, -sent/ n [C] the way in which people in a particular area, country, social class, etc. pronounce words • *He's got a strong French/Scottish/Birmingham/upper-class accent.* • *He speaks with a* **broad/pronounced/thick** (=strong) *Yorkshire accent.* • *Although French is her native language, she* **speaks** *with an impeccable English accent.* • *I tried to get rid of my Coventry accent when I went to university.* • *I thought I could detect a slight West Country accent.* • LP **Pronunciation, Varieties of English** ①

cli·ché /£ˈkliː·ʃeɪ, $-ˈ-/ n a form of expression that has been so often used that its original effectiveness has been lost • *Every time I ask my dad for some money, he always comes out with the old cliché, "It doesn't grow on trees, you know."* [C] • *You should always try to avoid the use of cliché.* [U] • *His speeches tend to be boring and cliché-ridden* (= contain a lot of clichés).

col·lo·cation /£ˈkɒl·əʊˈkeɪ·ʃᵊn, $ˈkɑː·lə-/ n specialized • A collocation (also **collocate**) is a word or phrase which is frequently used with another word or phrase, in a way that sounds correct to people who have spoken the language all their lives, but might not be expected from the meaning: *In the phrase 'a hard frost', 'hard' is a collocation of 'frost' and 'strong' would not sound natural.* [C] • A collocation can also be the combination of words formed when two or more words are frequently used together in a way that sounds correct. *The phrase 'a hard frost' is a collocation.* [C] • Collocation is also the frequent use of some words and phrases with others, esp. in a way which is difficult to guess: *Awareness of collocation is essential for fluency in a foreign language.* [U].

jar·gon /£ˈdʒɑː·gən, $ˈdʒɑːr-/ n [U] *disapproving* special words and phrases which are used by particular groups of people, esp. in their work • *military/legal/computer jargon* • *Some school prospectuses contained jargon and unexplained acronyms which parents found hard to understand.* • Compare TERMINOLOGY.

plat·i·tude /£ˈplæt·ɪ·tjuːd, $ˈplæt̬·ə·tuːd/ n [C] *disapproving* a remark or statement about something that, although it might be true, is boring and meaningless because it has been said so many times before • *We'll get the usual politicians who'll* **mouth** *the usual platitudes about 'the glories of democracy.'*

sar·ca·sm /£ˈsɑːkæz·ᵊm, $ˈsɑːr-/ n [U] (the use of) remarks which clearly mean the opposite of what they say, and which are made in order to hurt someone's feelings or to criticize something in an amusing way • *"You have been working hard", he said with* **heavy/biting** *sarcasm, as he looked at the empty page.* • *(saying)* 'Sarcasm is the lowest form of wit' means that sarcasm is the most unkind type of humour. • Compare IRONY FIGURATIVE SPEECH.

slo·gan /£ˈsləʊ·gən, $ˈsloʊ-/ n [C] a short easily remembered phrase intended to bring an idea or a product to public notice • *'Coke, it's the real thing' is an example of a slogan.*

from *Cambridge International Dictionary of English*

Index

Grammar review and Advanced grammar

Vocabulary development

Writing skills and Composition

Verbs, idioms and collocations

Exam practice